A social history
of psychology

A social history
of psychology

Edited by Jeroen Jansz and Peter van Drunen

BLACKWELL PUBLISHING
350 Main Street, Malden, MA 02148-5020, USA
9600 Garsington Road, Oxford OX4 2DQ, UK
550 Swanston Street, Carlton, Victoria 3053, Australia

First published 2004 by Blackwell Publishing Ltd

5   2007

Library of Congress Cataloging-in-Publication Data

A social history of psychology / edited by Jeroen Jansz and Peter van Drunen.
    p. cm.
Includes bibliographical references and index.
  ISBN 978-0-631-21570-7 (alk. paper) — ISBN 978-0-631-21571-4 (pbk. : alk. paper)
  1. Psychology—History—20th century. 2. Psychology—Social aspects.
I. Jansz, Jeroen, 1958– II. Drunen, Peter van.

BF105.S63 2003
150'.9—dc21

                            2002155248

A catalogue record for this title is available from the British Library.

Set in 10 / 12pt Galliard
by SNP Best-set Typesetter Ltd, Hong Kong
Printed and bound in Singapore
by Markono Print Media Pte Ltd

For further information on
Blackwell Publishing, visit our website:
www.blackwellpublishing.com

Contents

Preface

In recent decades, the image of the history of psychology has changed dramatically. Formerly considered a somewhat stuffy subject, it has developed into an exciting field of research and intellectual debate, with important ramifications for many of the issues which are at the heart of contemporary psychology: its theoretical diversity, the continuing debates on proper methodology and, last but not least, the impact of psychology on society at large.

These changes in the history of psychology are partly related to changing conceptions of psychology as a science. Rather than being considered the logical outcome of an intra-scientific accumulation of knowledge, it is increasingly viewed as a social enterprise, firmly embedded in wider social practices and preconceptions. This viewpoint has led to an increasing awareness of the importance of "practical" or "applied" psychology as an important nexus of psychology and society at large.

As teachers in the history of psychology, we have both been engaged in the development of courses that reflected and incorporated these recent developments. In this respect, we found that most existing textbooks on the history of psychology were not very helpful, especially in their coverage of practical psychology. This book is the result of a long-standing endeavor to develop an alternative that would suit our own needs as well as the interests of our students and, we hope, those of many of our colleagues and their students.

The "roots" of this book date back to the mid-1980s, when an increased interest in the history of psychology was witnessed at both Leiden and Groningen Universities. In the early 1990s, we decided to join forces in conceiving an introductory textbook, which would reflect our mutual interest in the social history of the discipline. With the enthusiastic help of colleagues both from our own departments and from other universities, this resulted in a book which to a large extent reflected current Dutch scholarship on the subject: *Met zachte hand. Opkomst en verbreiding van het psychologisch perspectief* ("The gentle force: genesis and dissemination of the psychological perspective," Jansz and van Drunen, eds, 1996). To our delight, this book found a ready and enthusiastic audience, as evidenced by the fact that it is currently part of the curriculum in about half of Dutch psychology departments.

The present book is to a large extent based on our experience with the preceding text, both as authors and as teachers using it. On the one hand, we have tried to incorporate recent historical research, as well as new insights within the field of historiography, both in Europe and the United States. On the other hand, we have tried to remain focused on the primary criteria for textbooks, that is, presenting the subject matter in a clear, consistent, and attractive way, which aims not only to convey information but also to kindle enthusiasm among the readers.

Like its predecessor, this book focuses on "practical psychology." This includes not only "applied psychology" as professional practice, but also the numerous other ways in which psychology is brought to bear on society, including popularization and the use of psychology by other disciplines, such as psychiatry, education, criminology, and cultural anthropology.

Despite its origin, the focus of this book is definitely not exclusively on Europe. On the contrary, given the prominence of American psychology, developments in the United States are generally covered more extensively than European ones. Often, developments in various countries are presented comparatively, to highlight historical contingencies. Incorporating primary and secondary literature in French, German, and Dutch as well as English, we have tried to cross language barriers. For an English-speaking audience, the book may thus provide access to sources not readily available in English.

A social history of psychology is primarily intended for use in introductory courses in the history of psychology at colleges and universities. As such, it requires no previous knowledge of psychology or its history. However, many teachers may find it useful to combine our social history with a more "classical" text, which focuses on the history of psychological theory. Alternatively, it can be used in advanced, or Masters, programs, as a sequel to a "classical" historical introduction.

As teachers in the history of psychology, we have over the years developed a host of teaching aids relating to the subject of this book, including cases for discussion or further exploration and a large bank of test items. Teachers using this book are encouraged to consult with us on tools for teaching, as well as to share with us their own ideas and experiences.

This book is the result of the prolonged and enthusiastic cooperation of many people. It would not have been possible without the support of our respective departments: the theory and history sections of the Psychology Departments of Leiden University and Groningen University, and the Department of Communication at the University of Amsterdam. Even more important than this institutional backing has been the heartwarming and enthusiastic support of our colleagues. In our immediate environment, we wish to mention especially Sacha Bem (Leiden), Pieter J. van Strien, and Trudy Dehue (Groningen), who stimulated us in our attempts to create a text which is both accessible and up-to-date in its coverage. Next are our Dutch colleagues, both at our own departments and at other Dutch universities. Amongst them, we would specifically like to thank those who contributed to the Dutch predecessor of this book, but for various reasons could not contribute to the present volume, that is, David Bos, Agneta Fischer, and (again) Trudy Dehue. We hope the present text reflects the fruits of their intellectual input. Further, we would like to mention Cheiron-Europe or, as it is currently known, the European Society for the History of the Human Sciences. Since 1982, the yearly meetings of Cheiron/ESHHS have provided a platform for European as well as some American scholars in the field, facilitating intellectual exchange as well as providing a friendly and encouraging environment. As participants will recognize, many of the ideas in this book were first raised in papers presented at these meetings, giving us the opportunity to profit from the comments of our international colleagues. Finally, we would like to mention the successive generations of students who helped us to develop our ideas and present them in an articulate and comprehensible way.

Writing this book was an exciting adventure, not only because of the complexity of its subject, but also because of the diversity of backgrounds and perspectives of its authors. As editors, we aimed at a coherent volume. If we have succeeded in this respect, this is to a great extent due to the prolonged efforts of the various authors to tailor their contributions to the general format of the book. We also gratefully acknowledge the contributions of the anonymous reviewers of this project. Their critical appraisals proved to be a source of inspiration. Many thanks are also due to our editors at Blackwell, Martin Davies and Phyllis Wentworth, both for their practical assistance and for their enthusiasm and stimulating comments. Without them, this book would not have been possible.

A number of people helped us with the final preparation of the manuscript. We want to thank A. J. S. Fischer-Vahl, David Ingleby and Grace Westendorp for correcting our English. Sarah Coleman provided great help by guiding us through the maze of copyright regulations and permissions regarding the pictorial material used. Her expert help was crucial to our mission of supporting our text with relevant illustrations. In the final stage, the careful and sensitive text editing of Teresa Brady not only boosted the text's readability but also contributed to its accuracy and consistency.

While editing this book, we have seen the enthusiasm of everyone involved in our intellectual enterprise growing as the volume gradually took shape. It is our great hope to convey this enthusiasm to our readers.

Jeroen Jansz

Peter van Drunen

Amsterdam and Groningen

Acknowledgments

The editors and publishers would like to thank the following for permission to reproduce illustrations in this book:

1   *Self-portrait of Katharina Van Hemessen* (1548). Source: Öffentliche Kunstsammlung Basel, Kunstmuseum. Photo: Öffentliche Kunstsammlung Basel, Martin Bühler.
2   *London, c. 1870*, engraving by Gustave Doré. Source: G. Doré and B. Jerrold, *London: a pilgrimage* (London, 1872).
3   Frontispiece of *American Phrenological Journal* (1848). Source: Psychology Pictures.
4   *A court for King Cholera*, engraving by John Leech (*c.* 1855–60). Source: J. Leech, *Later pencillings from Punch* (1864).
5   The first psychological laboratory. Source: Psychology Pictures/Archives of Dutch Psychology.
6   Francis Galton's Anthropometric Laboratory at the International Health Exhibition, London, 1884. Source: Psychology Pictures/Archives of Dutch Psychology.
7   A psychologist administering an intelligence test, *c.* 1930s. Source: Psychology Pictures/Archives of Dutch Psychology.
8   The child as mini-adult, *c.* 1750. Source: Psychology Pictures.
9   *Inside the mill* and *Supplementing factory rations*. Source: engravings from F. Trollope, *Life and adventures of Michael Armstrong, the factory boy* (London: Colburn, 1840).
10 A school classroom in the mid-nineteenth century. Source: Psychology Pictures/Archives of Dutch Psychology.
11 Granville Stanley Hall (1844–1924). Source: Clark University Archives; reproduced by permission.
12 Questionnaire results from the Child Study Movement. Source: *Pedagogical Seminary*, 1911. Reprinted by permission of Clark University Archives.
13 Experimental research for education, *c.* 1910s. Source: Psychology Pictures/Archives of Dutch Psychology.
14 Examination of child with experimental apparatus, *c.* 1910s. Source: Archives of the History of American Psychology, University of Akron.

15   French psychologist Alfred Binet (1857–1911). Source: Psychology Pictures/Archives of Dutch Psychology.

16   Binet–Simon test, Dutch version, 1919. Source: Psychology Pictures/Archives of Dutch Psychology.

17   *The menace of the feeble-minded* (1919). Source: Archives of the History of American Psychology, University of Akron, Goddard papers, File M614.

18   John B. Watson with "Little Albert." Picture courtesy of Benjamin Harris.

19   Illustration from Benjamin Spock's *Pocket book of baby and child care* (New York: Pocket Books, 1946). Reprinted by permission of Pocket Books, an imprint of Simon & Schuster Adult Publishing Group.

20   Cartoon reflecting the advance of psychological testing in the American educational system. Source: *American School Board Journal*, 1922. Reprinted by permission of the Department of Special Collections and University Archives, Stanford University Libraries.

21   A teaching machine, *c.* 1950s. Source: B. F. Skinner, *The technology of teaching* (New York: Appleton-Century-Crofts, 1968).

22   *Career of a madman*, engraving by William Hogarth (1735). Source: Psychology Pictures.

23   *Pinel et les aliénés de Bicêtre* ("Pinel and the insane of the Bicêtre"), painting by Charles Müller. Courtesy of the Bibliothèque de l'Académie national de Médecine, Paris. Photo: J. L. Charmet.

24   Meerenberg, a "modern" Dutch psychiatric hospital founded in 1849. Source: Psychology Pictures.

25   "Tranquillizing" chair, *c.* 1810. Source: National Library of Medicine, Bethesda, Maryland. Reprinted by permission of Visual Image Presentations.

26   *The clinical lesson* (1887). Source: Assistance Public Hôpitaux de Paris.

27   Sigmund Freud (1856–1939). Source: Archives of the History of American Psychology, University of Akron.

28   Freud's visit to the United States, 1909. Source: Clark University Archives.

29   Rorschach testing, *c.* 1930s. Source: Archives of the History of American Psychology, University of Akron.

30   Series of cartoons on the psychological impact of fear. Source: *War Medicine*, 5 (February 1944). Reprinted courtesy of the American Medical Association Archives.

31   Carl R. Rogers (1902–1986). Source: Carl R. Rogers Collection, Department of Special Collections, Davidson Library, University of California, Santa Barbara. Reprinted with permission.

32   Jack Nicholson in *One flew over the cuckoo's nest* (1975), produced by Fantasy Films/United Artists. Source: Kobal Collection, London.

33   Military drill, *c.* 1700. Six illustrations from a Dutch handbook on the use of the musket. Source: Psychology Pictures.

34   The "ergograph," *c.* 1880s. Source: Psychology Pictures/Archives of Dutch Psychology.

35   Time study. Source: Psychology Pictures/Archives of Dutch Psychology.

36   Motion study of bricklaying (1909). Source: F. B. Gilbreth, *Motion study* (New York: Van Nostrand, 1911).

37 First World War testing practices: Europe Sources: (a) Institute for the History of Psychology, Passau; (b) Psychology Pictures/Archives of Dutch Psychology.

38 First World War testing practices: United States Source: National Archives, Washington DC (111-SC-386 and 111-SC-385).

39 Changing expert models and methods in personnel selection. Source: Psychology Pictures/Archives of Dutch Psychology.

40 Hawthorne experiments, relay assembly testroom. Source: F. J. Roethlisberger and W. J. Dickson (eds.), *Management and the worker* (Cambridge, MA: Harvard University Press, 1949).

41 Job enrichment and the humanization of work. Source: Philips Company Archives.

42 Military origins of the assessment center method. Source: Archives of the History of American Psychology, University of Akron.

43 The "savages" of the island of Marie. Source: Collection Musée de l'Homme, Paris.

44 Typical illustration from a nineteenth-century textbook, suggesting "negroes" to be halfway between Caucasians and chimpanzees. Source: J. C. Nott and G. R. Gliddon, *Indigenous races of the earth* (Philadelphia: Lippincott, 1868).

45 Cambridge Torres Strait expedition (1898). Courtesy of the Cambridge University Museum of Archaeology and Anthropology, no. UMCAA.P.754.AXH1.

46 Psychological examination of immigrants on Ellis Island (1917). Source: Archives of the History of American Psychology, University of Akron.

47 Differences in "native" intelligence between various ethnic groups. Source: C. C. Brigham, *A study of American intelligence* (Princeton, NJ: Princeton University Press, 1922).

48 "Stimulation and frustration": mother–child interaction in Balinese culture. Source: G. Bateson and M. Mead, *Balinese character: a photographic analysis* (New York: New York Academy Press, 2nd edn., 1962); original copyright Special Publications of The New York Academy of Sciences (1942).

49 Drawing used in a famous study by Gordon Allport (1947). Source: G. W. Allport and L. Postman (eds.), *The psychology of rumor* (New York: Russell & Russell, 1965); copyright Thomas Learning, for the authors.

50 Graphs from *The bell curve*. Source: R. J. Herrnstein and C. Murray (1994), *The bell curve: intelligence and class structure in American life* (New York: Free Press); copyright *c.* 1994, by Richard J. Herrnstein and Charles Murray.

51 Cartoon on the monomania defense, by the famous French cartoonist Daumier (1846). Source: Psychology Pictures.

52 Agricultural colony for juvenile delinquents, Mettray, France (*c.* 1845). Source: Psychology Pictures/Archives of Dutch Psychology.

53 "Brigand of the Bastille" (1876). Source: Psychology Pictures.

54 A "stereograph," devised by the French surgeon and anthropologist Paul Broca. Source: Psychology Pictures/Archives of Dutch Psychology.

55 A lie detector test (*c.* 1930s). Source: W. M. Marston, *The lie detector test* (New York: R. R. Smith, 1938).

56 The Picture Completion Test. Source: Archives of the History of American Psychology, University of Akron.

57 Psychologist Kenneth Clark (1952). Source: Archives of the History of American Psychology, University of Akron.

58 Psychology of advertising, *c.* 1920s. Source: Psychology Pictures.

59 Ethnocentrism scale. Source: T. W. Adorno *et al.* (eds.), *The authoritarian personality* (New York: W. W. Norton, 1950).

60 (a) Purdue eye-camera. Source: Archives of the History of American Psychology, University of Akron. (b) Media research, *c.* 1950s. Source: A. Anastasi, *Fields of applied psychology* (New York: McGraw-Hill, 1964); copyright, Columbia Broadcasting Company.

Introduction

Peter van Drunen and Jeroen Jansz

> Practical psychology, which has done so much and will do far more in grading intelligence and in fitting men to their jobs, will transcend the fields of business and school and address itself to a more comprehensive program. … All the great problems of our age are becoming more and more psychological the better we understand them. The world needs a new psychology larger in all its dimensions more than it needs anything else.[1]

Thus wrote Granville Stanley Hall, one of the founding fathers of American psychology, in his autobiography, published shortly before his death in 1924. At the beginning of a new century, we can conclude that Hall's expectations have to a great extent come true. The sheer rise in the number of psychologists speaks for itself: if Hall had seen this tally rise from a handful to more than two thousand, the figure pales in comparison with recent estimates, which for the United States alone amount to more than 200,000. Other western societies have witnessed a similar development, making psychology one of the most rapidly expanding professions of the twentieth century.[2]

This increase in numbers has gone hand in hand with a steady expansion of the professional domain of psychologists. Psychological testing, already well established in Hall's day, has become a booming industry. Even more dramatic has been the rise and expansion of that other hallmark of the discipline – psychotherapy. Moreover, the psychological expert has found his (or her)* way into a host of other fields, from neonatology to gerontology, from professional sports to training of the physically handicapped, and from our intimate relationships to public policy and world affairs. Nor is the influence of psychology confined to the professional activities of its practitioners. Notions and concepts derived from psychology – "repression," "introvert," "extravert," "IQ" – have left their mark on the way we experience and understand ourselves and each other. Even the goals and values which guide us are increasingly

---

* With respect to the gendered nature of language, we generally employ the plural in this book in order to avoid using either "his" or "her." For reasons of elegance we sometimes deliberately use "her" or "his."

formulated in a psychological idiom: "mental health," "self-actualization," "openness," "emotional stability."

This book examines the rise of psychology and its growing influence on society. In other words, it focuses on what is generally called "applied" or practical psychology. We deliberately chose to call it a "social" history – not just because of its subject matter, but also because of the viewpoint and interpretative framework employed. To put this in perspective, we will first briefly discuss some major developments with respect to the historiography of psychology (section 1). This is followed by a short introduction to the subject matter and general approach of the present book (section 2), and a presentation of some of the key concepts employed (section 3). Finally, the overall plan of the book is presented (section 4).

1 The "new" history of psychology

Accounts of the history of psychology date back almost as far as the discipline of psychology itself. However, only in the last 35 years or so has the historiography of psychology (as it is formally called) developed into a specialized field of research. This "professionalization" of historical work has gone hand in hand with a radical shift in the perspective and methods employed. This shift is reflected in a frequently made distinction between "old" and "new" history.[3]

Generally, "old" history stems from psychologists themselves. Sometimes, it is the product of a curiosity not unlike that involved in attempts to construct a family genealogy. Sometimes, it is undertaken for celebratory reasons, or didactic purposes, to inform members of the discipline or aspiring students about the veritable tradition in which they stand. As such, "old" history is anything but dead: to this very day, typical examples can be found in jubilee publications, such as those published on the occasion of the centennial of American psychology (in 1992), and in historical chapters in psychology textbooks.[4]

Typically, "old" historians take the current state of psychology as their starting point. That is to say, they tend to highlight those theories and ideas which anticipated present-day psychology. Moreover, their description and evaluation of these developments is implicitly or explicitly colored by current notions, as is apparent from the identification of "progressive" and "erratic" elements, in other words those that tally with current thinking and those that do not. In their interpretation of historical development, they tend to conform to the idea of psychology and science in general as an intellectual endeavor: a succession of progressively better theories, with development primarily attributed to cognitive factors: the analytic and experimental power of scientific procedure, that has allowed us to weed out misconceptions and bring us closer to the truth. By and large, they thus take our current conceptions of both psychology and science in general for granted, rather than questioning them.

Although, as indicated, "old" history is still very much alive, it is increasingly challenged by a new generation of historians, who have come to the fore in recent decades. Rather than taking the present self-image of psychology as their starting point, "new" historians see it as their task to investigate its underlying assumptions. Is the evolution of psychology indeed as progressive as psychologists tend to take for granted? Is its development indeed primarily driven by cognitive factors, or should social circumstances and the influence of society be taken into account as well? And can psychology's impact on society indeed be seen as generally beneficial, as "old" historians tend to assume?

The "new" approach does not only involve a different approach to psychology's past. It also has implications for our perspective on the present status of the discipline. If "old" historians generally adhere to the premises and viewpoints of modern psychology, "new" historians tend to take a more detached, and sometimes even critical stance. Thus, history acquires a new meaning: rather than just tracing the roots of present-day psychology, it invites us to take a fresh look at it.

Among specialized historians, the "new" approach is almost universally favored over the "old" one. Unfortunately however, most introductory textbooks on the history of psychology still adhere to the "old" approach (although some do try to incorporate the results of "new" historical research[5]). This may well relate to their intended purpose: many authors see it as their primary duty to familiarize students with historical theories, as is evident from the frequent combination of "theory" and "history" courses.[6]

2   General perspective

In this book, we have not only tried to incorporate the findings of "new" historiography, but also to remain true to its main tenets, with respect to focus, perspective, epistemology, and explanatory schemes.

FOCUS: PRACTICAL PSYCHOLOGY

Whereas "old" history generally emphasizes academic psychology, the focus of this book is on "applied" or, as we prefer to call it, practical psychology. On the one hand, this choice was motivated by our primary interest: rather than merely reconstructing psychology's development, it has been to examine critically the impact of psychology on modern society. How can one account for psychology's tremendous expansion, and its growing influence? And should this development be evaluated simply as a blessing to society, as many psychologists would see it, or more critically, as a development which may also have its drawbacks?

In addition to this, our choice of practical psychology as our subject matter also had historiographic motives. "Old" historians tend to adhere to a concept of scientific development, in which the academic discipline takes precedence over practical psychology. Recent research has shown this notion to be highly problematic.[7] Practical psychology, it suggests, has a dynamic of its own. Not only does it often entail major adaptations of theories developed in academe, but sometimes it even engenders the development of radically new theories, methods, and instruments. In their turn, these can influence academic psychology: through psychological practice, new social issues and new concepts about man are introduced, which may seriously alter the course of research. A prominent example of this is psychoanalysis: developed outside academe, with assumptions radically different from those held by contemporary academic psychologists, Freud's theory not only captured the hearts and minds of practitioners and the lay public, but also influenced academic research.

Because of the relative autonomy of practice, we favor the concept of "practical psychology" over the more traditional notion of "applied psychology." We use this concept not only to refer to the professional practices of psychologists, but also to other ways in which psychology has been brought to bear on society, including the popularization of psychological concepts and the incorporation of theories and methods by other professions, such as psychiatry and education.

PERSPECTIVE: HISTORICISM

Perhaps the most fundamental difference between "old" and "new" history concerns their perspective on the way previous development should be evaluated: as a preliminary stage of psychology as we know it today ("presentism"), or as a subject meriting attention in its own right ("historicism").[8]

As we saw, "old" historians tend to take the presentist stance. Among "new" historians, this is generally considered to be unacceptable. According to them, historical developments should be understood within their own context, rather than from the perspectives of our own time. This is not to say that historical inquiry should not be inspired by present-day motives. The current rise of neuropsychology, for instance, may be an impetus to take a closer look at some of its historical predecessors, such as nineteenth-century phrenology, in which the skull was examined to obtain insight into underlying brain functions. However, our present notions about the brain add nothing to our understanding of the why and how of phrenology's success, or, for that matter, of its later demise. After all, nineteenth-century scientists were not privy to our current knowledge, so we should seek to know on what grounds they evaluated phrenology. In this respect "new" historians, as it were, forsake the benefit of hindsight.

Historicism is not without problems. For one thing, it is virtually impossible to free ourselves from current conceptions. Nevertheless, we have consistently tried to adhere to the historicist stance. Among other things, this means that we have tried not to restrict our focus to those developments which preceded current thinking, but also to examine theories, methods, and practices, which are now considered obsolete. Furthermore, we have tried to present psychology's past in a non-evaluative way.

EPISTEMOLOGY: CONSTRUCTIVISM

The difference between presentism and historicism has a wider significance than that of historical method. It is related to different concepts of what science is about and how it proceeds, in other words, to different epistemologies.

Implicitly or explicitly, "old," presentist historians generally adhere to some form of realism: scientific theories reflect the world as it is. Through empirical study, guided by rigorous method, psychology has succeeded in acquiring a progressively better understanding of its subject, i.e. mental processes and human behavior. From this standpoint, presentism is to a certain extent admissible. For psychologists of the past may not have been aware of current theories, but they faced the same subject that we do. So, assuming that our present knowledge reflects the "true" nature of this subject, we may indeed use it as a point of reference. Perhaps, to return to our example, phrenologists were ignorant of modern neuropsychology, but they faced the same human brain that we do. So that may indeed have dictated their search, erratic as it may have been on some points. The hallmark of this line of thinking is the notion of "discovery": literally "uncovering" the true nature of something.

"New" historians generally take a different point of view. Inspired by modern philosophies of science, they question the allegedly decisive role of "reality" in scientific development. Perhaps it is not true that "anything goes," but reality certainly leaves room for more than one concept of psychology's subject matter. (Just consider, for example, the different "schools" of psychotherapy, ranging from psychoanalysis to behavioral therapy.) In fact, even the subject matter itself may be prone to change: behaviorism concentrates on human behavior, whereas cognitive psychology takes mental processes to be the "core business" of psychology. In the light of this, there is no reason to assume that our current concepts (what we now consider to be "knowledge") can serve as a criterion for past theories. The resulting approach is often identified as relativistic, but might perhaps be characterized more adequately as "methodological agnosticism": judgment is not so much ruled out, as suspended.

In this book, we have tried to adhere to this constructivist perspective. Among other things, we have tried to avoid notions such as "discovery" and "invention" (suggesting the validity of theories and methods under discussion), as well as "error" and "misconception" (suggesting the opposite). This of course includes contemporary developments as well as historical ones: from a constructivist perspective, there is no reason to accord a different status to current theory and methods.

EXPLANATION: CONTEXTUALISM

How should one interpret and explain the historical development of psychology? In their emphasis on cognitive factors, "old" historians tend to concentrate on academic psychology and, more specifically, on the work of the most prominent historical representatives ("pioneers") of the discipline and their philosophical predecessors. In this respect, their accounts tend to be "personalistic," a history of "great men" (and, very occasionally, women). Insofar as non-rational factors are supposed to be involved, these are either of a very general nature (such as *Zeitgeist*, i.e. ideas that were "in the air") or biographical (the peculiar background, interests or habits of an individual scientist, which contributed to his work).

"New" historians, on the other hand, tend to take a broader perspective. Their agnostic stance prevents them from relying on cognitive progress as an explanatory concept. Instead, they tend to consider the development of psychology as the result of a complex interplay of various processes, within psychology as well as outside of it: social demands on psychologists, culturally prevalent conceptions of human behavior, and so on. Rather than capturing all these "external" forces under an evanescent concept such as the *Zeitgeist*, they tend to try to show in detail which specific influences contributed to the development of psychology. In this respect, their approach can be characterized as "contextual."

Again, we have tried in this book to adhere to the "new" approach. Specifically, we have attempted to relate the development of practical psychology to more encompassing developments in the social domains in which psychologists made their appearance.

3   Key concepts

As will become apparent in the following chapters, the number of links between practical psychology and its surroundings is practically limitless. At a microscopic level, we might look at the immediate social surroundings of leading practitioners: their biographical antecedents; the problems that were presented to them and guided them in their work; and the influence of colleagues, representatives of other professions, and the wider "public," and so on. On a somewhat larger scale, other aspects of context enter into the picture: the general state of the discipline, and the constraints and opportunities this implies; rivalry between psychology and neighboring disciplines; and specific developments within society, such as processes of industrialization and urbanization, wars breaking out and coming to an end, or new social problems coming to the fore. At a macroscopic level, finally, we might look for even more general patterns: how was the rise of psychology related to the general evolution of western society?

On the one hand, we have tried to do justice to the contingency of historical developments. On the other, we have tried to bring some unity to our account by focusing on two general social developments, which we consider germane to the development of practical psychology: individualization and social management.

INDIVIDUALIZATION

Individualization is a notion which almost invariably pops up in reflections about the relations between psychology and society. It is a concept which is used to describe a wide variety of phenomena, ranging from the loosening of social ties and structures (liberating individuals from their social embeddedness) to a growing awareness of "self," in particular with respect to the emotional interior. In our analysis, we have been primarily inspired by the work of the German sociologist Norbert Elias, who considers individualization and the increasing attention paid to emotions as essential elements of what he calls "the civilizing process": as societies become more complex, the lives of their members become increasingly intertwined, which calls for a more careful regulation of emotions and behavior.[9]

The relevance of individualization for our topic hardly needs clarification. Whether defined as the science of behavior, consciousness or cognition, psychology is clearly focused on the individual. This attention to the individual is especially prominent in the "applied" or practical manifestations of psychology. On the one hand clearly rooted in sociocultural conceptions and concerns about the individual, it also substantially contributed to these conceptions and concerns, as exemplified by the measurement of individual differences in intelligence and other mental attributes, and the treatment of individuals suffering from mental illness or emotional problems.

Although there is no complete agreement on the relations between various aspects of individualization, nor on the exact chronology of their occurrence, most authors agree on at least two points: first, that individualization is a characteristic feature of modern western society, as distinct from earlier phases of western civilization and from other civilizations. And second, that it is by no means a recent phenomenon, with early manifestations dating back as far as the late fourteenth century. In this book, we will focus on three aspects of the individualization process. First, the shift from the collective to the individual, which occurred both in social reality and in its various (ideological, philosophical, artistic) representations. Second, the growing awareness of individual differences in character, personality, and mental capacities. And third, psychologization: the development of a sense of "inwardness," presupposing that every individual possesses some form of private "inner space" of motives, thoughts and feelings, constitutive of his very being as a unique person and wholly or partly accessible through introspection.

SOCIAL MANAGEMENT

As will be shown in more detail in chapter 1, processes of individualization created the general cultural background for the rise of psychology in the nineteenth century. However, they do not in themselves account for the widespread and systematic employment of expert knowledge, which would become characteristic for the late nineteenth and twentieth century. This can only be understood in conjunction with another development, which we will refer to as *social management*.

In its broadest meaning, social management denotes all attempts to organize and direct social life. This may include administrative and political organization, as well as the organization of functions such as conflict resolution and the administration of justice, production and economic life, reproduction, socialization and family life, etc. In this book, however, we will employ the term in the more restricted sense of all planned and systematic attempts to monitor, influence, and control the behavior of individuals and social groups.

Both in its broadest sense and in the more specific sense employed here, social management is an essential element of social life: no society can exist without some form of organization and some form of control over the behavior of its members, however rudimentary. This certainly holds for early western society, with its relatively elaborate systems of, for instance, justice, religion, and political power. Nevertheless, there are marked differences between these older practices and arrangements and the new forms of social management, which emerged in nineteenth- and twentieth-century western societies. In particular the French philosopher Michel Foucault and his followers have called attention to these differences, and to their relevance for an adequate understanding of the development of psychology and the social and medical sciences.[10]

First, social management has become much more encompassing, bearing on hitherto untouched aspects of social life and behavior. From the early nineteenth century onward, changing economic and social conditions began to demand an ever greater degree of social organization and regulation, varying from urban planning to institutionalized forms of health care, education, and care and guidance for all those not meeting the requirements of "modern life." Existing institutions of social management – schools, madhouses, facilities for the poor and the sick – started to grow dramatically, and new ones evolved, such as special schools for the mentally and physically disabled and institutions for juvenile or mentally deranged criminals.

Secondly, the agency of social management gradually shifted from private organizations, such as guilds, charities, and philanthropic societies, to the public realm. From the second half of the nineteenth century onward, more and more aspects of human conduct became a matter of public concern and public policy. This provided the groundwork for what in the twentieth century would become known as the welfare state. Typically, these new interventions were firmly rooted in middle-class conceptions about what constituted "proper behavior," and targeted at other groups in society which did not conform to these norms, thus creating a new form of sociopolitical domination, described by some historians as "the civilizing offensive."[11]

Thirdly, social management was subject to a process of *professionalization* and *scientification*. At a general level, the very expansion of social management was deeply rooted in the ideology of the Enlightenment, which held that social processes were to be brought under the control of reason and science. This was reflected in its various domains, especially from the second half of the nineteenth century onward: areas such as poor relief, which had hitherto been the domain of the church and charities, saw the development of new helping professions, such as the social worker. And in domains where some degree of professional involvement had developed earlier (education, health care), standards of professional training were raised substantially. This process went hand in hand with the inception of new scientific disciplines related to the various fields of intervention, such as pedagogy, criminology, and sociology.

Fourthly, and perhaps most importantly, social management evolved from systems of brute external control to more intricate and subtle forms of influence, in which social norms were translated into systems of expert knowledge, which in their turn gradually became incorporated into the way people experience themselves and their outside world – just as our view of the natural world was shaped by the natural sciences, so our conception of ourselves is increasingly influenced by psychology and related sciences.

4   Scope and organization of the book

Practical psychology constitutes a heterogeneous field: evolving at different times, geared toward various groups of individuals, embedded in a diversity of societal arrangements, performed by a wide-ranging variety of agents, and employing a multitude of theories, methods, and instruments. In the organization of the present book, we have tried to do justice to this diversity, rather than attempting to "homogenize" these widely varying developments into one chronological account.

Chapter 1 provides the general background for the chapters that follow. Focusing on the key processes identified above – individualization and social management – it sketches the transformation of Western society which provided the "fertile soil" for the genesis of psychology in the late nineteenth and early twentieth century. In addition, it gives a brief overview of general developments in the twentieth century, considering both society at large and the development of psychology.

The following chapters explore in detail the development and impact of psychology with respect to six fields. Chapters 2 to 4 cover what are generally considered the main fields of "applied psychology": education and child-rearing, mental health, and work and organization. Chapters 5 to 7 cover three domains which from the standpoint of the history of the discipline are often considered to be more peripheral, but which nevertheless have been strongly influenced by psychology: ideas and interventions regarding members of other cultures, the realm of justice (more specifically, criminal law), and the rise of public opinion and consumer behavior as an object of psycho-scientific intervention.

Apart from a somewhat longer excursion in the first chapter, our historical focus is on the periods in which, respectively, the stage was set for the rise of psychology (roughly, the nineteenth century) and in which the discipline found its place within modern Western societies (roughly, the twentieth century). Although historical research on the post-Second World War era is still scarce, we have tried to cover developments up to the late 1960s and early 1970s, with occasional reference to even more recent developments.

Geographically, our focus is on north-western Europe and the United States. This is to some extent a matter of expediency: the rise of psychology has by no means been limited to these parts of the globe. In particular, in middle, southern, and eastern Europe, France, Italy, Spain, and Russia have also been home to long and influential psychological traditions. Insofar as ideas, techniques and practices developed in these countries have become part of "mainstream" international psychology, we have tried to take account of them. Generally speaking, however, the course of developments in these countries has been so different from that in the US or north-western Europe, that we have chosen not to try to incorporate them. The same holds for the occasionally viable traditions of psychology in "developing" countries in Latin America, Africa, and Asia, interesting as the mix may be, in these parts of the world, of indigenous intellectual traditions and "western" psychology.

Differences exist, of course, even within this delineated geographical domain. We have concentrated on developments which "led the way," i.e. became incorporated in the international mainstream. Occasionally, abortive or divergent developments are considered, primarily for purposes of elucidation by contrast. Generally speaking, the geographical focus shifts with time: from Europe (especially Germany), which led the way in the nineteenth century, to the United States, which became the birthplace of much of psychology as we know it today.

The development of psychology and its neighboring disciplines has not affected every citizen and social stratum to the same extent and in the same way. Nor was it meant to: especially insofar as psychology was embedded in more general practices of social management, it was more often than not directed toward specific social groups, such as children, workers, or criminals. Sometimes, this entailed explicit attention to gender, ethnic, or class differences: theories and practices of child-rearing, for instance, clearly differentiated between the roles of mothers and fathers, and sometimes between boys and girls as well. In other cases, these differentiations were implied, rather than spelt out: thus, psychiatry tended to deal with female patients, whereas interventions in the domain of work were generally aimed at men. Although these implicit emphases are by their very nature harder to uncover (and consequently often invisible in historical treatises), we have tried to do justice to them.

Like any book, this volume has its limitations. The domains considered by no means cover the whole range of psychology and its impact on contemporary culture and society. Nor was this our primary intention: although we aspired to cover the main fields and developments, our primary goal was not comprehensiveness, but the presentation of a coherent perspective for understanding the history of psychology.

This book emanated from the conviction that history is not just about the past: it also reflects on discussions about the current status of psychology and its social and cultural impact. In the Epilogue, we will return to some of the main themes addressed in the following chapters. History, however, does not dictate normative judgment. In this respect, we do hope the book will be used as we have intended it: not as a collection of facts to be stored in memory, but as food for thought and debate.

NOTES

1 G. Stanley Hall (1923), *Life and confessions of a psychologist* (New York: Appleton), pp. 437–8.

2 Figures for the US from J. H. Capshew (1999), *Psychologists on the march: science, practice and professional identity in America, 1923–1969* (Cambridge: Cambridge University Press), p. 1. Other sources cite even higher estimates. Cf. V. S. Sexton (1992), *International psychology: views from around the world* (Lincoln: University of Nebraska Press), pp. 479–80.

3 The classical discussion of the relation between "old" and "new" history of psychology is L. Furumoto (1989), The new history of psychology, in: L. S. Cohen (ed.), *The G. Stanley Hall lecture series, vol. 9*, 9–34.

4 See for a general discussion of didactic and ceremonial functions of history L. Graham, W. Lepenies and P. Weingart (eds.), *Functions and uses of disciplinary history* (Dordrecht: Reidel). An example of a ceremonial study is R. D. Parke et al. (eds.), *A century of developmental psychology* (Washington, DC: American Psychological Association). Examples of the use of history for didactic reasons can be found in virtually any introductory textbook, see for instance C. F. Graumann (2001) Introducing social psychology historically, in M. Hewstone and W. Stroebe (eds.), *Introduction to social psychology* (Cambridge, UK: Blackwell), pp. 3–23.

5 For example, T. H. Leahey (1991), *A history of modern psychology* (Englewood Cliffs, NJ: Prentice Hall).

6 See C. J. Goodwin (1999), *A history of modern psychology* (New York: John Wiley), p. 14.

7 See for a discussion of the relation between theory and practice, P. J. van Strien (1999) The impact of practice on the development of psychology, in W. Maiers et al. (eds.), *Challenges to theoretical psychology* (North York, Ontario: Captus University Publications), pp. 91–9, and H. V. Rappard et al. (1993), *Annals of Theoretical Psychology, vol. 8* (New York/London: Plenum), especially chs 2 and 4.

8 The classic text on presentism and historicism is G. W. Stocking (1965), On the limits of "presentism" and "historicism" in the historiography of the behavioral sciences, *Journal of the History of the Behavioural Sciences, 1*, 211–18.

9   See N. Elias, *The civilizing process. Sociogenetic and Psychogenic Investigations*, vols. *I and II* (Oxford: Basil Blackwell, 1978/1982), originally published in German as *Ueber den Prozess der Zivilisation* (Basel: Haus zum Falken, 1939). Elias' theory was originally developed to account for changes in manners during the transition from traditional to modern European society. For attempts to apply his insights to the development of modern society, see: J. Kasson, *Rudeness and civility: manners in nineteenth-century urban America* (New York: Hill and Wang, 1990); and C. Wouters (1995), Etiquette books and emotion management in the 20th century: the integration of social classes, *Journal of Social History, 29*, 107–24, and (1996), Etiquette books and emotion management in the 20th century: the integration of the sexes, *Journal of Social History, 29*, 325–40.

10 See in particular M. Foucault (1974), *The order of things: an archeology of the human sciences* (London: Tavistock Publications, originally published in 1966 as *Les mots et les choses* (Paris: Gallimard)) and *Madness and civilization: a history of insanity in the age of reason* (1965, London: Tavistock, originally published in 1961 as *Histoire de la folie* (Paris: Plon)). Of the many studies inspired by Foucault most pertinent to our subject are: J. Donzelot (1977), *La police des familles* (Paris: Minuit); N. Rose (1990) *Governing the soul. The shaping of the private self* (London: Routledge) and (1996) *Inventing our selves* (Cambridge: Cambridge University Press); and F. Castel, R. Castel, and A. Lovell (1982), *The psychiatric society* (New York: Columbia University Press).

11 A. Mitzman (1987), The civilizing offensive: mentalities, high culture, and individual psyches, *Journal of Social History, 20*, 663–88. See also A. de Swaan (1988), *In the care of the state: health care, education and welfare in Europe and the USA in the modern era* (Cambridge: Polity Press).

1 Psychology and society: an overview

Jeroen Jansz

It is generally considered that psychology was born as an independent discipline in 1879. In that year Wilhelm Wundt founded the first psychological laboratory in the world, at the University of Leipzig, Germany. Attempts to apply psychology to practical problems soon followed. As early as the 1890s, psychologists in various countries became involved in different social issues. In Germany, the psychologist Herman Ebbinghaus undertook studies regarding the question of fatigue among school children, and the psychiatrist Kraepelin put psychological instruments to use in examining psychiatric patients. And in Vienna, Sigmund Freud started a small private practice for patients with psychological problems, which would prepare the ground for psychoanalysis and psychotherapy. In the United States, Lightner Witmer opened a "psychological clinic" for diagnosis and treatment of children with educational problems.

What started out as isolated local initiatives soon became a veritable movement. By the 1910s, practical psychology was well underway, and in the early 1920s it already overshadowed academic psychology, especially in the United States. As a contemporary observer put it in 1924: "There is now not only psychology in the academic or college sense, but also a Psychology of Business, a Psychology of Education, a Psychology of Salesmanship, a Psychology of Religion. . . . In all our great cities there are already, or soon will be, signs that read 'Psychologist – Open Day and Night'."[1]

Why did practical psychology strike root so rapidly? Before turning to the various fields of psychological practice in the chapters to follow, in this chapter we will try to put the general early success of the discipline into perspective. In the Introduction, we presented two general socio-historical trends, which we consider to have been crucial for the success of psychology: individualization and social management. "Individualization" covers a number of changes in people's "life-world," in particular the shift from group to individual, the interest in individual differences, and a focus on the inner world of feelings. "Social management" refers to the concerted efforts to monitor and control the behavior of individuals and groups. Taking these phenomena as our leads, we will begin with a review of early processes of individualization, starting around 1400 (section 1). In subsequent sections, we will focus on what is generally known as "the long nineteenth century": the period starting with the industrial and political revolutions of the late eighteenth century, and ending with the outbreak of the First World War in 1914. Section 2 provides a general sketch of the period, with emphasis on the major social transformations which set this period off from earlier times. Section 3 discusses the transformation of the life-world from the perspective of individualization. Section 4 concentrates on the rise of practices of social management. In section 5, we turn to our subject proper: the inception of psychology as a practical field of expertise. Finally, in section 6 we will briefly discuss some general trends in the twentieth century, which set the stage for more recent developments in psychology, to be examined in greater detail in the chapters to follow.

1   Early western individuality (*c.* 1400–1800)

It is impossible to pin down a moment, or even a period, in which the western focus on the individual originated. Some historians point to philosophy in Greek antiquity, or focus on the emergence of private property around 1250. Here, we will follow common practice among historians and take the Renaissance at around 1400 as our starting point.[2]

Historical changes with respect to the concept of the individual have always been connected with economic, political, and legal developments. Mobility, for example, was an important factor. In the rural village, individual identities were tied up with jobs and positions held in the community and family. When people had to flee from their birth ground, or decided to move to town, they generally lost their traditional anchors.[3] Another relevant macro-development was the legal domain. For instance, when serfage ended it was easier for farmers to follow their own life course. For centuries, mobility, the law, and other macro-factors had a rather diverse and local impact on the population. Therefore we postpone our discussion of economy, politics, and law to the next section which is devoted to the nineteenth century. This section concentrates on the ideas about individuality that emerged early in history.

1.1   Early manifestations (c. 1400–1600)

The social and cultural developments of around 1400, generally labeled briefly as "the Renaissance," occurred first in Italian city-states such as Florence, and a little later in the cities of north-western Europe. The general tendency in these "urban" areas in this period was a gradual shift toward the individual among the societal elites. A self-conscious view of man emerged, that pictured the individual as less dependent on, for example, tradition and the church. Farmers and others in the Third Estate had probably less room for individuality, but they were not entirely excluded. The individual person as a point of reference was already presupposed in the practices of Christian faith and in legal systems based on Roman Law which affected the general population.[4] The growing emphasis on individuality manifested itself in diverse domains such as art, Protestantism, and Humanism, and was also discernible in ordinary life.

Art and literature. From the Renaissance onward, the scale in which individuality was expressed in artefacts was far larger than in the preceding ages. Paintings and sculptures bore the hallmark of the artist, which was exemplified by the addition of the artist's signature. The works they made were now seen as their personal product, expressing the artist's unique capacities. Many wealthy citizens had their portraits painted. Their individuality was thus represented on canvas, in the individual style of the painter. The new genre of the self-portrait crowned the sense of individuality (see figure 1). In writing, individual life histories were documented, with for example the publication of biographies of Dante and Petrarch. Collections of biographical essays concerned specific classes of people; Giovio, for example, described the lives of princes and generals (1514), and Vasari (1550) and Van Mander (1604) published the life histories of famous painters. Politicians, famous artists, and others from wealthy strata, including some women, published autobiographies, and so did many craftsmen, soldiers, and clerks. The goldsmith Cellini underlined the aims of the autobiographies when he wrote in the 1570s:

> No matter what sort he is, everyone who has to his credit what are or really seem great achievements, ought to write the story of his own life in his own hand.[5]

In other words, successful individuals ought to publish accounts of their own lives in order to provide a model for their readers.

Protestantism. The criticism of Roman Catholic theology voiced by Luther and Calvin in the early sixteenth century also contributed to an individualized concept of man. The individual's exclusive relation to God in matters of faith was central to the Protestant Reformation. Believers were urged to read the Holy Bible themselves, which contrasted sharply with common religious practice. Sins must be confessed in the private isolation of prayer, and Protestants thus became their own judge in determining the gravity of their transgressions. They could not rely on a priest who would give them penance after confession. This religious individualism prompted the examination of one's conscience in order to determine whether one had been virtuous and had refrained from committing sin. Many diaries written by devout Protestants bear witness to the inner loneliness that resulted from this doubt-ridden self-exploration.[6]

Humanism. The "free will" was the cornerstone of many Humanist writings in the sixteenth century. Erasmus, for example, criticized the Catholic clergy for keeping people ignorant. Although he did not join the Reformation, he urged believers to choose their own course of faith. Montaigne expressed a humanist spirit in his emphasis on the autonomous authority of man. The human psyche held a central position in his *Essais* (1580), in particular his own psyche: "I am myself the substance of my book. . . ."[7] The Humanism of the men of letters in the sixteenth century had a golden future, especially in its secular version, the Enlightenment, that came to dominate later centuries.

Ordinary life. In ordinary habits, individuality appeared in the guise of "privacy," for example among the educated and wealthy classes where people started to eat from

Figure 1 Self-portrait of Katharina Van Hemessen (1548). An example of early artistic expression of individuality, showing that this was not confined to men. Source: Öffentliche Kunstsammlung Basel, Kunstmuseum. Photo: Öffentliche Kunstsammlung Basel, Martin Bühler.

their own plate, rather than from a common dish, and sat down on chairs rather than on benches. The emergence of privacy coincided with that of etiquette. It was, for example, considered impolite to offer a guest an apple of which a part had already been eaten.[8]

We can conclude that an individualist concept of man emerged in the western world in the fifteenth and sixteenth centuries. It should be kept in mind, however, that these early forms of individualism were quite different from the perspective on the individual that came to dominate western culture in the twentieth century. As the historian Lyons has put it: "individuality was based on respect for talent, or property and legal rights, but invariably stopped short of an interest in the drama of an *idiosyncratic inner life*."[9] Instead of connecting individuality with reflection, contemplation, or the inner world of feelings, it was rather identified with one's effect on the community.

1.2 *The rational individual (c. 1600–1700)*

In the seventeenth century, individualism received a forceful new impetus from philosophy, most notably the work of the Frenchman René Descartes and the British philosopher John Locke. Descartes' contribution was epitomized in his famous dictum "cogito ergo sum" – "I think, and can therefore conclude that I am" (1637). With this statement, he asserted that the source of knowledge rested within the mind (*ratio*) of the individual.[10] This implied a self-sufficient, and competent I, capable of initiating and conducting well-reasoned thought. Through introspection the individual was able to gain knowledge and control over his own mind, and consequently over the external world, including his own body. The emphasis on the powers of the *ratio*, or *cogito*, echoed earlier humanist writings, but it was Descartes' account that contributed to a new western standard for defining individuality. If people had to answer who they were, they would now seek that answer in their own, rational minds.

Locke added another element to individualism, by conceptualizing the mind as a *tabula rasa*, that is, a blank slate. In the life course, Locke argued, this slate would be filled by the accumulation of learning experiences. This meant that "individuality" was permanently in the (re)making: new experiences led to new inscriptions on the "slate" of mind. On the one hand, this social construction of mind came with feelings of insecurity, because traditional identities waned, and citizens could no longer rely on having an immortal soul as a determinant of who they were. On the other hand, (re)construction contributed to individual freedom. The rational powers of "mind" enabled individuals to reflect on what they had experienced, and who they were as persons.[11]

The seventeenth-century philosophical notions about rationality and individuality were formulated in a general climate of "disenchantment." Galileo's conflict with the Church in 1633, and Newton's publication of a radical, mechanistic world view (1687) underlined the fact that, as explanations of nature, magic and religion were beginning to lose ground in favor of science.[12]

1.3 Enlightenment and Romanticism (c. 1700–1800)

In contemporary terminology we could characterize the eighteenth century as the era in which philosophy and science were popularized on an unprecedented scale. In philosophy, the secular way of thinking about the human individual reached its provisional completion in the Enlightenment. A secular intelligentsia of scientists and philosophers was now large enough and powerful enough to challenge the clergy, and promote widely its scientific and mechanistic account of nature.[13]

Faith in the powers of reason was voiced in a type of publication that became very popular in this century: the encyclopedia. In England, Chambers published his *Cyclopaedia* in 1728, but real fame for the genre came a little later with the French *Encyclopédie* (1751–1765) edited by Diderot in collaboration with D'Alembert. The *Encyclopédie*, and other examples such as the *Encyclopaedia Britannica* (Edinburgh, 1768–1771), offered the educated public a systematic survey of practical knowledge and thus were important instruments in convincing the readership of the capacities of the rational mind.

The emphasis on rationality was countered by a diversity of tendencies that can be subsumed in retrospect under the banner of Romanticism. In eighteenth-century France, for example, in cultivated circles the necessity of *sensibilité* was stressed, partly in reaction to the alienating aspects of rationality. People were urged to express their feelings, and be sympathetic to each other.[14] The French philosopher and pedagogue Rousseau appealed to this cult of sensibility with his vivid accounts of his own feelings and those of his protagonists. He deliberately propagated the notion of the nobility and depth of the lives of "uncivilized" individuals, such as savages and little children. French Romanticism temporarily lost its hold as a result of the Revolution in 1789, which favored rationality over emotionality. However, it resurfaced around 1800, both in France and elsewhere.

The eighteenth-century interest in individuality was also expressed in the considerable popularity of *physiognomy*, the science and art of inferring capacities and character from the outward appearance of individuals. In the late 1870s, the Swiss clergyman Lavater published his four volumes of *Physiognomische Fragmente*, which attained a wide readership. His books were illustrated with engravings of famous contemporaries whose faces provided ideal models of a particular character. The practical nature of physiognomy contributed to a general awareness about individual differences, and the way in which inner feelings could be read from facial display.[15]

1.4 Conclusion

In western culture, the societal and cultural focus gradually began to shift from the collective to the individual from the late fourteenth century onward. This happened first in the powerful elites, and then spread to wider educated and cultivated circles. Common practices of religious self-exploration and rational self-reflection in Humanism and seventeenth-century philosophy were important for the creation of notions of individuality. Romanticism added an important dimension: a growing part of the population now linked their individuality to an inner domain of feelings, and came to experience their interior as having *depth*. Thus, the stage was set for the further rise of individualism in the centuries to come.[16]

2   Toward "modern" society (*c.* 1775–1920)

In the nineteenth century, individualizing tendencies that had previously emerged were further intensified. "Traditional" society with its emphasis on the family and the village was gradually replaced by a "modern" society that emphasized the individual rather than the collective. In this section we will document this transition by discussing the rapid, if not revolutionary, transformations in demography, industry, and politics, and also in religion, philosophy, and the sciences.

Demography. Agricultural reform in the eighteenth century resulted in a decrease in crop failures, and an increase in produce. A larger number of people could be fed properly, so fewer people died of hunger and disease. There was a steady growth in population, and in the nineteenth century this was further assisted by better hygiene and the prevention of contagious diseases. Between 1750 and 1900, the European population increased from about 140 to 420 million souls. Population growth was most clearly discernible in the cities. In England, for example, in 1800 there were 106 cities with more than 5000 inhabitants; by the end of the century, there were 622. The social mobility toward the cities is illustrated by the fact that by 1850 half of the British population lived in cities. Germany reached this degree of urbanization at around 1900, and France only in 1930. Urbanization in the United States was characterized by the contrast between giant metropolises of more than a million citizens, on the east coast (New York) and in the midwest (Chicago), and a thinly populated, vast countryside.

From the middle of the eighteenth century, most of the people who migrated to the city did so in order to find work in trade, commerce, or industry. People from different backgrounds lived together in overcrowded dwellings because they could not afford anything else. Many were uprooted, because the ties with their original community were cut. The conditions in the slums at the urban periphery contrasted sharply with the inner city districts (see figure 2). The center of the city was the domain of the middle classes, or *bourgeoisie*. Many had their roots in civic urban life, because their families had been part of the urban elite of administrators and professionals. The lower middle classes, for example shopkeepers, had smaller financial resources, but most of them were able to cope successfully with the demands of daily life.[17]

Industry. The industrial mode of production grew steadily in the nineteenth century. In the first decades, Great Britain kept the leading position it had attained in the eighteenth century through its pioneering role in the mechanization of production and the use of steam-power. Cotton and iron were the most important new industrial products. In the later decades, British industries lost their leading position to German and North American manufacturers, especially in new fields such as the chemical industry. As a result of industrial expansion, wealth increased between the

Figure 2 London, *c.* 1870, an engraving by Gustave Doré, showing monumental buildings side by side with humble lodgings. Industrialization and urbanization changed both the physical and the social landscape. Source: G. Doré and B. Jerrold (1872), *London: a pilgrimage* (London).

early 1800s and 1914. At the same time, social inequality also became greater, especially in the United States where the wealth of a Carnegie or a Vanderbilt was beyond all comparison with the meager wage of a laborer. At all layers of society, people had to cope with the insecurities of nineteenth-century capitalism. Economic "booms" coexisted with crises. The mid-century prosperity ended abruptly with the *krach* of 1873. The effects of the following economic downturn were felt across the whole world, thus underlining the new status of capitalism as a global enterprise. Trade between the western powers and their colonies had boomed from about 1850 onward, but it remained very unbalanced. In almost all cases, it was one-way traffic, with colonies supplying raw materials such as mineral oil and rubber at low prices to western industries.

Politics. The emerging middle class manifested itself as an important political agent in the nineteenth century. It continued the program of the civil political revolutions in the United States of America (1776) and France (1789). There, the traditional power of the aristocracy and clergy had been broken, to the benefit of the middle class. Bourgeois politics in the nineteenth century was generally characterized by liberal individualism. It held that the nation's inhabitants enjoyed their political rights and duties as individuals, rather than as groups or corporations. Middle-class citizens agitated against the class voting system, because they aspired to a political position that would match their economic power. Their claims for the vote were successful in the long run. Political participation did not mean, however, that the middle classes had enough power to control the state. In many European states, the largely conservative aristocracy held a strong base in parliament well into the twentieth century.

Secularization and scientification. Perhaps less visible, but at least as important as the changes discussed above, were transformations within the ideational realm. Religion gradually lost its place as the principal frame of reference, in favor of a secularized and scientific world-view. In everyday life, religious institutions remained important agents, and political authorities continued to refer to religious values and to the church as the bearer of moral authority. However, the position of religion and church as the ultimate authority was no longer self-evident. In former times, even the work of philosophical and scientific dissenters such as Newton and Descartes had been imbued with a religious spirit. In contrast, the nineteenth century saw the emergence of wholly secularized systems of thought, which augmented the spirit of the Enlightenment; religious elements were minimalized or even explicitly shunned.

One of the earliest expressions of systematic secular and scientific thought was *positivism*, developed in the 1830s by the French philosopher Auguste Comte. According to Comte, the religious world-view reflected a primitive state of social evolution, which was to be superseded by scientific analysis, not only in the realm of the natural sciences, but also with respect to social phenomena. This resulted in his proclamation of a science of society or *sociologie*, which would replace both religion and political philosophy and provide the basis for political stability. In Comte's own words: "In political philosophy from now on there can be no order or agreement possible, except by subjecting social phenomena, like all other phenomena, to invariable natural laws that will limit in each epoch . . . the extent and character of political action."[18]

Comte's ideas rapidly lost influence when he elaborated them into a kind of secular religion, with a church-like hierarchical power structure of its own. However, the general idea of a scientific analysis of social life quickly took root. It found its most forceful expression in a theory which was developed in the 1850s by the English philosopher Herbert Spencer. The starting point for Spencer's philosophy was social conflict, which he considered a prerequisite for progress. He argued that social living was hampered by scarcity. Therefore, people had to struggle for resources, and came into conflict with each other. In this struggle for life, only those individuals would survive who were well adjusted to their environment.

Spencer's account received a forceful impetus from the publication of Darwin's theory of evolution (1859), which apparently corroborated his analysis. As *social darwinism*, it became the favored ideology of the upper strata of society, who understood "survival of the fittest" as a moral principle, which legitimized both social order in general and their own privileged social position. Moreover, it served as an important argument against social reform, which stood in the way of progress because it was at odds with the driving force of progress, "survival of the fittest."[19]

If social darwinism provided a scientific legitimation of the existing social order, social protest also came to be based on a scientific footing, with the work of the philosopher Karl Marx. Fulminating against morally inspired proposals for social reform ("utopian socialism"), in *Das Kapital* (1867) Marx elaborated a scientific theory of society which aimed to demonstrate both the transitional nature of capitalism and the inevitability of its eventual supplanting by a new social order. As *scientific socialism* this theory would develop into a powerful source of inspiration for the labor movement and others advocating social change.

3   Individualization (*c.* 1800–1900)

The social transformations of the nineteenth century gradually brought the individual citizen to the fore in, for example, politics and production, but also in science and education. Middle-class citizens in particular focused increasingly on their individual being, rather than on the groups to which they belonged. From now on, public discourse about one's societal position emphasized individual accomplishments and personal characteristics. Group membership and birth status largely lost the determining power they had held in traditional society. Generally speaking, individualism opened up possibilities for those who had been constrained by the traditional frames of church and community. On the other hand, it also contributed to feelings of insecurity, in particular in people who felt uprooted and alienated in the course of the rapid social changes.

In the middle classes, the private world of the family became a refuge from public life. The sense of *privacy* acquired prestige, and thus the middle-class "home" was screened from interference from outside. The family was seen as a "haven in a heartless world" where intimate feelings could be expressed freely. In the public world of work and business, intimate expressions were avoided because they were understood as a sign of weakness.[20] The separation of public and private spheres was connected with a rather strict division of labor between the sexes. Men went out to work and the private world of reproduction was the domain of women. It was generally considered improper for a lady to work. Her children were taken care of by a wet-nurse, and the household tasks were done by domestic servants if the family could afford it.

3.1   Mapping individual differences

The societal changes of the nineteenth century and the concomitant ideologies of liberalism and social darwinism emphasized the relative success of individuals. In all social layers it was hard to ignore the fact that some individuals were better competitors than others. When the winner's demographic and economic background could not account for his success, a different explanation was needed, focusing on mental characteristics. The growing fascination with mental differences was exemplified by the tremendous popularity of phrenology: the science of inferring mental characteristics from the shape of the skull. Phrenology was developed around 1800 by the Viennese neuroanatomist Gall. He was able to convince large audiences across Europe of the scientific benefits of phrenology. However, it was in the United States that phrenology had a sweeping breakthrough, and in the second half of the century it became big business. This was largely the result of initiatives by the Fowler family (see figure 3), who opened consulting firms, published popular accounts, and sold china busts of the skull with the sites of the faculties marked on them. Despite the fact that the credibility of phrenology sank under the weight of neurological counterevidence, it continued for a long time to enjoy the confidence of large sections of the public. The New York Institute of Phrenology, for example, remained in business until 1912.[21]

In Europe, French *craniométrie* gained a reputation in the 1860s. Broca claimed in 1861 that the volume of the brain predicted the magnitude of the individual's intellectual capacities. He theorized that eminent men had large brains, and that the small brains of women and "savages" accounted for their intellectual inferiority. Craniometry was discussed extensively in the press which undoubtedly contributed to its popularity. The public imagination was however really seized when Lombroso's *L'uomo delinquente* (*Delinquent man*, 1876) became accessible across Europe and the United States. Although Lombroso discussed in detail the social and psychological causes of delinquency, his theory of the born criminal and the physiognomic indications of criminality were remembered better.[22]

There were of course many other ways in which nineteenth-century individuals sought to determine their own unique qualities. The tendency to identify with the pursuit of individual, material well-being was particularly strong in the United States. Practical guides like, for example, *Dollars and sense, or how to get on* (1890), and *The keys to success* (1898) instructed the public on how to reach the top. These success manuals attracted a large readership, in particular among the lower middle class. Obviously, they believed in the liberal ideology of success, although their economic position was generally far from fortunate.[23]

The interest in individuality also manifested itself at quite a different level. Feelings were increasingly seen as the foremost source of individuality. As a direct sequel to the Romantic reaction against the rationalism of the Enlightenment in the late eighteenth century, the focus on feelings found a powerful expression in nineteenth-century Romantic art. For example, Coleridge, Shelley, and Wordsworth articulated unprecedented sensibilities in their poetry. Outside poetry and art, a large segment of the public was increasingly preoccupied with the inner world of feelings. Many assumed that feelings originated in a "deep interior" that lay beneath a thin layer of conscious reason. Rationality came under suspicion. Some held that it was nothing but an artificial mask that tried to cover what really mattered "inside": emotions as the source of an authentic self. Many were engaged in sensitive self-scrutiny, for example by writing diaries, autobiographies, and poetry.[24]

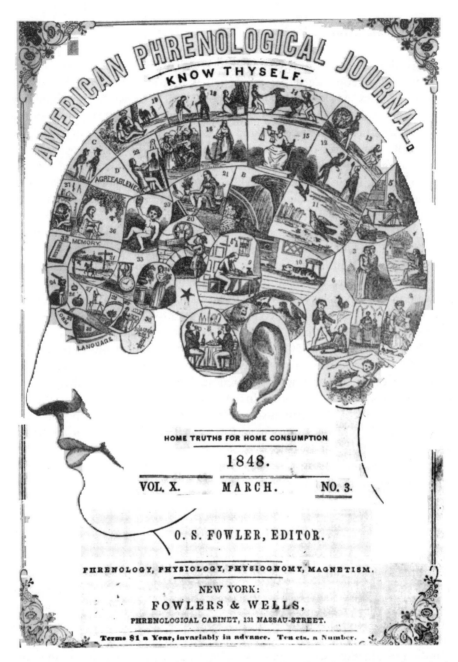

Figure 3 *Know thyself: home truths for home consumption.* Frontispiece of a phrenological journal (1848), illustrating the location of the 37 "organs of the mind." Source: Psychology Pictures.

3.2   *Conclusion*

In the last decades of the nineteenth century, individualistic values were embraced widely in society. People were keen to assess their individuality, and understood their personal emotions as a defining characteristic of their "selves." The popularity of individualism could not, however, hide its problematic nature. "The individual" was in fact a rather strictly circumscribed kind of person. The first feature of the individual was a middle-class background. Members of the lower strata were approached as a different category of persons, and their way of life was generally viewed with suspicion. The second feature of the nineteenth-century individual was masculine gender. This was particularly noticeable with respect to the rationality that was attributed to individuals. Men were assumed to be rational and women emotional, if not irrational. This stereotype was further supported by the sexual division of labor in middle-class families, and had consequences beyond the private domain: female emotionality was an important argument for withholding the vote from women and for denying them admission to university.[25] Finally, "the individual" had a white skin, and the differences of non-white peoples were readily translated into a judgment of inferiority. The colonial rulers proudly expressed confidence in their own race. In Great Britain, for example, at the end of the century it was applauded that some 6000 British officials successfully governed about 300 million people on the Indian subcontinent.[26]

The obvious differences between individuals from the white, male middle class and people from other backgrounds prompted an interest in those "others" at home (women and workers) and abroad (colonial subjects). The questions about the others' nature were often coupled with anxieties about what they were up to. The demonstrations and strikes of the labor movement, as well as the marches of the feminists, provoked fear among the middle-class elite. It stimulated the development of new forms of social management as a means to regulate, if not control, the behavior of the uncomprehended other(s).

4   Social management (*c.* 1800–1900)

"Modern" society in the nineteenth century not only generated new forms and conceptions of individuality. It also witnessed a dramatic expansion of attempts to monitor and control the populace or, as we earlier defined it, of social management. Next to individualization, this was a second major development which would prove to be crucial as a breeding ground for the social sciences in general, and psychology in particular.

In the Introduction, we presented social management as all planned and systematic attempts to influence and control human behavior. As we observed, this is by no means a typically "modern" phenomenon: no society can exist without some form of organization and some form of control, however rudimentary, over the behavior of its members. This certainly holds for early western society, with its relatively elaborate systems of, for instance, justice, religion, and politics. However, the nineteenth century witnessed both a marked increase in social management practices, and a gradual shift in underlying motives, organization, and methods employed.

First, we will briefly review some major manifestations of nineteenth-century social management. After that, we will discuss some characteristic changes that took place, in motives, organization, and method.

4.1 Practices

In the course of the nineteenth century, the scope of social management increased dramatically. Changing economic and social conditions began to demand an ever greater degree of social organization and regulation, varying from urban planning to institutionalized forms of health care, education, and care and guidance for all those not meeting the requirements of "modern life." Sometimes, these initiatives were primarily inspired by humane motives, sometimes by concerns about social stability or even by downright fear of social unrest and revolution.

Many of the practices that evolved will be discussed in detail in subsequent chapters. Here, we will confine ourselves to a short discussion of some of the major manifestations.

Education. The traditional situation of the schools changed rather drastically in the nineteenth century. In the previous centuries, schooling had been the prerogative of the clergy. In the seventeenth century, local elites appeared on the scene, particularly in the towns: influential citizens organized a basic kind of schooling for an expanding number of pupils. In the nineteenth century, two changes stand out: the Church lost influence to secular authorities, and a national curriculum came to replace the patchwork of local programs. All children were taught reading, writing, and arithmetic. Often, the ambitions of the curriculum went beyond these basics. History and geography lessons, for example, were meant to instruct pupils in national values. General primary education was profitable for industry. Technical changes required literate workers who could read the directions for using machines, and comprehend the complexities of the production process. In addition, schooling was seen often as an instrument to regulate the social order, especially where neglected children were assumed to be potential criminals (see chapter 2). By the end of the century, most countries had passed laws on compulsory education. Now, all children were legally obliged to attend school.[27]

Poor relief. For centuries, Christian charity had inspired the clergy and wealthy believers to take care of the poor, disabled, and ill. From the sixteenth century onwards, poor relief was expanded. Town councils and societies of citizens established communal almshouses as a kind of institutional support. From the late eighteenth century, groups of "enlightened" middle-class individuals engaged in philanthropic support. They were convinced that a large part of the working class suffered from serious social handicaps and would not be able to gain a solid position in society. As the century progressed, relief was increasingly combined with attempts to "educate" and "civilize." Support was individualized which meant that a poor individual or family was first scrutinized in order to determine whether they were decent enough to receive help and whether they would be able to support themselves in the future. The examples of philanthropic societies in Britain and the Netherlands showed that the poor had to comply with the norms of the philanthropists. In the 1890s, for example, the British Charity Organization Society deliberately expressed a bourgeois "evangelism" in order to transform the habits of the working class.[28]

Exclusion. With social organization becoming more complex, the room for deviance gradually shrank. In earlier days, the number of people considered "deviant" was limited. Many were cared for by the community, and only if they were considered dangerous were they locked away, mostly in prisons. Only a few cities had a custodial institution for socially deviant people, in particular for the mentally disturbed. Bedlam in London and the Bicêtre in Paris were notorious examples of such lunatic asylums. From the beginning of the nineteenth century, the number of asylums rose sharply, on both sides of the Atlantic. These new institutions were in most cases the result of private initiatives, although the state attained a prominent pioneering role in Germany. The psychiatric asylums were overcrowded in the course of the century. Actual psychiatric treatment was not very successful: many people were confined to mental hospitals, few were released.[29]

Institutionalized care of children also intensified in the nineteenth century. Institutions for children were not a new phenomenon, of course: examples of orphanages dated back as far as the late middle ages. However, from the 1830s onward custodial care was expanded and came to include new classes of dependent children, such as, for example, the handicapped, and the disturbed, but also "street children," and young delinquents. The focus on delinquents was partly due to new regulations, which resulted in separate treatment for juveniles: rather than being sent to prison, these young offenders had to be re-educated. Finally, the increasing standardization of education generated its own kinds of deviants: those children who for one reason or another could not meet the requirements of the regular curriculum.

Hygienism. Christian reform and philanthropy were forerunners of a wide range of activities that came to be known as "hygienism." The cholera epidemics which spread after the 1830s confronted everyone with the consequences of the urban concentration of people (see figure 4). In medical circles, a debate unfolded about the cause of epidemics. The "contagionists" held that diseases were passed on from individual to individual, the defenders of the "miasma theory" argued, by contrast, that the emanations from excrement, dirt, and filthy water were the primary cause. Both positions were translated into practical proposals. Contagionists published a steady stream of brochures in which the public were persuaded to change their ordinary habits, for example, to wash their clothes regularly, and clean their hands and bodies with water and soap. Miasma theorists embraced the proposal of the British reformer Chadwick to build fresh water supplies and sewer systems in the overcrowded cities. From the end of the 1840s, miasma theory was put into practice. Local authorities started expensive infrastructural operations to supply cities with the basic sanitary services of running water, and sewage and rubbish disposal.[30] The so-called hygienic "offensive" successfully addressed the population at large, thus reaching a wider range of people than philanthropic efforts. The hygienists directed their advice both to their fellow

Figure 4   *A court for King Cholera.* Engraving by John Leech (*c.* 1855–60), reflecting the growing influence of "hygienistic" ideas about the link between sanitation and disease. Source: J. Leech (1864), *Later pencillings from Punch.*

citizens in the middle classes and to the masses in the lower social strata. Contagious diseases, it was argued, were very democratic: they were not hindered at all by the invisible border between social classes.

Social security. The new forms of social management were generally products of private initiative and local authorities. National governments generally confined their role to the establishment of a juridical frame for the regulation of behavior. In the later decades of the century, legislative activity intensified. In a climate of revolts and political agitation, legislation was initiated that aimed to protect citizens against the exploitations of capitalism. Child protection legislation, for example, was passed in most countries. In addition, many governments followed the example of the German *Reich* that had installed national social insurance in the 1880s. On the eve of the First World War, almost all European countries had provided national and compulsory insurance against illness, accidents, and old age. Child labor was forbidden, and children were legally obliged to attend school for about six years. The American situation was different. For decades to come, the US government consistently adhered to the liberal idea of the state as a "night-watchman," and so federal social legislation was postponed. American society was generally more reluctant to accept an active role for the government. In due course, however, many of the European examples were followed, especially in the industrialized midwest and east coast.

Eugenics. Launched in 1883 by the English scholar Francis Galton, eugenics took biological endowment as the key to improving society. Galton derived the word "eugenics" from a Greek root meaning "good in birth." Inspired by darwinism, Galton held that both mental and physical characteristics were to a great extent – if not exclusively – inherited. From this viewpoint, he proposed the design of selective programs of marriage and reproduction, analogous to the breeding of, for example, racehorses. After 1900, this idea would find a wide audience, especially in England and the United States. British eugenicists generally confined themselves to so-called "positive eugenics" which aimed at more prolific breeding among those of excellent stock. American eugenicists propagated in addition "negative eugenics," that is, preventing the procreation of what they considered to be "unfit" individuals. They supported the establishment of sterilization laws that aimed at, in the words of the Iowa law (1913), "the prevention of the procreation of criminals, rapists, idiots, feeble-minded, imbeciles, lunatics, drunkards, drug fiends, epileptics, syphilitics, moral and sexual perverts, and diseased and degenerate persons."[31] Eugenicists also campaigned for immigration restriction. They argued that intermarriages of "superior" Nordic individuals with "inferior" ones from the Mediterranean and eastern parts of Europe would seriously damage the quality of the "American race."[32]

4.2   New characteristics

The extension of social management practices was not just "more of the same." It went hand in hand with some major changes with respect to its nature. These can be summarized under three headings: governmentalization, individualization, and scientification.

Governmentalization. Philanthropists, hygienists, eugenicists, and other social reformers were largely responsible for the increase in social management during the nineteenth century. In the second part of the century, the private initiatives of "enlightened" citizens were often backed by the state, as we have seen for example in the case of education, social legislation, and eugenic laws. In the last decades, private forms of social management were gradually incorporated into national government initiatives. From that time, social management became an instrument in national politics. Some attempts at behavior regulation were aimed at the population at large, as was the case, for example, in education, health care, and urban planning. Other attempts, such as social work, were directed toward specific groups. In western Europe, the state would finally outstrip private initiatives of social management, thus laying the foundation for what would become known as the "welfare state."

Individualization. As the century progressed, schemes of social management became increasingly individualized. The changing modes of poor relief are a case in point: material help was increasingly combined with detailed scrutiny of the lifestyle of those in need, and attempts to "civilize" and "re-educate." A similar trend was visible in other domains. With respect to psychiatric patients and delinquent or pre-delinquent children, mere exclusion was increasingly replaced by ideals and practices of "treatment" or "re-education," entailing detailed scrutiny of individual "cases." And within education, detailed recording of individual pupils' achievements became standard practice.

Science. The links between social management and (social) science also gradually intensified. As we have seen, in the 1840s, with his "sociologie," Comte pioneered a science devoted explicitly to societal issues. Demography was another example of a new science concerned with social issues: statistics about, for example, birth rate, marriage and occupations were crucial for a rational analysis of society. By the end of the century, various domains of social management could rely on a specific scientific contribution. Education, for example, could benefit from pedagogy, regulation of disturbed behavior from psychiatry, and the tracing of deviant behavior could benefit from criminology. At the turn of the century, the expansion of social management became an important factor in the further development of interventionist sciences, psychology included.

American "Progressivism" was an important example of the articulate translation of scientific ideas into proposals for social reform. The philosophy of pragmatism was the major source of inspiration for the Progressives. William James and John Dewey developed this truly American philosophy in the last decade of the century. They shunned philosophical debate about the nature of truth and knowledge, and claimed quite bluntly that ordinary practice was the final criterion: "true is what works." A "Progressive Movement" emerged that based its practices of social management on pragmatist ideas. The Progressives propagated, for example, school reform, and they also established "settlement houses" in the slums in an attempt to ameliorate living conditions. When Theodore Roosevelt became president in 1901 the Progressive program was turned into official politics. The Progressive Era ended on the eve of the First World War.

4.3 Conclusion

In the course of the nineteenth century, the new and reconstructed forms of social management were targeted eventually at the entire population. Rather than brute imposition of social order or religiously inspired charity, social management became infused with notions of rational, scientific social planning. From now on, every individual, irrespective of his or her position, could in principle be advised, observed, registered, and compared with other individuals. This expansion did not, however, change the power structure behind social management. Often, dependent citizens from the lower strata were subjected to the directives of middle-class professionals. When the social distance between the professionals and their "subjects" was large, subjects had to comply with the norms of social management. The societal elite, by contrast, received advice rather than directives.

5 Psychology (*c.* 1880–1910)

Academic psychology was developed and institutionalized in the last decades of the nineteenth century. The systematic reflection on individuals and their consciousness, however, had a far longer history in western thought. All kinds of "psychologies" had been developed in the preceding centuries. Often, psychological notions were part of philosophy, inside and outside the universities. The eighteenth-century *Encyclopédie*, for example, had an entry "Psychologie" in which it was defined as the part of philosophy that teaches all we can know about the human soul.[33] In the nineteenth century a number of monographs and textbooks appeared with "psychology" in the title. Herbart, for example, proposed in his influential *Psychologie als Wissenschaft* ("Psychology as Science," 1824–5) a formal system of "mental dynamics" with the inclusion of perception, thinking, feeling, and volition. Spencer's *The principles of psychology* (1855) also reached a large audience. He took issue with the notion of the *tabula rasa*, by emphasizing hereditary determination. Both books (and many others) addressed "psychological" topics a couple of decades before psychology had taken root as an academic discipline at the universities.

Around 1850, the study of mental processes became an issue within Dutch and German physiology. Donders, Helmholtz, and Fechner initiated laboratory research on the topic, and in his experimental papers of 1850–52, Helmholtz demonstrated that it took time for an impulse to travel through a nerve. For him and his fellow physiologists, this meant that mental processes could be measured quantitatively. A decade later, Fechner coined "psychophysics" as a branch of science dedicated to the study of the relation between physical and mental phenomena. The future of psychological research seemed to be linked to the discipline of physiology, until Wilhelm Wundt appeared on the scene.

5.1   A new discipline

In 1879 Wilhelm Wundt established in Leipzig the first psychological laboratory of the world. In the positivist climate of the nineteenth century, a laboratory conferred the status of a genuine science to an academic discipline. Consequently, Wundt came to be seen as the "founding father" of academic psychology (see figure 5).[34]

Wundt's establishment of a psychological laboratory was not an impulsive act. In his *Grundzüge der physiologischen Psychologie* ("Foundations of physiological psychology") of 1873–4 he already had made a case for psychology as an independent science. Psychology should be dedicated to the *empirical* study of mind, or rather *Bewußtsein* (consciousness), and should therefore distance itself from both philosophy (which was not empirical) and physiology (which did not center on consciousness). Wundt's scientific program and his laboratory attracted students and scholars from Germany and abroad. Many researchers followed his example and opened research facilities at home. In 1890 there were fifteen psychological laboratories, in 1900 about sixty. Most were based in Germany and the United States. Laboratories were also opened in, for example, France, Italy, the Netherlands, Russia, and even Japan.

A number of other initiatives contributed to psychology's status as a truly academic discipline, including the founding of scientific journals about psychology. In Germany *Philosophische Studien* ("Philosophical Studies"), founded by Wundt in 1881, first appeared, and the *Zeitschrift für Psychologie und Physiologie der*

Figure 5   The first psychological laboratory: Wilhelm Wundt (*sitting*), surrounded by some of his students. Source: Psychology Pictures/Archives of Dutch Psychology.

Sinnesorganen ("Journal for the Psychology and Physiology of the Sense Organs") in 1890. Across the Atlantic, the *American Journal of Psychology* (in 1887), and the *Psychological Review* (founded in 1894) were published. The new field expanded its institutional base by means of scientific societies such as the American Psychological Association, which was established in 1892, and the Deutsche Gesellschaft für Psychologie (Society for Psychology), founded in 1904.[35] Scientific congresses also testified to the foundation and expansion of psychology. The first international congress for psychophysiology in 1889 attracted about thirty participants; ten years later the first international congress of psychology hosted about 500 delegates, mainly from Germany, the United States, and France. A final indication of the establishment of psychology was the publication of introductory textbooks such as Külpe's *Grundriss der Psychologie* ("Principles of psychology") in 1893, and James' *Principles of psychology* in 1890.

From its inception, psychology was characterized by theoretical diversity and argument between opposing views. The self-acclaimed "psychologists" of the nineteenth century came from very different backgrounds. Some had been trained as natural scientists, and embraced a positivist, quantitative philosophy of science. Others felt inspired by German phenomenology and defended an interpretative approach. Positivist ideals were clearly discernible in Wundt's experimental program. Empirical research in the laboratory would unfold the universal laws of mental functioning, on which general theories of the human mind could be built. However, the structural focus of Wundtian psychology soon ran into discord with the functional approach of American psychologists. Functionalism was an important step toward the behaviorism that came to dominate American psychology from the 1920s onwards.

Outside the universities, the Viennese *nervenartzt* (neurologist) Sigmund Freud developed one of the most influential psychologies ever: psychoanalysis. Like Wundt, Freud aimed at the discovery of the universal laws of the psyche, but his trajectory was radically different from the one followed in academic psychology. From about 1890, Freud combined therapeutic work in his private practice with the construction of theory. This enabled him to use interpretative analyses of the material provided by his patients, for example when they talked about their dreams, in the development of his psychoanalytic theory.[36] With regard to theory, Freud also followed a course of his own, countering the Wundtian emphasis on consciousness with a concern with unconscious processes.

5.2 *Practical psychology*

According to its founder, Wilhelm Wundt, psychology was first and foremost an academic, theoretical enterprise. Many of his colleagues were of a different opinion. The idea of the study of the human mind neatly fitted with both the growing prominence of individuality and the attempts to systematize practices of social intervention. From the early 1890s onwards, the new discipline was brought to bear on an almost limitless variety of social domains and problems: education and child-rearing (Stanley Hall, 1891), sex differences (Havelock Ellis, 1892), politics (Le Bon, 1895), witness testimony (Cattell, 1895), psychiatric diagnosis (Kraepelin, 1896), anthropology (Rivers, 1898), religion (James, 1902), and even economics (Tarde, 1904). Within years, "psychology" became a household word among the intellectual elites, as well as professionals working in various domains of social management. In 1903, the first journal was published which was exclusively dedicated to "applied psychology." This was *Psychologie der Aussage* ("Psychology of Testimony"), renamed *Zeitschrift für angewandte Psychologie* ("Journal of Applied Psychology") three years later. In another three years, the Dutch psychologist Heymans would confidently express his belief in a future "century of psychology": if nineteenth-century science had brought technological advance and prosperity, so psychology would prove to be the key to what mattered most, that is, happiness and peace of mind.[37]

Apart from referring to "psychology" or "the new psychology," all these attempts originally had little in common. Although Wundt's ground-breaking work was frequently mentioned, few of the attempts at "application" actually made use of his theoretical concepts or empirical results. Even more than academic psychology itself, the practical manifestations represented a wide range of methods and theoretical concepts. To a great extent, this reflected the widely varying background of its main advocates: some were trained as psychologists, but the majority of them primarily identified with other disciplines, such as sociology, criminology, psychiatry, and pedagogy. Late nineteenth-century practical psychology was a thoroughly interdisciplinary affair, with its advocates and practitioners sharing little more than the conviction that the study of the human mind held the key to many of society's problems.

5.3 *Psychology as a profession*

If early practical psychology was predominantly an interdisciplinary affair, as early as the mid-1890s the contours had begun to emerge of the more clearly defined expertise of the professional psychologist. The starting point of this development is generally located to 1896, when the American psychologist Lightner Witmer started a psychological clinic for the diagnosis and treatment of children with learning difficulties. However, it was only after 1900 that the new profession began to take shape. An important impetus was the development of a specialized form of expertise, which distinguished the new profession from other disciplines – psychological testing.

Whereas academic psychology concentrated on the human mind in general, psychological testing emanated from attempts to map out individual differences. Originally the domain of physiognomists and phrenologists, this theme had in the 1870s and 1880s received a new impetus from the work of the British *homo universalis*, Francis Galton, whom we have previously encountered as the founding father of eugenics (see section 4). Just as in eugenics, Galton's interest in individual differences stemmed from his fascination with Darwin's theory of evolution. Galton reasoned that if evolution proceeded by variation and selection, then it was of the utmost importance to develop the means by which to measure human variability. In 1884 this resulted in the establishment of the Anthropometric Laboratory, at the International Health Exhibition in London, which later transferred to the South Kensington Museum in London where it was to remain for six years (see figure 6). Unlike phrenologists and physiognomists, Galton was interested in human functions, rather than bodily appearance. For his laboratory, he devised equipment for monitoring no fewer than 17 different physical and mental capacities, including breathing power, strength of pull and squeeze, quickness of blow, hearing, seeing, and colour sense.[38]

Galton's work received wide attention, among both the lay public and psychologists. In all, more than 9000 persons subjected themselves to examination at the laboratory. Inspired by this success, the American psychologist McKeen Cattell in 1890 proposed to elaborate upon Galton's work, concentrating on mental capacities. This resulted in a more limited series of ten measurements, as well as the introduction of a concept which would become the hallmark of professional psychology: *mental* or *psychological testing*.

Though attracting wide interest, Cattell's efforts were not very successful at first. Of the various tests he and others devised, virtually none proved to be of much practical value. The same held for attempts to transform psychological apparatus developed in the Wundtian tradition of research on human consciousness into instruments for measuring individual differences. Nevertheless, many psychologists remained convinced that the notion of individual differences and their measurement held the key to the successful application of psychology. In 1905, this finally resulted in the invention of an instrument, which would become a symbol of psychological expertise for decades to come: the intelligence test, devised by the French psychologist Alfred Binet and his co-worker Theodore Simon.

Originally devised for the rather restricted purpose of screening children suspected of feeble-mindedness, the test quickly found its way into other areas of practice.

Figure 6   Francis Galton's Anthropometric Laboratory at the International Health Exhibition, London, 1884. Source: Psychology Pictures/Archives of Dutch Psychology.

Together with other types of tests developed in subsequent years, it provided the basis for the evolution of a distinct professional identity for practicing psychologists, as experts in diagnosis and mental measurement. This provided the basis for them to gain access to a wide variety of societal practices (see figure 7).

5.4   *Conclusion*

In the later decades of the nineteenth century, psychology took root in the fertile ground of western, individualistic society. The new science of the individual was in keeping with earlier attempts to theorize about and measure individuality, for example phrenology, but its contribution was more diverse. The earliest decades of psychology show its development, from its very inception, as a *practical science*. The close links between theorizing and practical intervention were highlighted by the work of Galton and Binet. Psychoanalysis was another instance of cross-fertilization between theory and practice. Freud's work held a special position, however, because it was developed outside a university context. The non-academic nature of its base did not impair its influence: psychoanalysis became one of the most famous psychological theories.

Figure 7 A psychologist administering an intelligence test, the Netherlands, *c*. 1930s. As the hallmark of professional expertise, psychological tests laid the foundation for the entrance of psychologists into a wide range of professional domains. Source: Psychology Pictures/Archives of Dutch Psychology.

As we saw, psychology owed much initial success to representatives of other disciplines, who quickly embraced the new science as a useful contribution to their work. It was only in the early twentieth century that psychologists managed to carve out a professional niche of their own, in psychological testing. Together with psychoanalysis, this constituted the basis of much of the expansion of psychology expansion in the decades preceding the Second World War.

6 "Psychological society" (*c.* 1920–present)

The twentieth century saw an unprecedented expansion of psychology in western countries, as well as a massive increase in social management. The closing section of this chapter sketches the emergence of a "psychological society" as the product of the interaction between individualization, social management, and the expansion of psychology.[39] Discussion here will be confined to some general trends, as background for the more detailed analyses in subsequent chapters.

6.1   *Individualization*

In the course of the twentieth century, there was an intensification of all the earlier tendencies toward individualization. Across different layers of society, the balance between the "individual" and the "collective" shifted radically toward the individual. In addition, individual differences were brought to the fore, with the measurement of individual characteristics and accomplishments becoming an integral part of societal organization. Finally, the inner world of feelings became a key aspect of social life, in the private as well as in the public domain.[40] The primacy of individualism, however, was not unchallenged. Throughout the century, the central position of the individual was contested by collectivist ideas and practices. In the first half of the century, these included communism and national socialism. After 1945 there was the appeal of various kinds of nationalism, although they never undermined the individualistic nature of western society.[41]

The prominence of individualism coincided with a gradual expansion of the middle class. The sharp distinctions between the various social classes blurred and individual social mobility increased, often as a result of better education. Secularization also contributed to individual mobility: in all layers of society people left the churches, and felt less constrained by religious dogma. After the Second World War, wealth increased for many. In due course, this enabled laborers to accumulate capital, for example, by purchasing private housing. In the same period, decolonialization intensified international mobility. The availability of radio, telephone, and television enabled worldwide communication, turning the world into a "global village."

Postwar social mobility inevitably led to a focus on individual differences: some people were successful, others were not. In the middle class, individual accomplishment was often expressed in a material way. Houses, automobiles, vacations, and numerous consumer goods bespoke individual wealth. In the Americas of the 1950s, this middle-class consumerism was attacked by the "beat generation," who broke with middle-class comfort and traditional family life. The "beats" voiced a rebellious mentality that was felt in wider circles on both sides of the Atlantic. The rebellion gained force in the course of the 1950s, when people increasingly started to question traditional authority in politics, as well as in family life.

The political protest movements of blacks, feminists, and students stressed individual "freedom" as an inalienable right, and challenged the authority of the white, male elite. This contributed to a gradual eradication of the barriers between the sexes and peoples of different ethnicity, albeit formally, given that in everyday life both women and non-whites still experience discrimination and unequal access to many of society's resources.

Instead of accepting the directives of superiors, the assertive citizens of the 1950s and 1960s engaged themselves in a negotiation with those in charge. This was reflected in the private domain, where the "youth culture" of the late 1950s fueled rebellion against parental authority. As some sociologists have observed: at all levels, "command" gave way to "negotiation" as the principle governing relationships between people.[42] In general, this liberated citizens from many traditional constraints, and opened new options for action. But it also generated doubt. The directives of religious and political authorities lost their cohesive power, and there were no solid anchors to replace them.

The cultural focus on the individual assumed a different quality in the 1970s. During this "me decade", emancipation was defined less and less in political terms, as people trusted that they would find the sources of liberation inside themselves. Many "turned inward" in the most literal sense when they started meditation or took psychedelic drugs. Some heralded this cultural shift as a new step toward the liberation of the individual; others considered it to be narcissism. Whatever the evaluation, the self-focus implied an increased emphasis on personal, emotional life as the ultimate reference point, rather than on wealth and social status.[43] In due course, the cultural "inward turn" weakened the distinction between the private and public domain. It became common to express personal feelings in public contexts, such as, for example, human interest journalism, and television talk shows.

6.2 Social management

Increasing individualization went hand in hand with a further expansion of arrangements and institutions for social management. Especially after the Second World War, social management practices received a strong impetus from the new concept of the "welfare state." In north-western Europe, this concept was almost universally adopted in the 1950s and 1960s. In the United States, it met with fierce opposition from conservatives who lauded the free market. Nevertheless, even there welfare provision gradually expanded, especially as part of the "unconditional war on poverty" of the Johnson administration.

The introduction of the welfare state implied an enlarged responsibility of the state and its government for the well-being of its citizens. Next to material safeguards (full employment, social insurance), health care and education, this increasingly encompassed mental well-being also. This found its clearest expression in the concept of "mental health," which quickly gained currency after the Second World War in both the United States and Europe.

Apart from the shift from private initiative to state interventionism, social management changed in other respects as well. With divisions between various social strata gradually becoming less important, corresponding divides within social management also disappeared. Many of the practices originally targeted at the lower classes expanded to encompass all citizens, irrespective of social background.

This "democratization" of social management corresponded with a gradual shift in its primary goals. Although humanitarian motives had not been totally absent from nineteenth-century social interventionism, its primary focus had been on control and discipline, guided by motives of social order rather than individual well-being. With the advent of the concept of the welfare state, emphasis shifted. "Care," rather than "control" became the dominant theme; rather than being forced upon people in the interests of social order, programs of social management were advocated as services offered to them, for the sake of their own well-being.

Partly, this shift in emphasis was rhetorical, as the motives of social order, control, and discipline did not disappear, although the promotion of individual well-being was emphasized. This is exemplified in education. On the one hand, schooling was promoted as a social right and an instrument for individual welfare, rather than as a means of social control. On the other hand, both its compulsory nature and numerous regulations regarding the curriculum reflected the persistence of many of the social functions which originally had inspired it, such as the transfer of socially relevant values.

The professionalization of social management practices which had begun in the nineteenth century continued to accelerate in the twentieth century, resulting in a tremendous expansion of the "helping professions." This was combined with a subtle but significant change in the relationship between professionals and their clientele.

On the one hand, the change from "control" to "care," and the general democratization of society resulted in a more "horizontal" relationship: the authority of doctors, social workers, teachers and the like was no longer self-evident, and clients claimed a say in what was going on. On the other hand, prospective clients learned to attune to the helping arrangements offered, a process which is termed "proto-professionalization."[44] Increasingly, they linked their problems to the various professional approaches, and took over many of their core concepts, from "health" to "school readiness," and from "mental well-being" to "maladaptive behavior."

In the consulting room, these changes were reflected in a gradual change in the techniques employed, as rather than unidirectionally imposing expert knowledge, professionals tended to redefine helping processes as a joint endeavor of expert and client. Earlier authoritarian forms of interventionism and behavior regulation were superseded by humanistic techniques of counseling and advice, characterized by cooperation between professionals and clients.

6.3   *Psychology*

As early as the mid-1920s, an American social critic observed that his country had experienced "an outbreak of psychology."[45] However, it was only after the Second World War that the discipline would really gain momentum, not only in the United States but also in Europe. From the 1950s onward, academic psychology ranked among the bigger scientific disciplines, with an appeal to students and researchers alike which has continued to grow until this very day. The development of practical psychology is even more impressive: if professional psychology had succeeded in acquiring its own niche alongside academic psychology before the war, in the postwar period it became increasingly dominant, at least quantitatively.

Partly, the expansion of practical psychology reflected processes of individualization and developments in social management. Aptitude testing, for instance, became increasingly important in schools and occupational life, due to increased social mobility and emphasis on individual merit. In the emotional realm, psychoanalysis captured the hearts and minds of both professionals and the public at large, offering new means of self-reflection and a new interpretative framework for understanding a wide range of social phenomena. From the late 1950s onward, it was joined in this area by a host of new clinically based theories, varying from humanistic psychology to transactional analysis and rational-emotive therapy, which both reflected and reinforced the "turning inward" of the late 1960s and 1970s. This was reflected in a tremendous expansion of mental health provision, which after the war became the main professional domain of psychologists.

Apart from riding the waves of individualization and the expanding activities of social management, psychologists also managed to extend the boundaries of their own professional expertise in relation to other groups of experts. Most significant in this respect was their entry into the field of psychotherapy. Primarily due to a lack of qualified medical doctors, this field opened up to psychologists during the Second World War. Postwar psychology further strengthened its position by developing new techniques of therapy and treatment. Similar developments took place in other fields, such as work and education, where psychologists managed to acquire new roles within, for instance, organizational consultancy and curriculum development.

But if the profession became more prominent, it was by no means the only agent of the growing influence of psychology on society. Perhaps as important was the gradual adoption of psychological methods and more generally, a psychologized perspective, by other professionals. Almost without exception, psychology was introduced as part of the training in the "helping" professions. In particular, the basic technique of "counseling," developed in the early 1950s by psychologist Carl Rogers, became a widely used tool among professionals of various disciplines. Focusing on the articulation of clients' needs and encouraging a supportive and advisory, rather than directing, role of professionals, it fitted perfectly with the change from an authoritarian, disciplinary style of intervention to more subtle ways of influencing behavior.

Finally, psychology also gained a prominent position in the public imagination. Movie directors such as Hitchcock and Bertolucci, as well as numerous literary authors, expressed a profound fascination with psychoanalysis in their works. In addition, the media offered an easy access to psychological analysis. In 1957, for example, the influential magazine *Life* featured a series of articles on "The age of psychology." An important step in popularization was taken in 1967 when the American periodical *Psychology Today* was first published. Many prominent psychologists used this forum to inform the general public about their research. Its success led to the publication of similar magazines in Europe. In American and European bookshops, the shelves gradually filled with pop psychology. Television further enhanced the public visibility of psychology. In the United States, Joyce Brothers hosted her own psychology show from the mid-1950s onward. Her impact was captured in the words of a contemporary observer who noted, "She not only brings the lessons of psychology, for better or worse, she *is* psychology to millions of Americans."[46]

This is not to say that everybody was happy with the way in which psychology developed. In the United States, for example, black psychologists attacked the discipline for its white, or Caucasian, biases. This finally led to the foundation of the Association of Black Psychologists in 1968. In a similar vein, feminists took issue with psychology's male bias. Naomi Weisstein argued in 1968 that psychology had nothing to say about what women were really like, what they needed, and what they wanted, because psychology simply *did not know*. Her line of argument was taken on board by American and European women who developed a feminist psychology under the banner of "women's studies."[47] In Europe, many inside and outside the student movement embraced Klaus Holzkamp's Marxist psychology as an emancipatory tool. A critical psychology could contribute to political emancipation, they argued, by its detailed analysis of the subjective conditions of existence under capitalism.[48]

Although critical of "mainstream psychology," black psychologists, feminists, and critical psychologists did not oppose the wide proliferation of psychology in western culture. On the contrary, as their initiatives suggest, they too considered psychology to be a potential ally in their political struggle. This psychologization of politics became most apparent within feminism. The feminist slogan "the personal is political" aptly expressed the idea that humanist emancipation was concerned with both the public and the private domain.

7   Conclusion

In this chapter we have sketched the psychologization of western culture against the background of a growing historical emphasis on the individual. The historical relation between psychologization and individualization has always been dialectic. On the one hand, a psychological perspective was the outcome of individualization: when the emphasis shifted from the collective to the individual, an interest in individuality emerged, which provided a fertile ground for knowledge about individual minds and behavior. On the other hand, "psychology" contributed to individualistic ideas and practices in western society. From its earliest days, the practical science of psychology provided both authorities and citizens with instruments to pin down individuality, and in particular, individual differences.

In the twentieth century, psychology gained a prominent position within social management. Professional regulation of behavior as such was far older than the science of psychology, but twentieth-century psychologists succeeded in convincing their clients and colleagues of the value of their contribution. From that time, all kinds of professionals used psychological terminologies, theories, and tests to guide, advise, and help their clients.

After 1945, the psychologization of society reached new heights as a result of the radical psychologization of social management, the prominence of psychology in the public imagination, and an unprecedented popularization. At the cultural level, the general focus shifted from social adjustment to the possibilities for personal growth. Now, managing one's individuality became a matter of personal interest. Individuals would scrutinize their inner world in order to understand how they could develop their own hidden potentials. For many, pop psychology and therapeutic practices such as counseling and therapy contributed to this quest for "self-realization."[49] The dialectic between the availability of psychology and the public's interest gradually turned most western nations into "psychological societies."

PRINCIPAL SOURCES AND FURTHER READING

For a general account of western social history in the nineteenth century, see E. J. Hobsbawm's multi-volume work *The age of revolution, 1789–1848* (New York: Vintage Books, 1962/1996), *The age of capital, 1848–1875* (New York: Vintage

Books, 1975/1996), and *The age of empire, 1875–1914* (New York: Vintage Books, 1987/1989). For (social) historical facts about the United States, see: G. B. Tindall and D. E. Shi (2000), *America. A narrative history* (New York: Norton), and D. J. Monti Jr (1999), *The American city: a social and cultural history* (Malden, MA: Blackwell). For Europe, we profited from the classical text by P. N. Stearns (1975), *European society in upheaval. Social history since 1750* (New York: Macmillan), and P. N. Stearns, ed., (2001), *Encyclopaedia of European social history from 1350 to 2000* (Detroit: Scribner).

Among the sources for the sketch of the historical process of individualization were: N. Elias (1987), *Die Gesellschaft der Individuen* (Frankfurt am Main: Suhrkamp); J. Jansz (1991), *Person, self, and moral demands. Individualism contested by collectivism* (Leiden: DSWO Press); C. Taylor (1989), *Sources of the self: the making of modern identity* (Cambridge: Cambridge University Press). R. Smith (1997), *The Fontana history of the human sciences* (London: HarperCollins) presents in a very accessible way detailed knowledge about the position of philosophy and the human sciences in the process of individualization. Three titles covered individualization with a focus on changing mentalities: R. Porter, ed. (1997), *Rewriting the self. Histories from the Renaissance to the present* (London: Routledge); R. Sennett (1977), *The fall of public man* (New York: Vintage Books); and W. McClay (1994), *The masterless. Society and self in modern America* (Chapel Hill: University of North Carolina Press).

The notion of social management and the description of its historical development owes much to M. Foucault (1970), *The order of things. An archaeology of the human sciences* (London: Tavistock); N. Elias (1978/1982), *The civilizing process. Socio-genetic and psychogenic investigations, vols. I and II* (Oxford: Blackwell); N. Rose (1996), *Inventing our selves. Psychology, power, and personhood* (Cambridge: Cambridge University Press); and A. de Swaan (1988), *In the care of the state. Health care, education and welfare in Europe and the USA in the modern era* (Cambridge: Polity Press).

A good textbook on the history of academic psychology, including some reference to psychological practices and their impact on society is T. H. Leahey (1991), *A history of modern psychology* (Englewood Cliffs, NJ: Prentice Hall). Other useful sources on academic psychology include: S. Koch and D. E. Leary, eds., (1985), *A century of psychology as a science* (New York: McGraw-Hill); and the special issue of the *American Psychologist, vol. 47(2)* (1992) about the history of American psychology (guest editor, L. T. Benjamin Jr). H. F. Ellenberger (1970), *The discovery of the unconscious: the history and evolution of dynamic psychiatry* (New York: Basic Books) details the historical context for the emergence of dynamic psychologies in the nineteenth century, in particular psychoanalysis.

For the interaction between society and culture on the one hand, and psychology on the other see: J. C. Burnham (1987), *How superstition won and science lost* (New Brunswick: Rutgers University Press); K. Danziger (1990), *Constructing the subject. Historical origins of psychological research* (Cambridge: Cambridge University Press); and N. Rose (1990) *Governing the soul. The shaping of the private self* (London: Routledge). With respect to the professionalization of psychology, see D. S. Napoli (1982), *Architects of adjustment: the history of the psychological profession in the United States* (Port Washington, NY: Kennikat). Particularly valuable sources with respect to the post-Second World War era in the United States are: J. H. Capshew (1999), *Psychologists on the march. Science, practice and professional identity in America, 1923–1969* (Cambridge: Cambridge University Press); and E. Herman (1995), *The romance of American psychology* (Berkeley: University of California Press).

NOTES

1   As quoted in Napoli, *Architects of adjustment*, p. 42.
2   P. Burke (1998), *The European Renaissance: centres and peripheries* (Oxford: Blackwell); Porter, *Rewriting the self.*
3   This complex shift has often been phrased as a change in historical ideal types, from *Gemeinschaft* (community) to *Gesellschaft* (society). See F. Tönnies (1969/1887), *Gemeinschaft und Gesellschaft: Grundbegriffe der reinen Soziologie* [Community and Society. Fundamental Concepts of Pure Sociology] (Darmstadt: Wissenschaftliche Buchgesellschaft).
4   Elias, *Die Gesellschaft der Individuen*, p. 138; Smith, *Fontana history of the human sciences*, p. 143.
5   P. Rietbergen (1998), *Europe: a cultural history.* (London: Routledge), p. 189.
6   L. Dumont (1985) "A modified view of our origins: the Christian beginnings of modern individualism," in M. Carrithers, S. Collins, and S. Lukes, (eds.), *The category of the person: anthropology, philosophy, history* (Cambridge: Cambridge University Press), pp. 93–122; S. Lukes (1973), *Individualism* (Oxford: Blackwell), p. 94. For diaries see P. Burke (1997) "Representations of the self from Petrarch to Descartes," in Porter, *Rewriting the self*, pp. 17–29. For autobiography see K. J. Weintraub (1978), *The value of the individual: self and circumstance in autobiography* (Chicago: University of Chicago Press).
7   As quoted in Smith, *Fontana history of the human sciences*, p. 146.
8   P. Burke (1987), *The Renaissance* (Basingstoke: Macmillan), p. 81.
9   J. O. Lyons (1978), *The invention of the self* (New York: Feffer and Simmons), p. 70.
10 Lukes, *Individualism*, p. 107.
11 K. Danziger (1997), *Naming the mind. How psychology found its language* (London: Sage), pp. 46–7; Taylor, *Sources of the self*, p. 171.
12 "Disenchantment" is a translation of Max Weber's concept *Entzauberung*. M. F. Cohen (1995), *The scientific revolution: a historiographical inquiry* (Chicago: University of Chicago Press).
13 R. Porter (1990), *The Enlightenment* (London: Macmillan); Rietbergen, *Europe*, p. 311.
14 Rietbergen, *Europe: a cultural history*, ch. 12; B. Russell (1979/1946), *History of western philosophy* (London: George Allen & Unwin), p. 651.
15 Smith, *Fontana history of the human sciences*, pp. 211–13.
16 R. F. Baumeister (1997), The self and society: changes, problems, and opportunities, in R. D. Ashmore, and L. Jussim (eds.), *Self and identity: fundamental issues* (Oxford: Oxford University Press), pp. 191–218. Taylor, *Sources of the self*, pp. 389–90.
17 See P. Gay (1995), *The naked heart. The bourgeois experience, vol. 4* (New York: Norton), p. 7.
18 Smith, *Fontana history of the human sciences*, p. 430.
19 The label "social darwinism" suggests that Spencer translated darwinian principles to society. Historically, this is not accurate: Spencer developed his evolutionary account of society in the 1850s, that is, a couple of years before Darwin published his *Origin of species* (1859). In addition, Darwin did not have much to do with the competitive ideology that bore his name (Smith, *Fontana history of the human sciences*, p. 467).

20 Gay, *The naked heart*, p. 171.

21 J. D. Davies (1955), *Phrenology: fad and science. A 19th century American crusade* (New Haven: Yale University Press); J. M. O'Donnell (1985), *The origins of behaviorism: American psychology, 1870–1920* (New York: New York University Press), p. 77. E. G. Boring (1950), *A history of experimental psychology* (Englewood Cliffs, NJ: Prentice Hall), p. 57.

22 S. J. Gould (1984), *The mismeasure of man* (London: Pelican Books), p. 82. For Lombroso see: J. van Ginneken (1992), *Crowds, psychology, and politics, 1871–1899* (Cambridge: Cambridge University Press), p. 62.

23 J. Hilkey (1997), *Character is capital: success manuals and manhood in gilded age America* (Chapel Hill: North Carolina Press).

24 Gay, *The naked heart*. K. J. Gergen (1991), *The saturated self* (New York: Basic Books), p. 20. Weintraub, *The value of the individual*.

25 R. Rosenberg (1982), *Beyond separate spheres. Intellectual roots of modern feminism* (New Haven: Yale University Press), and S. Shields (1975), Functionalism, Darwinism, and the psychology of women: A study in social myth, *American Psychologist, 30,* 739–754.

26 Hobsbawm, *The age of empire*, p. 81.

27 For early primary education in the seventeenth century, see De Swaan, *In the care*, ch. 1.

28 For the "modern" approach, see K. Woodroofe (1962), *From charity to social work*. (London: Routledge). For the evangelism of the C.O.S. see J. Weeks (1981), *Sex, politics, and society* (London: Longman), p. 75. In the USA, *The National Conference of Charities and Corrections* was founded in 1874. Its name illustrated, again, the combination of support and scrutiny.

29 E. Shorter (1997), *A history of psychiatry. From the era of the asylum to the age of Prozac* (New York: John Wiley), ch. 2.

30 L. Benevolo (1993), *The European city* (Oxford: Blackwell), pp. 166–9. A. Corbin (1982), *Le Miasme et la jonquille: l'odorat et l'imaginaire social, 18ᵉ–19ᵉ siècle* (Paris: Aubier). De Swaan, *In the care*, ch. 4.

31 H. H. Laughlin in 1922, as quoted in L. J. Kamin (1974), *The science and politics of IQ* (Harmondsworth: Penguin), p. 27.

32 D. J. Kevles (1985), *In the name of eugenics* (New York: Knopf); for positive and negative eugenics, see p. 85.

33 Smith, *Fontana history of the human sciences*, 238. L. J. Pongratz (1967/1984), *Problemgeschichte der Psychologie* (München: Francke Verlag) describes in detail the early uses of "psychology" and related terms. He recorded the first use of "psychologia" in the work of the German professor Goclenius in 1590.

34 As Smith, *Fontana history of the human sciences*, pointed out in detail (ch. 14), the origin myth of psychology was created by Boring in *A history of experimental psychology*. Origin myths focus on one specific event and tend to neglect the complex interplay of societal and cultural factors.

35 Capshew, *Psychologists on the march*, p. 16.

36 The development of psychoanalysis is placed in a wider context in Ellenberger, *Discovery*. Another classical source is P. Rieff (1961), *Freud: the mind of the moralist* (New York: Anchor Books).

37 G. Heymans (1909), *De toekomstige eeuw der psychologie* [The future century of psychology]. (Groningen: Wolters).

38 Boring, *A history of experimental psychology*, p. 487.

39 Sigmund Koch, the senior editor of *A century of psychology as a science*, aptly christened the twentieth century as "the psychological century" (p. 32).

40 R. N. Bellah et al. (1986), *Habits of the heart. Individualism and commitment in American life* (New York: Harper and Row), p. 334.

41   Individualism was always contested by collectivism. Therefore it is far too simple to rewrite political history as a triumph of individualistic liberalism as was done by F. Fukuyama (1989), The end of history, *The National Interest, 16,* 3–13.

42   A. de Swaan (1990), The politics of agoraphobia, in A. de Swaan, *The management of normality. Critical essays in health and welfare* (London: Routledge), pp. 139–68.

43   The term "me decade" was coined by Tom Wolfe. The bestseller by C. Lasch (1979), *The culture of narcissim* (New York: Norton) was particularly critical of emotionalization. For the alleged authenticity of feelings see A. H. Fischer and J. Jansz (1995), Reconciling emotions with western personhood. *Journal for the Theory of Social Behaviour, 25,* 59–81; C. Lutz (1996), Cultural politics by other means: gender and politics in some American psychologies of emotion, in C. F. Graumann and K. J. Gergen (eds), (1996), *Historical dimensions of psychological discourse* (Cambridge: Cambridge University Press), pp. 125–45.

44   A. de Swaan (1990), From troubles to problems, in Swaan, *The management of normality* (London: Routledge), pp. 99–108.

45   As quoted in Burnham, *How superstition won and science lost,* p. 95.

46   The popularization of psychology is covered in detail in Burnham, *How superstition won and science lost,* ch. 3; Capshew, *Psychologists on the march,* discusses Brothers' career (pp. 247–9; quote on p. 248). The observer is quoted in Herman, *The romance of American psychology,* p. 304.

47   R. V. Guthrie (1976), *Even the rat was white. A historical view of psychology* (New York: Harper and Row); N. Weisstein (1968), *Kinder, Kirche, Küche as scientific law: psychology constructs the female* (Boston: New England Free Press).

48   R. Abma, and J. Jansz (2000). Radical psychology institutionalized: a history of the journal Psychologie & Maatschappij (Psychology & Society). *Journal of the History of the Behavioral Sciences, 36,* 1–14; T. Teo (1998). Klaus Holzkamp and the rise and decline of German critical psychology. *History of Psychology, 1,* 235–253.

49   Nikolas Rose summarized the effects of psychologization as "the birth of a new type of person." N. Rose (1997), Assembling the modern self, in Porter, *Rewriting the self,* pp. 224–49, in particular pp. 233–4.

2 Child-rearing and education

Peter van Drunen and Jeroen Jansz

Introduction

The year 1900 saw the publication of *The century of the child*, written by the Swedish feminist Ellen Key. Her prospective view of the central position of children seemed to touch a nerve: the book became a worldwide bestseller. Key's title referred to the century that had just begun, but her writings also confirmed the public concern with children's welfare that had emerged in the previous decades. In the course of the nineteenth century, "the child" increasingly became the object of intervention, for example, through institutional care for delinquent and marginalized children, the ban on child labor, and the enforcement of compulsory schooling. These new forms of social management supplemented earlier philosophical ideas about children. The treatises of, for instance, Locke and Rousseau had contributed to notions about the particular nature of the child, and about "childhood" as a distinct episode in life. The impact of social management on the ordinary life of nineteenth-century children and families powerfully enhanced the construction of childhood as a lengthy period devoted to play and education.

This chapter presents nineteenth-century social management with regard to children as a pertinent background to the emergence of a psychological perspective on children. It shows how children and their development and education were increasingly "psychologized." We will document the role of psychologists in this process, but we will also show that psychologization was frequently the result of efforts by physicians, teachers, social workers, and others. More often than not, these professionals had already embraced a psychological perspective before psychology was established as an academic discipline.

The chapter concentrates on the psychologization of the normal child, although we will see that professional attention was often initially directed toward specific groups of children and was subsequently generalized to all children. Before we document the pervasive psychological expertise about children, we present a brief sketch of the historical developments in western society which contributed to the central position of children by the end of the nineteenth century.

1   Early history of "childhood" (*c.* 1500–1900)

While there have always been children, it took several centuries of social change before the first decades of life became what we currently call "childhood" (see figure 8).

1.1   *Family, work, and school*

From the beginning of the sixteenth century, the nuclear family gradually became the dominant family type in the Western world. This household of two generations living together was first discernible in north-western Europe and the city-states of middle and southern Europe. In almost all instances, labor within the nuclear family was divided according to gender: fathers worked outside the house to earn a wage, and mothers stayed home to run the household and supervise the children. Upper-class families generally had enough resources to assign men and women to their "separate spheres" of life. Thus, the public world of work became dominated by men, which reinforced male dominance in society. Women dominated the private sphere of family relations and household arrangements. This gave mothers ample opportunity to engage themselves with their offspring, but it also made them responsible for the behavior of their children in private and public. Lower-class families faced an entirely different situation. They could not survive on one income: capitalist exploitation forced working-class mothers, as well as their children, to earn a wage. Industrial production separated the place of work from the home; the family members spent long days in the factory. As a result there was very little time to focus on private life and the well-being of children.

Family size decreased over the centuries at all social levels, although this was most conspicuous in the lower strata where large families had been common. Well into the nineteenth century, many newborns died before the age of one, and older children often fell victim to contagious diseases. It was not uncommon for parents to die before their children reached maturity. Consequently, the family composition might change twice in the lifetime of one generation. In the lower classes, the effect of a family member's death extended beyond the emotional consequences: the family's meager resources were reduced significantly. Over a long historical period, children contributed to the family income. In agricultural economies, they started as young as six, looking after the cattle or collecting silkworms. A couple of years later they did their full share of manual labor in the fields, which integrated them fully into the social world of adults. The first phases of industrialization starting in Great Britain in the eighteenth century resulted in an upsurge in domestic industries, where children in the lower social strata executed simple, monotonous labor, often supervised by their own mothers.

Thus, until the late eighteenth century children tended to be integrated in the social world of adults, rather than having a definite social identity of their own. This was reflected in early industrial practice, in which children were considered to be part and parcel of the regular workforce. So, for instance, as late as 1835, 43 percent of the labor force in the British cotton industries was under eighteen years of age (see figures 9a and b). Subsequent decades, however, saw a rapid decline in these

Figure 8 The child as mini-adult, *c*. 1750. It was only in the course of the eighteenth century that "childhood" became a separate phase of life. Source: Psychology Pictures.

(a)

Figure 9   (a) *Inside the mill* and (b) *Supplementing factory rations*. Engravings depicting the miserable conditions of lower class children in mid-nineteenth-century England. From: F. Trollope (1840), *Life and adventures of Michael Armstrong, the factory boy* (London: Colburn).

practices. Influenced by new pedagogical theories, the idea took hold that children should enjoy a relatively undisturbed period of development. This inspired forceful protest against child labor, and moreover, the nineteenth century saw equally vigorous campaigns for general education. Rather than being ancillary to work and other social duties, schooling came to be considered the central element of children's lives.

(b)

Figure 9 *Continued*

These transitions did not take place overnight. In most European countries it was not until the late 1890s that child labor was prohibited and compulsory education introduced. The United States lagged even further behind: here, it was 1918 before there was a federal ban on child labor. But if the transition was slow, its impact was little short of revolutionary: rather than being considered "small adults," children in the course of the nineteenth century acquired a social status of their own. This was reflected in a vast extension of practices aiming at guiding, correcting, and educating them, as well as their parents.

1.2   Child-rearing advice

Religious authorities were important voices with respect to children and correct child-rearing. From the sixteenth century, the number of published educational ideas increased steadily, with Protestant authors being most prolific in presenting guidance about education. From that era onwards, Luther's doctrine of original sin was generally embraced; this held that every human being was born wicked, if not evil. The advisory literature urged parents to "break the will" of the "little tyrants" as soon as possible. Any delay in discipline would be very unwise, it was thought, because of the risk of an early death before the child had repented. The advice was directed to the father because he represented religious authority in the family. He could exert patriarchal power using every means, including corporal punishment. However, in 1833, the Reverend Abbott addressed the audience of mothers. His popular guide, *The mother at home*, argued that piety and a clear conscience required the child's will to be broken, but the disciplinary method shifted from physical force to that of withholding love. This psychological discipline was considered to be more effective than corporal punishment in creating a guilt-ridden conscience.

In the eighteenth-century spirit of the Enlightenment, the number of secular treatises about child-rearing increased. John Locke's *Some thoughts concerning education* (1693) served as an outstanding example for many. This was a compilation of letters sent to a friend who had asked Locke's advice about his son. It was no coincidence, of course, that the empiricist philosopher put his faith in education as a means to improving individual qualities. The training of proper habits from the earliest age was presented as an effective pedagogic procedure. In addition, Locke continued to express the humanism of the Enlightenment by advocating reasoning with the child as an educational method. If corporal punishment was necessary, it should be carried out rationally, that is without passion.[1]

Locke's *Thoughts* were followed in 1762 by an equally influential publication by the French philosopher Jean Jacques Rousseau, *Émile, ou de l'éducation* ("Émile, or about education"). Although he acknowledged Locke as his predecessor, Rousseau opposed his rational faith. Children, he argued, should be approached as children *per se* rather than as young, rational individuals. Virtue was embedded in the child's nature, and its unfolding demanded that the child was temporarily kept innocent of artificial society. Mothers were to be the prime educators. According to Rousseau, the alleged "blind affection" of mothers did less harm to the child than the common "harshness," "ambition," and "neglect" practiced by fathers.

Rousseau's more or less Romantic view of the child's nature became very influential from the end of the eighteenth century. His emphasis on "childhood" as a distinct period was embraced widely, and so was his emphasis on the natural capacities of mothers. Religious educators were critical because the doctrine of original sin could not be reconciled with a natural goodness in children, but they had to accept the expansion of Romantic pedagogy. Halfway through the nineteenth century, the Romantic view of children and childhood pervaded many social milieus. Advisory texts urged parents to guarantee their offspring a happy childhood which would function as a rich resource in later life. The availability of toys and toyshops contributed to the ideal of happiness. In Germany, Fröbel translated ideas of an unspoilt childhood into proposals for school reform. The effects of the social construction of childhood in nineteenth-century society underlined societal inequality. In particular, children from middle-class and wealthy families could enjoy the fruits of an unspoilt childhood. Their poorer peers still had to create their own playtime in between the hours of work.

A new kind of popular guidance appeared in the course of the nineteenth century when religious and social philosophical treatises were supplemented by popular medical advice from physicians. The focus on children's health was a new development in European and American medicine. The establishment of children's hospitals halfway through the century in, for example, Paris, London, and New York contributed to the establishment of pediatrics as a subdiscipline. Pasteur's discovery of germs and the subsequent development of bacteriology also stimulated medical concern about children. Curing childhood diseases could now go hand in hand with prophylaxis, that is, preventing illness and early death. Publication of *The care and feeding of children* (1894) by the American physician Holt was a landmark in the popularization of pediatrics. This book made a strong case for hygienic prophylaxis, and emphasized proper nutrition as a prerequisite for physical well-being; it also addressed issues such as sleeping patterns and the necessity of exercise for development. Pediatricians emphasized an objective, scientific approach to child development which had nothing to do with the moralism of philosophers and the clergy. In their popular pamphlets and brochures, they urged their readership of middle-class mothers to take their duties more seriously. Mothers should feed and supervise their own children, it was said, instead of entrusting them to a wet nurse or domestic servant. Mothers were also expected to garner expert knowledge in order to educate themselves in medical matters.[2] Consequently, the popular medical accounts presented motherhood as an important duty, in fact as a profession. This did not imply, however, that mothers were held exclusively responsible for the development of their children. On the contrary, the increase in the volume of advice literature was accompanied by growth in other kinds of social interference with children's development. The most widespread and influential manifestation of this was the expansion of institutionalized systems of formal education.

1.3   The expansion of schooling

Schools as such were not a new phenomenon. Churches and monastic institutions, for example, had provided some kind of schooling in earlier centuries, and during the eighteenth century groups of "enlightened" citizens had opened so-called "parish schools." It was, however, only in the course of the nineteenth century that schooling came to be considered central to the world of children.

The first proposals for nationwide, general systems of education for all children were formulated in the second half of the eighteenth century. Although they clearly carried the hallmark of the Enlightenment, their focus was on preservation of the social order rather than change. To be sure, some of its proponents saw general education as a means of alleviating the lot of the lower classes, as well as of demolishing time-honored boundaries between the sexes. The majority of educational reformers, however, stressed exactly the opposite: general education was considered to be a means of instilling order, discipline and love of one's country, in short, as a way of turning the unruly lower classes into a law-abiding, hard-working population. In this respect, the movement for general education fitted within the general pattern of late eighteenth- and nineteenth-century reflections on social management. Inspired by notions about the importance of childhood as a formative period which could decisively influence future behavior, educational reformers were generally convinced that the home environment was inadequate and in need of a publicly controlled supplement: in other words, education.

Around 1800, almost all the countries of north-western Europe witnessed strong movements for general education. In some countries, this was reflected in legislation regarding the provision of schools, the education of teachers, and – in some instances – even compulsory school attendance by children of a specified age. Generally speaking, however, early nineteenth-century states were too weak to enforce these regulations. Consequently, it was not until the middle of the century that general education came into vogue – a development reinforced by increased state funding of schools and firmly established towards the end of the century by the introduction of compulsory education.

The educational systems that evolved during the nineteenth century reflected their intended purposes. For one thing, they tended to be multi-layered rather than uniform, providing well-defined and different curricula for pupils of different social backgrounds. Some countries even had formally separate systems of "lower," "middle," and "higher" education, not reflecting the age of pupils or intellectual differences, but the layer of society for which they were intended. For children from the lower classes, a few years of basic schooling were considered sufficient; too much knowledge might fuel dissatisfaction with their lot, creating social unrest rather than order. The syllabus encompassed little more than a basic knowledge of the three Rs (reading, writing and arithmetic), supplemented by a little history and geography, which were supposed to instil a sense of national identity and pride. The disciplinary function of schooling was reflected in classroom organization, which was characterized by "simultaneous methods," centered around the teacher, with children's responses being regimented in an almost military fashion (see figure 10).

The development of general education as a new social practice was reflected in the emergence of educational theory. As early as the late 1700s, education or "pedagogy" became a specialized field of study, and educationalists such as Fröbel, Pestalozzi, and Herbart developed their theories in the early 1800s. Perhaps more decisive was the gradual evolution of teacher training. In the course of the nineteenth century, teaching developed into a well-defined profession, and the so-called "normal schools" were created to prepare aspiring teachers for their task. Generally speaking, the emphasis in these schools was on a thorough knowledge of elementary school subjects, and on techniques of instilling order and discipline. Even before 1840, however, books began to appear which aimed to acquaint teachers with "modern" ideas about children's minds.[3] In the final decades of the century, acquisition of a rudimentary knowledge of psychology became a regular part of teacher training. In some countries, this even evolved into a statutory requirement. As a Dutch educator put it in 1889: "The idea that one can teach pedagogy without psychology is as absurd as the idea that medicine could be taught without prior knowledge of the biology of the human body."[4]

Figure 10 State-sponsored education in mid-nineteenth-century Europe. Its regimented layout reflects the educational goals of order, discipline, and obedience. Source: Psychology Pictures/Archives of Dutch Psychology.

1.4 Saving the child

If education was by far the most far-reaching and influential form of social management, it was by no means the only one. In chapter 1, we described the general advance of social management in the nineteenth century. In almost all its manifestations, from religious charity and philanthropy to state interventionism, children featured prominently. This stemmed primarily from the belief in the malleability and vulnerability of the child. The latter idea especially was reinforced by the Romantic view of childhood, which became prominent from the late eighteenth century onward. Children should and could be protected from bad influences, and corrected rather than punished when wandering astray. Although this was considered primarily the responsibility of the parents, other agents became increasingly involved as well, either assisting parents or taking over their role.

Thus, next to the political movements for banning child labor and promoting general education, the nineteenth century saw a plethora of other initiatives aimed at promoting the welfare of children. Within philanthropic welfare schemes for the poor, increasing attention was paid to the child-rearing practices of those in need of assistance. So for instance, Amsterdam welfare workers in the 1880s routinely saw it as their duty to advise families about proper child-rearing practices, with the possible sanction of withdrawing or reducing financial assistance when elementary norms were not observed.[5] Thus, the lessons taught by child-rearing manuals were passed on to the lower strata of society. Toward the end of the century, this would result in a massive movement for improving the lot of children, partly by medical advice (as provided at child welfare clinics) and partly by legislative measures which protected children against parental abuse and neglect.

An even more conspicuous form of social interventionism was the rapid expansion of institutionalized care for those children who, in one way or another, were in need of particular care; this included handicapped children, but more prominently orphans, "street children," and young delinquents. Institutions for children were not a new phenomenon at the time, especially for orphans, as provisions can be dated back as far as the late middle ages. However, from the 1830s onward the number of children in institutionalized care began to rise sharply. This was partly due to new laws, which provided for separate treatment for juvenile delinquents: rather than being sent to prison, these children should be re-educated (see chapter 6). However, arrangements for other categories of children expanded equally rapidly. In the US, for instance, the number of private orphanages rose from 77 in 1851 to 613 in 1880.[6]

The expansion of institutionalized care went hand in hand with the development of new models of education or re-education, which in many respects foreshadowed the approach that in the twentieth century would become the hallmark of psychology. Characteristic of this approach was a highly individualized system of guidance and control, modeled on the nuclear family, and consisting of an intricate mix of close surveillance, severe discipline, and affection. This approach found its most manifest form in the so-called agricultural colonies, which by mid-century had become the favored form of institution for delinquent and pre-delinquent youth (see chapter 6).

1.5   Conclusion

Societal developments from the sixteenth century onward resulted in the gradual, but decisive construction of "childhood" as a transitional phase between the infant's total dependency and the adult's autonomous functioning. The tendencies toward compulsory education and the bans on child labor reflected the idea that children had much to learn before they could participate in the world of adults. In addition, religious, philosophical, and scientific treatises highlighted the unique nature of the child, sometimes to the extent of emphasizing the child's vulnerability. The gist of popular educational advice was that child-rearing was anything but simple and self-evident. It required serious attention from parents, more specifically from mothers. This view reached its most cogent expression in the concept of "motherhood as a profession," which was introduced in the late nineteenth century. This conveyed both the importance of bringing up children as a duty of mothers and the necessity of specific skills and knowledge, either in addition to maternal instincts or as a correction thereof. When nineteenth-century mothers doubted their abilities, or failed in their duties, increasingly they could enlist the help of medical and pedagogic professionals. By the end of the century, the implications for the lives of children of the construction of "childhood" had spread from children of prosperous families to the young population at large. Extended schooling and the prohibition of child labor postponed the integration of chidren into the world of adults, thus extending the transitional phase of "childhood" into "adolescence."

2 Psychological perspectives (*c.* 1890–1920)

The central social position children had gained in the course of the nineteenth century was strengthened around 1900 by the steady decrease in family size. The small nuclear family was well on its way to becoming the standard in most western countries, notwithstanding important differences between religious groups, particular regions, and social strata. Social management with respect to children was intensified further in the earliest decades of the twentieth century. Many perceived the improvement of children's welfare as a powerful tool for social reform. Through their children, it was thought, the "worthy" poor would be lifted up, and children from dubious backgrounds could be disciplined in order to prevent their taking to crime.

The idea of social reform through education was particularly strong among American Progressives. Their earliest concern with marginal groups was gradually widened to include, for example, immigrant children, and finally embraced the "normal" population in its entirety. This extension of interventionism was mirrored in a growing interest in child-rearing advice among parents, as indicated by the popularity of advisory literature on child-rearing and of parental organizations such as the American National Congress of Mothers, established in 1897.

In the earliest decades of the twentieth century, most western countries deliberately increased governmental efforts targeted at children. Such public programs of child welfare were motivated generally by the need to prepare children to assume adult economic roles, but also by the need to assimilate young citizens into a community of shared values and ideals. By the eve of the First World War, most western governments had established national agencies to coordinate the private and public practices of social management regarding children and families; in the United States, for instance, Congress established the federal Children's Bureau in 1912.

2.1 *The Child Study Movement*

In the later decades of the nineteenth century, a psychological perspective on children and their development found an enthusiastic audience among scientists and professionals as well as the lay public. It seemed that a psychological account of development was welcomed as a useful supplement to the medico-hygienic treatises which dominated public discourse. The pioneering work in the psychology of infants was in fact done by non-psychologists. Both Darwin and the French sociologist Taine published detailed and influential observations of the physical and psychological development of their own children.[7] The most famous study, however, was *Die Seele des Kindes* ("The soul of the child") (1882) by the German physiologist Preyer. In the following decades, many child psychologists took to heart Preyer's emphasis on meticulous observation. They also embraced his biogenetic theory, which gave biological processes a prime role with the claim that maturation determined psychosocial development.

The American psychologist Granville Stanley Hall aimed to make an empirical contribution to a psychological perspective on development (see figure 11). In his paper "The Contents of Children's Minds" (1883) he reported what children of a particular age really knew and understood, and found, for example, that urban children had an astonishingly meager knowledge of nature. After a brief interlude, Hall returned energetically in the early 1890s to the scientific study of children and their

Figure 11   Granville Stanley Hall (1844–1924), founding father of the Child Study Movement. Source: Clark University Archives.

development. From that time he employed psychological knowledge to create a science of pedagogy, which resulted in a practical application of his scientific work.[8] Close links were established between him, his colleagues at Clark University, school-teachers, and other educationalists. This collaboration resulted in what came to be known as Hall's "Child Study Movement." In the 1890s, the Movement dedicated much of its energy to large-scale surveys of children and their development. This project, spanning years, involved sending out thousands of questionnaires to parents, teachers, and other professional educators. They were asked to supply Hall with their systematic observations about diverse aspects of development, such as children's anger, nervousness, or self-image, but also about children's food preferences and religious experiences (see figure 12).

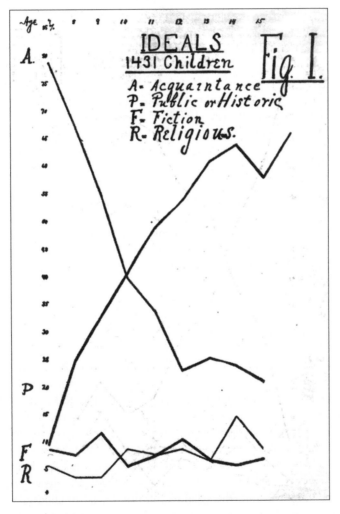

Figure 12 An example of results from a Child Study Movement questionnaire: the ideal figures of children of various ages. Younger children tended to mention an acquaintance as their ideal, older children favored public figures. Source: *Pedagogical Seminary*, 1911.

The results of the questionnaire project were published in *Pedagogical Seminary*, a journal Hall had established in 1891. Parents and teachers enjoyed reading the reports, and replicated some studies informally in class or at home. The Child Study Movement grew quickly: by 1900 it covered about three-quarters of American states. It also inspired people across the Atlantic. The British Child Study Association, for example, was established in 1898, and the German *Verein für Kinderpsychologie* in 1899. In France, *La Societé Libre pour l'Étude psychologique de l'Enfant* (1899) was directly modeled on Hall's examplar. The experimental psychologist Alfred Binet presided over the society, which contributed enormously to the prestige of child study.[9]

Stanley Hall's popular fame extended beyond his own Child Study Movement. He had, for example, become the favored psychologist of the National Congress of Mothers, the nationwide parent-education organization mentioned above, which was established in 1897. The concerns of the Congress neatly kept in step with the subjects Hall covered; this is illustrated by the shift in focus from infants and young children to adolescents after the publication of Hall's magnum opus *Adolescence* (1904). At his own Clark University, Hall established a Children's Institute in 1909 to merge scientific research with wider concerns for children's welfare. The Institute never functioned, partly as the result of the stern criticism Hall received from psychologists outside Clark University. In the 1910s Hall had moved into the margins of American psychology, which coincided with the gradual demise of the Child Study Movement. His pupils, however, were more successful. One of them, Arnold Gesell, established a psychological clinic at Yale University in 1911 with the aim of translating scientific research into practical applications. Technical innovations such as the one-way screen and cinematographic recording enabled him to be as precise in his observations as his exemplar, Preyer. Gesell constructed normative scales to assess children's physical and mental development. This standardization attracted a large following: the tabulated and graphically displayed "landmarks of development" found their way into the psychology textbooks, but also into numerous popular baby books and teacher manuals.[10]

2.2   Educational reform

Within education, the Child Study Movement dovetailed with a general spirit of educational reform, which gained strength from the 1890s onwards. Traditional education was found wanting in many respects and in need of radical transformation. Both in the United States and in Europe, movements for educational reform developed.[11] Their programs combined a number of motives. First, it was thought that schools were not responding appropriately to societal demands, which increasingly required more than the rudimentary knowledge described in section 1.3. Secondly, the traditional system was considered ill-suited to children's needs: with its emphasis on formal knowledge and rote-learning, the syllabus did not appeal to children's interests and made poor use of the "natural curiosity" that they were supposed to have. Moreover, classroom conditions left too little room to allow for individual differences, in interests and in style and speed of learning. Thirdly, traditional schools were criticized for their ineffectiveness, a theme which was especially prominent in the American reform movement. Disparate as these motives were, they shared one common theme: education was grounded too much in tradition and outdated pedagogical theory, such as Herbartianism. If it was to change, it should be based on research and take new scientific findings into account. This led to a strong interest in the twin fields of pedagogy and psychology.

Generally speaking, it was pedagogy rather than psychology which led the way. In the United States, for instance, the ideas of philosopher and pedagogue John Dewey would become the beacons of the reform movement. In Europe, so-called "reform pedagogues" such as Decroly (Belgium), Kerschensteiner (Germany), and Montessori (Italy) played an important role. Insofar as their reforming proposals invoked psychology, this was only in a very general way, as a "new look" on learning and education rather than an incorporation of specific theories or research findings. However, in their wake, specific psychological expertise also claimed a place. In Germany, the psychologist of memory, Herman Ebbinghaus, had pioneered educational research in 1895 when he studied the mental effort and "fatigue" of pupils. In other countries, psychologists such as Claparède (Switzerland) and Binet (France) used the new child psychology in their proposals for experimental forms of education (see figure 13).

On the continent of Europe, psychology would remain second to pedagogy until the 1950s. In the United States, however, psychologists fared much better. This resulted in the emergence of a new subdiscipline, which developed in the wake of the progressive reform movement – educational psychology. This new field quickly became established in teachers' colleges and departments of education which were created in the early twentieth century at various universities.

The champion of the new discipline was Edward Lee Thorndike. Originally trained as an animal psychologist, in 1899 Thorndike moved to Teachers College at Columbia University, New York, by that time the epicenter for educational research in the United States. In 1903 he published *Educational psychology* (1903), a book that would become the authoritative reference for the contribution of psychology to education in the first half of the twentieth century. Thorndike favored a quantitative, strictly empirical approach to learning and education, as epitomized by his motto "whatever exists at all exists in some amount."

Despite its pretensions, psychology did not have very much to offer when it came to learning processes, and perhaps even less with regard to teaching. Thorndike's learning theory, for instance, was to a large extent a matter of old wine in new bottles. Its central idea was that learning amounted to the formation of connections in the brain. The actual development of these mental connections followed scientific laws. The *law of exercise*, for example, indicated that repetition was a prerequisite for learning, and the *law of effect* emphasized the role of positive reinforcement. Both laws did little more than corroborate the timeworn method of rote learning, which was considered to be the best technique for fixing the nascent stimulus–response connections.

If educational psychology was hardly revolutionary with regard to theories of learning, it did succeed in carving out another niche within the educational domain – that of assessment, measurement, and experimentation, both with respect to indi-

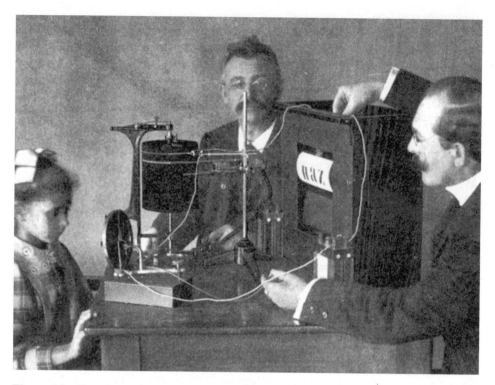

Figure 13 Experimental research in education, Germany, *c.* 1910, showing an attempt to measure the time needed to reproduce a presented word. Source: Psychology Pictures/ Archives of Dutch Psychology.

vidual pupils and to the effectiveness of educational programs as a whole. Both issues were at the core of the educational reform movement. As the emphasis had moved from moral education and discipline to qualification, the measurement of achievement had gradually gained prominence within education. Moreover, with public expenditure on education rising quickly, both the general public and policymakers began to question the effectiveness of educational programs. Both themes were taken up zealously by Thorndike and his colleagues, resulting in ambitious programs for the development of achievement tests and experimental comparison of various educational "treatments." Although "neutral" on the subject of grander pedagogic ideas and reforms, American psychologists thus created their own "niche" within the educational system.

2.3 Social management

In the wake of the Child Study Movement and the infusion of psychology into education, the new discipline also made its appearance in other areas of social intervention. As we have seen in chapter 1, the later decades of the nineteenth century saw a veritable boom in social interventionism, inspired by such diverse ideological backgrounds as the Progressive Movement in the United States and coalitions of social democrats and enlightened liberals in Europe. As in earlier periods, the welfare of children was among the prime concerns of interventionists. Previously established forms of youth care expanded rapidly, and in addition a number of new initiatives were developed. Within this flourishing sphere, psychologists also found their place, developing new services to cater for various problems.

The United States was in the vanguard of these psycho-educational practices. A major impetus was the introduction of compulsory education, which brought a new category of problematic children to the fore: those who, for one reason or another, did not fit within the regimented mold of general education.[12] As a response, a whole range of ameliorative programs developed, varying from rudimentary forms of remedial teaching to special classes and special schools for particular categories of "exceptional children." Generally, teachers and physicians led the way, but from the mid-1890s onward psychologists were also involved. In chapter 1, we have already briefly mentioned a decisive step in this respect, that is, the foundation of the first "psychological clinic" by Lightner Witmer (1896). Inspired by a request from a teacher regarding a child who could not keep up with his fellow-pupils, Witmer saw it as his mission to develop a form of psychology, which contributed to the welfare of individual children, rather than just studying mental processes in general. As he formulated this retrospectively in 1907: "It appeared to me that if psychology was worth anything . . . it should be able to assist the efforts of a teacher in a retarded case of this kind." The result was a flourishing practice, characterized by a strictly individualized approach and close cooperation between psychologists and teachers, and which set the example for a number of similar "psycho-educational clinics," to be founded throughout the country.[13]

In a more or less similar vein, psychology made its appearance in other areas of social intervention, such as the provision for juvenile delinquents (see chapter 6). This was in various forms: independent psychological practice (as in the case of Witmer); the inclusion of psychologists in teams (generally under medical supervision); or the incorporation of psychological tools and methods in the work of other professions. As far as the specific role of psychologists was concerned, the emphasis was, without exception, on examination rather than treatment (see figure 14). Making use of laboratory instruments borrowed from academic psychology as well as self-devised tests, psychologists thus carved out a professional niche for themselves in diagnosis and testing which would remain the cornerstone of their work for decades to come. This development was greatly enhanced by the invention of a new instrument, which would become one of the hallmarks of psychological expertise in the twentieth century – the intelligence test.

2.4 The "feeble-minded" and intelligence testing

The intelligence test emanated from yet another new field of social intervention: the identification and care of children with inherent learning difficulties. Its invention provides an elegant demonstration of the way societal changes may lead to new cat-

Figure 14   A child being examined with an experimental apparatus, United States, *c.* 1910. Source: Archives of the History of American Psychology, University of Akron.

egorizations of problems – and new scientific interventions. The severely mentally handicapped – "idiots," in the vernacular of the time – had already been identified as a special category in earlier days.[14] With the introduction of compulsory education, attention was focused on milder forms of retardation. Apart from children suffering from specific social, emotional, or cognitive problems, a large group was identified which included children who for no particular reason simply could not keep up with their fellow pupils; these children were categorized as "feeble-minded."

But how might these children with inherent learning difficulties be distinguished from those pupils who had other reasons for not being able to keep up with their classmates? Originally, this was considered to be a medical problem, falling within the jurisdiction of school physicians. Following diagnostic systems which had been developed for people with severe disability, most doctors tended to look for physical characteristics, such as the form and size of the head and bodily malformations. However, none of the diagnostic systems developed along these lines proved satisfactory. In fact, there was a growing consensus that, in contrast with more severe mental handicap, "feeble-mindedness" did not show up in physical characteristics. At the request of the French government, the psychologist Alfred Binet (see figure 15) explored a new avenue: rather than using educational and medical criteria, diagnosis

Figure 15 French psychologist Alfred Binet (1857–1911), inventor of the intelligence test. Source: Psychology Pictures/Archives of Dutch Psychology.

should proceed along psychological lines. The result was a "metric scale for the assessment of intelligence," published in 1905.

The items included in Binet's "scale" were anything but revolutionary.[15] By and large, they reflected well-known, basic operations, such as pointing out parts of the body, describing the content of pictures and answering specific questions such as "What's your age?" or "Where do you go if you want to buy a loaf of bread?" Nevertheless, the test constituted a major breakthrough, both compared with existing medical diagnostic systems and with earlier psychological tests. Previous test series, such as those developed by Galton, had begun by measuring discrete psychological functions (for example, acuity of the senses, memory, and attention), under the premise that the results would correlate with everyday performance. This assumption, however, time and again proved problematic. Binet and his collaborator Simon followed another route. Rather than taking different mental functions as their starting point, they tried to devise a test consisting of items of increasing difficulty. The result was an "age scale," consisting of items that had been empirically demonstrated to reflect the mental development of children of various ages (see figure 16).

Compared with the earlier tests Binet's approach had two decisive advantages. First, as a result of the way the test was constructed, its practical relevance was guaranteed from the outset; rather than the use of guesswork to decide how items would correlate with levels of intellectual functioning, this relation was "built in" by the

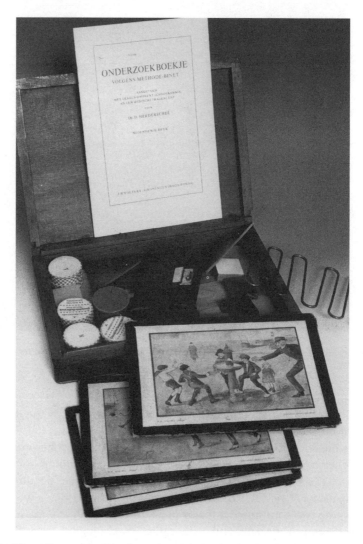

Figure 16   Binet–Simon test, Dutch version, 1919. Source: Psychology Pictures/Archives of Dutch Psychology.

selection of items on the basis of their demonstrated difficulty. Secondly, the test offered a clear standard of comparison: with items reflecting various age levels, the test offered a readily comprehensible formula for indicating levels of mental performance – the "mental age."

The merits of Binet's test were quickly recognized. The quantifiable results it generated were considered to provide a clear-cut distinction between "normal" and "feeble-minded" children, and between various levels of mental deficiency. Within a few years, the test was introduced as an integral part of the examination of slower pupils, on both sides of the Atlantic. Perhaps even more important, Binet scores gradually replaced the older medical definitions and diagnostic criteria for "feeble-mindedness," both in Europe and the United States. Thus, for instance, in 1910 the medically dominated American Association for the Study of the Feeble-Minded adopted the Binet scales as the basis for the classification of children with learning disabilities, defining as an "idiot" one with a test result below a mental age of three, and as an "imbecile" one with a test result between three and seven.

In everyday practice, psychologists would only gradually replace school physicians when it came to the examination of children suspected to be "feeble-minded." Nevertheless, the importance of the introduction of Binet's test can hardly be overestimated, in that both the definition and the assessment of mental retardation had been transferred from the medical to the psychological domain. If the problem of "feeble-mindedness" originated from changes in education and society at large, it was psychology which provided its definition and the means to identify it.

Not only did the discipline acquire a decisive and unprecedented role in determining which children should be sent to special classes or referred to special institutions, but this new concept was also brought to bear on a host of other social problems. According to the champions of American intelligence testing, Henry Goddard and Lewis Terman, people with mental retardation presented a silent threat to society at large, predisposed as they were, in the view of Goddard and Terman, to prostitution, criminality and other kinds of maladaptive behavior. Inspired by the eugenic idea that "feeble-mindedness" was a hereditary condition, they launched a vigorous campaign against "the menace of the feeble-minded" (see figure 17). One of the results of this campaign was the inclusion of "feeble-mindedness" among the grounds for sterilization. Laws to this effect would be passed in a number of American states, decisively influencing the lives of thousands of children and adults.[16]

Inspired by the rapid success of their test, it was but a small step for psychologists to try to enlarge their jurisdiction to all children. The full consequences of this expansion would become manifest after the First World War, and will be explored in section 4.2 of this chapter.

2.5 Conclusion

Between 1890 and 1915, social interest and interventions regarding children reached a new level. The ban on child labor and the introduction of compulsory education had marked out childhood as a separate stage of life, and this distinction was strength-

Figure 17   "The menace of the feeble-minded." Panel from a pamphlet (1919) on the dangerous social consequences of unlimited reproduction by people of low intelligence. Based on a famous study by psychologist Henry Goddard, *The Kallikak family* (1912). On the left are shown the legitimate offspring of Martin Kallikak, resulting from his marriage with a "worthy Quakeress," and on the right the results of his liaison with a feeble-minded tavern girl – "hundreds of the lowest types of human beings." Source: Archives of the History of American Psychology, University of Akron. Goddard papers, File M614.

ened by the gradual extension of education and the introduction of "adolescence" as a new phase between childhood and adulthood.

The growing interest in children and education was exemplified in the American Child Study Movement and similar coalitions between parents, educators, and academic researchers in Europe. Within these movements, psychology was accorded a prominent place, as shown by the prominent roles of, for example, Stanley Hall and Alfred Binet. Rather than religious, moral, or medical viewpoints, it was a psychological perspective which dominated the new movements. This was reflected in various interventionist practices, in which psychologists claimed their place alongside other professions. Within education, psychology developed into one of the cornerstones of teacher education, most markedly in the United States where "educational psychology" developed as a new subdiscipline, relatively independent from pedagogy. Apart from that, psychologists made their appearance in all kinds of ancillary social agencies, such as clinics for delinquent youth or centers for vocational guidance. With Witmer's "psychological clinic," they even created a new kind of institution, independent of other professions and helping services. Their greatest influence, however, involved a social group which was to a great extent defined by their very expertise, that is, people with mental handicap. From this context also emanated the tool that would play a considerable role in the advance of psychology in subsequent decades: the intelligence test.

The wide audience for Stanley Hall's ideas and the impact of the "menace of the feeble-minded" campaign are but two indications of the success of psychology in influencing public notions about childhood and development, and actually defining the issues which needed to be addressed by parents and educators. This laid the basis for the further increase, after the First World War, of the influence of psychology with regard to children. We will now turn to this subject, concentrating on the home environment in the next section, and on the child at school in section 4.

3   The child at home (*c.* 1920–1960)

Social management with respect to child-rearing expanded enormously in the decades after the First World War. The gradual decline in the number of children per family, dating back to the nineteenth century, continued, eventually resulting in a further proliferation of what one might call "the standard nuclear family" of father, mother, and two children. Also, a newborn's chance of survival was greater because of improvement in birth conditions and the successful prevention and control of contagious diseases.

A rather different tendency also emphasized the focus on children and families. A widespread concern for private life emerged after the First World War. In the United States this was partly reflected in the membership figures of the National Congress of Mothers, which rose from about 50,000 in 1910 to 190,000 in 1920, and to nearly 1,500,000 by 1930. Feminist organizations also contributed to a focus on private life. Now that female suffrage had been realized in most countries, attention moved from the legal and political domains to everyday life. Across Europe and the United States, young women manifested their independence, sometimes by deliberately transgressing sartorial conventions, as in the case of the American "flappers." At the same time, self-consciously married women explicitly cultivated motherhood and endorsed so-called "domestic science" as a way of keeping families together. These modern mothers became the dedicated readership of popular advice about marriage, family relations, and, of course, bringing up children. This was demonstrated by the circulation figures for the American *Parent's Magazine*, which sold about 100,000 copies a month in the late 1920s and the 1930s. In addition to such popular sources of advice, many institutes for child care opened their doors in almost all western nations. As a result, parents could rely on a network of educational advice, with expertise as varied as psychology, medicine, and social casework.[17]

3.1   Popular advice

As we have demonstrated earlier, in the course of the nineteenth century medical expertise came ro replace religious and moral convictions as the most important source of advice on child-rearing. After the First World War, the professional focus started to shift once again, with the emphasis on medical and hygienic aspects being gradually supplemented with psychological topics. This was evident, for instance, in later editions of *Infant care*, the publication of the US Children's Bureau. The 1920 edition, for example, addressed the psychosocial problem of discipline, advising parents to employ the approved traditional method of "habit training." The British *Mothercraft manual*, which started as a series in 1923, also embraced strict schedules of training.[18]

An explicit and detailed psychological perspective on infant development and child-rearing was expressed by the behaviorist John B. Watson. As a student of learning he had always been interested in developmental issues. His major contribution to popular advice on child-rearing came in the years after he was fired by his university because of an extramarital affair with a student. Watson emphasized, in many publications, the importance of a scientific approach to child-rearing. He argued that the traditional confidence in maternal (or parental) instinct was misplaced: a proper education needed the application of scientific psychology.[19]

Watson reached his largest audience of parents with *The psychological care of the infant and child* (1928). This popular book was written in collaboration with his former student who in the meantime had become his wife. Watson and Watson advocated a truly objective, scientific approach to matters educational. They were convinced that maternal love, however well-meant, inclined mothers to "smother" their child rather than mother it. This view of a natural female inclination toward sentimentality was apparently widely shared: many child-rearing manuals warned against female emotionality and emphasized an objective approach to motherhood.[20] "Scientific motherhood" as the Watsons saw it, distanced itself from confidence in feelings and based itself on a rational style of family interaction:

> There is a sensible way of treating children. Treat them as if they were young adults.
> . . . Never hug and kiss them, never let them sit in your lap. If you must, kiss them once
> on the forehead when they say good night. Shake hands with them in the morning. . . .
> Try it out. In a week's time you will find how easy it is to be perfectly objective with
> your child and at the same time kind. You will be utterly ashamed of the mawkish, sen
> timental way you have been handling it.[20]

Watson's objective approach to children and their development was popular, but it also repeatedly stirred controversy. This happened for example in the early 1920s

Figure 18 John B. Watson (*right*) with his most famous experimental subject, "Little Albert." To demonstrate the potential of learning and behavior modification, Watson induced Albert to learn to fear small animals such as mice by making a loud noise when the animals were presented to the baby. On the left is Rosalie Rayner, Watson's student and later his wife. Picture: courtesy of Benjamin Harris.

when people took issue with the way in which Watson had subjected a child to a psychological experiment. In this famous "little Albert" study, it was shown how a child could be taught to generalize his fear of a loud noise to harmless objects, such as a tiny rabbit or a soft cuddly toy (see figure 18). A little later, the American House-wives' League perceived *The psychological care of the infant and child* as an attack on the warm and affectionate American family. The public criticism did not impair the popular reception of Watson's books and his contributions to, among other periodicals, *Cosmopolitan* and *Harper's Magazine*. The large sale of *The psychological care of the infant and child* was probably also the result of its systematic coverage of day-to-day issues, such as toilet training, temper tantrums and childhood fears. What the Watsons advised here was far less sensational than their earlier statements, but turned out to be very practical.[22]

The impact of Watson's approach is discernible in the 1938 edition of *Infant care*. It explained in detail how learning principles could be applied to topics as varied as toilet training and food aversion. Watson's impact outside the United States is illustrated by Newson and Newson who quote a British college-educated woman saying about herself in the 1930s:

In my day we were instructed that frost never hurt a baby yet, and if the baby cried it must be *mastered*. Working-class women cuddled their babies up in the warm as women had done for millions of years. We, the young graduate law-abiding wives of the thirties, cried *ourselves* as our babies went blue with cold.

This woman felt obliged to commit herself to strict principles and assumed that bringing up children was far easier for mothers who did not carry the burden of scientific advice. In the United Kingdom, the earlier emphasis on habit training was continued in the 1930s by the famous Sir Frederic Truby King and his Mothercraft Training Society. He was convinced that "the leading authorities of the day – English, foreign and American – all agree that the first thing to establish in life is regularity of habits" (1937).[23] Like Watson, Truby King set out to propagate systematic training and an "objective" approach to child-rearing.

In the same period, other popular authors advocated a different approach. Susan Isaacs, for example, opposed the rigidity of the current "scientific motherhood," and supported an alternative, fairly liberal approach. Her views were based in psychoanalysis, and thus she argued in her popular book, *The nursery years* (1929) that "a good boiled sweet" could very well function as a "substitute pleasure" for thumb sucking. She also urged British parents to accept the noise, sloppiness, and disobedience of their children as a natural part of childhood.[24] In the United States, this new child-oriented attitude was stressed by Aldrich and Aldrich among others. In their book *Babies are human beings* (1938), they argued that the needs of babies should be respected rather than cast in the mold of discipline. The US Children's Bureau expressed the same spirit when it stated: "Babies want attention; they probably need plenty of it."[25] This relocated the baby to the central position it had occupied in nineteenth-century Romantic advisory literature; a large gap materialized between these child-centered approaches on the one hand, and the practices advocated by the Watsons on the other.

3.2   The Child Guidance Clinics

By the beginning of the 1920s, the pioneering work of Witmer and others had been followed in a number of ways in the United States. For example, about a dozen universities had established institutes for the assessment and treatment of disturbed children, and the Mental Hygiene Movement (MHM) had preached the necessity of prophylaxis at an early age and put this into practice. In 1921, the MHM opened the first "Child Guidance Clinic" (CGC) with financial support from the philanthropic Commonwealth Fund. This new type of clinic was intended to serve a clientele of disturbed and delinquent children, and mostly did so. The patients were often referred from juvenile courts, schools, and private physicians. The CGC proved to be a successful institution. In 1932 the National Committee for Mental Hygiene announced that 232 clinics were in operation, including part-time facilities. As a result of the expansion of the CGCs in the 1930s, the clientele changed from children at the margins of society to those from predominantly middle-class families. The new clients were often self-referred; for many parents, it seems that consulting a CGC was an attractive option alongside reading popular advice about child-rearing. The growth of the network of clinics coincided with a change in tone. The early CGCs advocated a strict approach in order to discipline the young clients; later the services aimed at an empathic understanding of children, and thus took account of children's own perspectives on their inner lives.

The model adopted by the Child Guidance Clinic combined prophylaxis, assessment and treatment, and used the concept of "mental health" as its dominant perspective. This implied an interdisciplinary approach in which each individual child was scrutinized from different professional perspectives: physicians investigated physical health and hygiene, psychologists assessed the child's capacities, and social workers mapped the child's domestic circumstances. Despite the general dedication to what was called "therapeutic teamwork," physicians were generally in charge of the clinic; thus they made the decisions concerning appropriate assessment and treatment. The position of psychologists was mostly weak, and they were obliged to confine themselves to rather circumscribed duties, such as administering psychological tests.

The fate of the psychological perspective was, by contrast, far more positive, with psychoanalytic accounts especially being widely employed in the clinics. Psychoanalysis had been used at a very early stage by the psychiatrist Healy in his treatment of young offenders, and it remained on the scene when the focus of the child guidance professionals shifted from delinquent youth to children suffering from mild "adaptational" problems at home and in school. The bio-historical method of psychoanalysis offered social workers a suitable framework for the compilation of case histories, and the therapists could use a psychoanalytic approach to family circumstances in their explanation of individual misbehavior and suffering.

In Europe, the institutional context had much in common with that of America. In England, for example, the Clinic at Tavistock Square in London (established in 1920) had both children and adults among its patients. The clinic treated mal-adjusted pupils and children with criminal records, but it was also concerned with "nervous" children from middle-class families. The American model of child guidance was imported in 1927 when the first clinic opened in London. Dutch hygienists kept pace with their Anglo-Saxon counterparts by establishing a child guidance clinic (*Medisch Opvoedkundig Bureau*) in Amsterdam in 1928. The network of British and Dutch clinics expanded quickly, and in less than a decade this kind of child guidance became one of the most important forms of social management. After the Second World War, Germany followed with the foundation of *Erziehungsberatungsstellen* ("educational advice bureaus"), modeled upon the child guidance clinics, but with the additional goal of re-educating German youth as democratic citizens.[26]

3.3 From discipline to "natural needs"

The Second World War had, of course, far-reaching consequences for children and their parents. In many countries fathers were sent away to the battlefields, and mothers labored in the munitions industry. Many children lost their parents as a result of wartime cruelties, such as bombings and the Holocaust. The British government established so-called "war nurseries" to provide care for urban children. Children, including orphans and some whose mothers worked untimely hours in munitions factories, were supported. Anna Freud was in charge of one of the London nurseries. She provided psychoanalytic therapy for the small victims of the *Blitzkrieg* using play as a way of entering into the orphan's mental world. She acknowledged the importance of the emotional ties between mother and child, but stressed in particular the profound positive contribution of emotional bonds among peers. Her fellow psychoanalyst Melanie Klein emphasized the primacy of the mother–child symbiosis and strongly opposed the separation of children from their biological mother. "Maternal deprivation," she argued, would generate unbridled aggression in nursery children which would be difficult to contain. Such psychoanalytic claims figured prominently in the postwar debate about these nurseries and finally contributed to the closure of the facilities.[27]

After the war, the advantages of the traditional family were proclaimed in almost all western countries. Rebuilding family life was generally seen as the key to children's welfare. The bond between mother and child was given primacy, and so mothers were pressed to concentrate exclusively on their reproductive roles.[28] Psychological arguments held a prominent position in the defense of traditional family values. The British psychiatrist John Bowlby expatiated upon the earlier notion of maternal deprivation. After the World Health Organization had asked him to report on the mental state of war orphans, in *Maternal care and mental health* (1951) Bowlby stated that many children in orphanages and refugee camps were emotionally withdrawn and lagged behind in development. According to Bowlby, this was caused by the separation of these children from their mothers. The children suffered from a lack of "vitamin A," that is, the affectionate attachment between mother and child, which was as important for development as vitamin D. The public at large, as well as many professionals, understood Bowlby's work as a scientific corroboration of the idea that a good mother stayed home with her young children.[29]

In the United States and the wealthier countries in Europe, economic growth in the 1950s improved material conditions for most families. It was easier to survive on one income, and so many married women could comply with the traditional role of mother. The availability of contraceptives enabled many young couples to limit the number of their children, which confirmed the demise of the large family. The nuclear family of the 1950s and 1960s gave parents, in particular mothers, ample room to focus their attention on the emotional well-being of their children.

Parents in the postwar period could turn for advice to a burgeoning array of literature. Specialized periodicals such as *Infant care* and *The mothercraft manual* continued to serve large audiences, and newspapers and magazines also regularly covered child-rearing issues. The advice given was by no means unequivocal. The American psychiatrist Levy, for example, continued to voice the prewar fears about maternal overprotection. As we have seen, Bowlby, by contrast, emphasized the dire consequences of maternal deprivation. As the psychoanalyst Winnicott put it, in his BBC radio talks of the 1950s: the "ordinary devoted mother" could be a source of both good and evil in the child's development.[30] One lesson could be drawn by the public: maternal instinct as such could not be trusted; women had to consciously learn how to be good mothers.

The American physician Benjamin Spock employed quite a different tone. In 1946 in *The common sense book of baby and child care* (soon retitled *The pocket book of baby and child care*) he urged parents, or rather mothers, to trust their own capacities, instead of addressing them as ignorant recipients of advice. Spock advocated a flexible approach to socialization based on a permissive attitude toward children. He was convinced that such flexibility would be more successful and pleasurable than the disciplinarian methods such as habit training which had been all too common in earlier decades (see figure 19). The chapter title "Enjoy your baby" aptly summarized Spock's basic philosophy: child-rearing could be greatly enjoyed by both parents and children as long as parents were not discomfited by their own uncertainties. In his advice, generally proffered as between equals, he employed a psychoanalytic frame, without however using explicitly psychoanalytic terminology. For example, while he informed his readers that girls of a certain age prefer to be boys and that infants may be very attached to their ordure, he did so without using the terms "penis envy" and "anal phase."[31]

The massive success of Spock's volume eclipsed all other popular parental advice books. In the next couple of decades, *The pocket book of baby and child care* appeared in many editions and was translated all over the world. In due course, other publications were also dominated by a flexible approach. *Infant care*, for example, advised the following about where the baby should sleep: "Do whatever way disturbs your

Be friendly and easygoing about the bathroom.

Figure 19 Illustration from Benjamin Spock's *Pocket book of baby and child care* (1946). In print for more than 50 years and translated into numerous languages, "Spock" is said to be the second best-selling book in the world (after the Bible). The drawing illustrates Spock's permissive attitude with respect to child-rearing, compared with the habit training advocated by earlier authors.

sleep least." This illustrates both the flexibility of the advice given and the notion that there was no need for parents to sacrifice their sleep in the baby's interest. A contemporary observer, Martha Wolfenstein, noted in 1951 that the widespread emphasis on flexibility and the joys of child-rearing marked the emergence of a new mentality. From now on, child-rearing would be dominated by what she called the "fun morality."[32]

3.4   Conclusion

The period roughly from 1920 to 1960 saw an expanding network concerned with the welfare of children and, with regard to popular advice, the gradual emergence of the advocacy of a flexible approach to the detriment of strict procedures. These developments left one structure almost untouched: western families were generally characterized by a gendered division of labor. Women had, of course, broken the traditional pattern during the Depression of the 1930s and during the Second World War, but the traditional maternal role was firmly restored after the war. Fears were voiced that mothers might deprive their children of maternal love, which was in a sense exactly the opposite of the interwar concern with maternal overprotection. Despite the conflicting thrusts of these psychological arguments, both attributed prime responsibility to the mother.

The gradual delineation of childhood as a separate phase intensified further, especially after the Second World War. Adolescence was recognized as a transitional phase between childhood and adult functioning. Parents were prompted to attend to the individual, psychological characteristics of children and teenagers in order to contribute to the full realization of their potential. They were also told that, if their children encountered problems, then child counseling or therapy would be available.[33] So, on the one hand, children gained a great measure of freedom to postpone their life choices, but, on the other hand, they were increasingly subjected to professional supervision.

4   The child at school (*c.* 1920–1960)

The "century of the child" was not only manifested in an increased interest in child-rearing practices in the home but also in social interventions to assist, guide, correct, and supplement parental efforts. Education flourished too, and in this area also the expertise of psychology played an increasingly important role. Around the turn of the century, the social goals of education gradually began to shift from those of instilling social discipline to a preparation for societal life or, to be more specific, for the world of work. The number of years children spent in school gradually increased to include a few years of secondary education. This partly reflected the greater complexity of society, which demanded a longer education. More importantly, education slowly began to replace social background as the dominant factor in the distribution of social position. This reflected the more general processes of individualization and increased social mobility. Individual capabilities ("merit") gained precedence over ancestry, and education was generally considered to be their main indicator. Thus, the traditional class society gave way little by little to the "schooling society."

Like parental child-rearing, education was subject to a process of professionalization and scientification, in which psychology had a prominent role. This was reflected both in its place within the training of teachers, and in the gradual proliferation of professional activity by psychologists within the educational system. In the United States, "educational psychology" developed into a discipline with a well-defined identity of its own, and direct links to both the training of teachers and educational theory and practice. Following the pioneering work of Thorndike before the First World War, the US saw the emergence of a strong, rather technologically oriented tradition of educational research. Amongst other things, this manifested itself in the development of new psychologically based teaching approaches. An early example was the *Thorndike arithmetics* (1917), a series of elementary textbooks produced according to the principles of Thorndike's psychology of learning. After the First World War other psychologists followed, with the development of new instructional methods for school subjects such as reading and mathematics. Although the changes these methods entailed were not at all as revolutionary as those advocated by Dewey and other "Progressive" pedagogues, they would deeply influence day-to-day educational practices.

Although there were some initiatives in Europe, involving the psychology of teaching and research into methods of evaluation, neither topic became really prominent before the Second World War. Because of the dominant position of pedagogy over psychology, and the strongly humanistic (*geisteswissenschaftlich*) orientation of pedagogy, the influence of psychology was both indirect and rather unspecific. Typically, as in the United States, psychology held a prominent place within teacher training. Thus, through courses in "pedagogical" or "educational" psychology," aspiring teachers became familiar with the current psychological theories of the day. When it came to specific advice or instructional methods, however, the impact of psychology in Europe was much smaller, overshadowed as it was by the more philosophical and anthropological conceptions of continental European pedagogy.[34]

The contrasts between the United States and Europe also manifested themselves in the most salient contribution of psychology to education – the measurement of individual differences. On both sides of the Atlantic, this subject gained a prominent place within educational theory and practice. However, there was great diversity in the way that it was tackled.

4.1   Meritocracy and the rise of mental testing

In sections 2.2 and 2.4, we discussed the early history of educational testing, including the invention of the intelligence test, and the rise of achievement testing in the United States. If intelligence testing was originally confined to "exceptional children," achievement testing had quickly become part and parcel of American education. By the early 1920s, there were already dozens of standardized achievement tests in print, for various school subjects, including the three Rs, geography, and history, as well as more outlandish tests such as a "Scale for Measuring Certain Elements in Hand Sewing." Indicative of their popularity were the sales figures of one of the more general tests, the Stanford Achievement Test, devised by psychologist Lewis Terman; published in 1923, its sales rocketed within two years to more than 1.5 million per year.[35]

Despite its widespread acceptance, achievement testing was overshadowed by a much more ambitious (and controversial) activity: the measurement of mental ability, more specifically, of intelligence. In 1908, Binet had already speculated about the future prospects for his tests:

> Countless applications are conceivable. Our ultimate dream is a future society better organized than ours, in which everyone will be employed according to his endowment, thus ensuring that no single part of mental endowment will be lost for society. That would be the ideal state.[36]

On the one hand, Binet's vision reflected the gradual change toward a "merito-cratic" society, based on individual merit rather than social background and ances-try. On the other hand, it spoke of the professional aspirations of psychologists: if ability was to be the decisive factor, and if they could measure ability, their expertise would be of vital importance in "modern" society.[37]

Between 1905 and 1911, Binet gradually extended the range of his test to include the assessment of higher levels of intellectual functioning. After his premature death in 1911, others continued his work along these lines. In 1912, the German psy-chologist William Stern proposed the concept and the mathematical formula, which would in time become almost synonymous with intellectual ability – the "intelligence quotient" or "IQ", defined as mental age divided by chronological age, multiplied by 100. Four years later, the American psychologist Lewis Terman published a test which, it was claimed, could also measure adult intelligence. This was the Stanford–Binet test, which would become the "gold standard" for intelligence testing for decades to come.

If European psychologists (including Binet himself) would long harbor some doubts regarding the validity of intelligence testing, their American colleagues were more confident. Not only did they unhesitatingly consider the test to be an adequate measure of intelligence, but influenced by eugenics and social darwinism, they also had a very definite concept about what was being measured. Intelligence was con-sidered to be: (i) a unitary phenomenon (rather than just a "sum" of various mental abilities), which (ii) exclusively or predominantly reflected genetic endowment (rather than upbringing, education or other "environmental" factors), and which (iii) not only reflected on educability, but also influenced the social functioning and worth of individuals in many other respects. As Terman expressed it: "Moral judgment, like business judgment, social judgment, or any other kind of higher thought process, is a function of intelligence."[38] Thus, intelligence-as-tested became almost synonymous with "fitness" as understood by eugenists and social darwinists, that is a measure of the genetic quality and social merit of an individual.

At first, the general public reacted with skepticism to these claims. This changed after the test was adopted by the military in 1917, when America entered the First World War. Within a year, a testing program had been devised and implemented which included intelligence testing of more than 1.7 million recruits for the army (see chapter 4). The result was a dual breakthrough. On the one hand, the army program resulted in a technological adaptation which made the test suitable for mass application: the paper-and-pencil test of intelligence, which did not require oral instruction, and thus was suitable for examining large numbers of people at one time. On the other hand, the apparent success of the program served to convince the public of the potential value of the tests. As one contemporary psychologist put it:

> Before the World War, the average intelligent layman probably had little confidence in the value or use of mental tests. After the war, he believed that psychologists had devised a simple and relatively perfect method of measuring intelligence.[39]

The purposes for which intelligence testing was promoted were almost limitless, varying from personnel selection to eugenic measurements (see chapters 4 and 6). It was, however, within education that the tests found their most favorable reception. The tests fitted in well with the general progressive themes of efficiency and adaptation of the curriculum to individual differences. This was reflected most prominently in the so-called "tracking system," which gained widespread acceptance within American schools in the course of the 1920s. Central to this system was the replacement of a uniform program by separate school tracks for "slow," "regular" and "fast" students. On the one hand, intelligence testing, with its strong emphasis on differences in ability and "mental endowment" provided an important impetus to the introduction of tracking (see figure 20). On the other hand, the introduction of the tracking system created a mass market for the test; where tracking was introduced, it was almost universally combined with the use of intelligence tests as the primary and sometimes even the only means of assessing and allocating children to the different tracks. In addition, the test was gradually introduced for other purposes, such as educational guidance, vocational guidance, and selection for higher education. Testimony to its rapid acceptance is the proliferation of the number of tests that were devised. In 1925, seven years after the war, there were already some 75 different intelligence tests in print.[40]

In the course of the 1930s, the consensus among American psychologists about the meaning and social importance of intelligence gradually dissolved. New studies cast doubt on the assumed overriding importance of "nature" over "nurture"; new models of intelligence stressed the diversity of various abilities rather than its unified character; and empirical research often failed to establish the alleged superiority of intelligence testing over other "predictors" of educational and social success. Thus, many of the presuppositions underlying the initial success of the testing movement came under siege, opening up an area of intellectual debate commonly known as the "nature–nurture controversy," which would periodically resurface in decades to come. As we will see in the next section, however, these disputes did not prevent the further proliferation of testing.

In Europe, the introduction of intelligence and related tests proceeded at a slower pace and in a less wholesale and pervasive way.[41] For one thing, in most countries the old class barriers in education continued to exist until the Second World War. In England for instance, where the tests were introduced as early as the 1920s, their impact was limited because of the divide between "elementary schools" (for the lower classes) and "preparatory schools" (for the middle and higher classes), which remained a major influence until after the Second World War. On the Continent, acceptance of the test was even slower. As well as being impeded by the persistence

Figure 20   Cartoon reflecting the advance of psychological testing in the American educational system. Source: *American School Journal*, 1922.

of class divisions, it was hampered both by rivalry between psychologists and pedagogues and by theoretical doubts among psychologists themselves. The common theme here was a deeply felt skepticism about the possibility of reducing something as complex as scholastic aptitude to a simple measure such as IQ. Insofar as tests were adopted, their use typically remained confined to the examination of "slow" children and within programs of educational and vocational guidance, rather than for institutional selection.

4.2   *The proliferation of psychology*

In the period between the two world wars the introduction of testing had given psychologists a place within the educational system. From this position they engaged in a myriad of other activities, such as the development of special educational and training programs for both slow learners and highly gifted pupils, and extensive "guidance" and "counseling" programs concerning both education and vocational choice.

After the Second World War, the involvement of psychologists in education increased even more. We will briefly review three of the most important manifestations of this expansion: the introduction of "school psychology" as a new professional identity, new forms of psychologically based instruction methods, and the further growth of testing.

SCHOOL PSYCHOLOGY

After the Second World War, the new concept of school psychology gained currency, describing and promoting the multifarious involvement of psychologists with education.[42] Again, the United States took the lead, but this time other developed countries were quick to follow. An important influence was the Mental Hygiene Movement which after the war (in the meantime having changed its name to Mental Health Movement) resumed its role as a major social influence, promoting all kinds of "welfare arrangements" to improve psychological well-being.

As we have seen, children and their development figured prominently as objects of concern within the Mental Hygiene Movement, as witnessed by the rapid expansion of Child Guidance Clinics. After the war attention gradually shifted from the clinics to schools. Whereas the Child Guidance Clinics had a limited reach, education provided an avenue for making every child subject to psycho-hygienic interference. As an American report put it:

> The schools enrol nearly all the children in the nation and so furnish each child's earliest contact with public authority . . . here in the all-important early years is the place where every opportunity should be seized for the promotion of good mental health – not just the prevention of mental illness, but the achievement of wholesome personality and happy, useful living . . . the schools have a major role in the promotion of good mental hygiene.[43]

The hygienists' interest in education thus clearly reflected their aspiration to become a major force of influence and intervention. School psychologists aligned with this movement, which provided them with a forceful rhetoric for promoting their services. Sponsored by leading agencies in the field of mental health, such as the US National Institute of Mental Health and Unesco, psychologists managed to obtain recognition for school psychology, resulting in the establishment of school psychological services in virtually all the countries of North America and Europe.

As well as a significant expansion of psychologists' involvement with education, school psychology also reflected a shift in emphasis from testing and educational technology to the emotional development and adaptation of the child. A new, clinical psychological perspective was introduced into education, exemplified by concepts such as "school readiness" and "fear of failure," and resulting in an extension of psychological activity to include a more or less therapeutic approach.

THE PSYCHOLOGY OF LEARNING AND EDUCATIONAL TECHNOLOGY

New developments also took place in the area of the psychology of learning, traditionally the theoretical heart of educational psychology. In the United States,
Thorndike's connectionism as the dominant paradigm was replaced after the war by
the behaviorism propounded by Burrhus F. Skinner.[44] In accordance with the central
tenets of behaviorism, Skinner regarded education as the acquisition of appropriate
behavior, and he strongly propagated the use in education of his "operant conditioning" model. According to Skinner, educational goals should be formulated
in concrete, well-defined terms of behavior. Subsequently, this behavior was to be
stimulated and rewarded ("reinforced") as efficiently as possible by means of the
principles of operant conditioning. To this end Skinner propagated the use of "teaching machines" for individualized instruction; these would present the subject matter
step by step and provide immediate feedback on students' responses (see figure 21).

Toward the end of the 1950s American educational research received a strong
impetus from the National Defense Education Act (1957). Enacted during the Cold
War, this law was a direct reaction to the launching of the first space rocket, the
Sputnik, by the Russians in 1957. If America was to keep up with the Soviet Union,
it was argued, it was of paramount importance to increase its scientific and technological potential. Education was seen as the most important means to this end. Enor-

Figure 21   Teaching machine, *c.* 1950s. Source: B. F. Skinner (1968), *The technology of teaching* (New York: Appleton-Century-Crofts).

mous amounts of new funding became available, as a result of which the number of educational researchers tripled within ten years.[45] Although psychologists were not the only group to profit, they did play a prominent part in this trend, partly as a result of the rise of cognitive psychology, which seemed to offer a fertile new paradigm for the development of more efficient and scientifically based educational methods.

In Europe too, the 1960s saw a revival of interest in empirically orientated educational research. Traditional, philosophically oriented pedagogy was waning, resulting in new opportunities for psychology and the application of empirical methods of investigation.

THE EXPANSION OF TESTING

Despite these new interests, testing remained by far the most influential aspect of psychology in education. In the United States, increasing participation in higher education created a new market, alongside the continuing use of tests in elementary and high schools.[46] Before the war, a couple of Ivy League universities had already experimented with the use of tests as selection instruments. To this end, a special test had been developed in 1927 – the Scholastic Aptitude Test (SAT). After the war, the SAT was promoted aggressively by its publisher, the recently founded Educational Testing Service, as a fair and effective way for the selection of aspiring students. These efforts met with success, as a growing number of universities, faced with rapidly increasing numbers of applicants, adopted the test as their main, and sometimes only, means of selection.

Intelligence and other tests were also being introduced on an increasing scale in Europe. Partly, this reflected the continuation of education beyond elementary school, which had also become increasingly common in postwar Europe. In contrast to the United States, however, the promotion of testing was inspired by motives of social justice, rather than efficiency. The most notable example of this was in Great Britain, where the so-called "eleven-plus" examination was introduced in 1945. Intelligence tests were central to this statutory examination, taken at the end of primary education and which served as a basis for admission into secondary education.Its most important aim was to remove traditional class barriers in British education, providing better educational and social chances to children from lower social backgrounds. In other countries, such as the Netherlands, the advance of psychological tests manifested itself in large-scale projects of educational and vocational guidance; children were tested toward the conclusion of primary education in order that advice could be given on the choice of secondary education.

Toward the end of the 1950s testing received a new boost, due to a growing emphasis on detecting ability. Society, it was thought, could not afford to leave talent and "human potential" unused. This conviction arose partly because of technological developments and economic conditions which had created a shortage of well-qualified personnel. Cold War motives were also involved, especially in the United States. As a consequence of the National Defense Education Act mentioned earlier, a large-scale testing and guidance program was instigated with the aim of identifying talented young people and encouraging their interest in technical and scientific studies.

4.3   Conclusion

In the middle decades of the twentieth century, psychology gained a definite foothold within education. Before the war it flourished primarily in the United States, through the establishment of solid traditions of research and teaching, combined with the wide-scale introduction of testing as its most salient contribution. After the war, its spheres of activity widened to include psychosocial care and new forms of educational technology, besides testing. And its influence spread geographically also, as European countries increasingly followed the example of the US in incorporating psychological practices and insights into their educational systems.

Despite the broadening scope of psychology, testing undoubtedly remained its important contribution to education. By stressing the importance of aptitude and individual differences, psychologists had played an important role in the transformation from nineteenth-century class education to a meritocratic educational system, with its emphasis on individual abilities as determinants in a child's educational career. Moreover, the introduction of testing also meant that the definition of aptitude and "merit" became to a large extent a matter for psychologists. Especially in the United States, tests came to determine children's educational careers to a large extent, and therefore their social perspectives. Thus, the meritocratic ideal increasingly evolved into what could be called a "psychocracy": a social structure in which psychology played a decisive role in the distribution of educational chances and social position – and therefore in the legitimization of social differences. As we will see in the next section, however, this role would not remain unchallenged.

5   New problems and perspectives (*c.* 1960–present)

During the 1960s and early 1970s, a sanguine social climate coincided with economic prosperity. The optimism of the time was reflected in the conviction that environmental factors determined individual development. In order to enhance its quality, formal education was further infused with refined psychological concepts and technologies. The civil rights movement and feminism translated ideas of environmental determination into political claims. Psychological arguments were often used to substantiate these demands, regarding, for example, gender-role socialization and educational opportunities.

5.1   Concern for disadvantaged children

In the course of the 1960s, a new theme emerged with respect to both child-rearing at home and school education: the problem of disadvantaged children. To a large extent, the objects of concern were the same groups of children who in the nineteenth and earlier twentieth century had been the prime targets for social and psychological surveillance and intervention, that is children from poor backgrounds, or of non-white ethnicity, or both. However, the perspective had markedly shifted, with the emphasis now on emancipation and improving social opportunities, rather than control and discipline.

Again, the United States led the way. From the 1950s, concerned organizations had urged the government to take action on the poor living conditions of blacks and other minorities. In the early 1960s, poverty among whites also became an issue. Within both the discipline of psychology and society at large, hereditary explanations of social differences had gradually given way to environmental ones, with social background rather than genetics considered to be the main determinant of social prospects. As part of the "unconditional war on poverty," the federal administration in 1965 launched "Operation Head Start," one of the largest programs of social management in American history. Child Development Centers were established in urban poverty areas where preschoolers were offered attractive courses to develop their potential. In the schools, Head Start was supplemented by various programs for so-called "compensatory education," aiming to make up for deficits in the home environment. Also, parents were drawn into programs of parental participation and families were provided with psychological counseling, nutritional advice, and health services; from the mid-1970s, this was developed as a semi-independent program, "Home Start."[47]

The American example was followed in Europe, although on a less extensive scale. In the United Kingdom, for example, "educational priority areas" were designated in 1968 where families were offered compensatory education. The need to compensate for social deprivation was also acknowledged in Dutch politics. Most large cities established educational programs for underprivileged children from the lowest social strata, in which school and the home environment were linked together.

The 1960s' belief in environmental determination also had implications for the use of intelligence tests as diagnostic and selective instruments within education. If intelligence was socially determined, then testing simply reproduced social inequality, it was argued. Moreover, empirical studies cast doubts on the alleged value of the tests as predictors of scholastic achievement. Consequently, in many countries intelligence testing was abolished or greatly reduced. In the United States, for instance, various court rulings prohibited the use of the tests as criteria for the assignment of pupils to different tracks within elementary education or special classes for those with severe learning disabilities.[48]

Psychology had a prominent role in compensatory education on both sides of the Atlantic. The effects of programs such as Head Start were studied in detail. Most researchers concluded that children certainly profited from this supplementation, but that the positive effects disappeared soon after completion. A public debate about this lack of lasting success developed in many countries. Critical sociologists argued that compensatory education left the capitalist structures of inequality untouched. The psychologist Arthur Jensen gave quite a different explanation for the failure of Head Start. In his 1969 paper "How much can we boost IQ and scholastic achievement?" he formulated a pessimistic answer. The manipulation of environmental factors would be of limited effect, according to Jensen, because about 80 percent of intelligence is determined by heredity.[49]

Jensen's claims gave rise to a heated controversy, including accusations of political bias and racism. The hereditary position received a serious blow when evidence suggested it was partly based on fraudulent research by the British psychologist Burt.[50] Nevertheless, the lack of lasting success was an important argument for reducing special provisions for underprivileged children when economic resources became less abundant in the 1970s.

In the mid-1990s, the issues addressed by Jensen would once again enter into the political debate, when psychologist Richard Herrnstein and political theorist Charles Murray published *The bell curve* (1994).[51] Subtitled "Intelligence and class structure in American life," this book by and large reiterated the position held by Jensen and earlier proponents of the hereditarian position: social differences are predominantly the result of genetically determined differences in intelligence, rather than differences in education or social background. The public attention generated by the book once again testified to the overriding importance attached to intelligence, and hence the impact of psychological theory on social issues.

5.2   Expert advice, families, and institutions

In the 1970s, new forms of child support were developed. Most did not involve the expensive establishment of separate institutions for the underprivileged. Efforts to compensate for societal disadvantage became part of projects directed toward the population at large. In most western countries infant welfare centers and child guidance clinics intensified their programs of early screening on such a scale that almost all babies and infants were monitored. The common practice of early medical diagnosis and educational advice was supplemented with psychosocial assessment. This kind of comprehensive screening became the new standard in many countries during the 1970s.[52] The notion of the "enriched environment," originally developed within the Head Start and Home Start programs, was generalized to large parts of the population. Childcare professionals advised parents to supply their children with rich stimuli and challenging toys in the playpen, and books such as Joan Beck's *How to raise a brighter child* (1968) offered popular kinds of instruction.

Preschool playgroups were assumed to offer a different type of enriched environment. The playgroup was run by volunteer mothers, and offered a safe environment where infants could interact with peers for a couple of hours weekly. In the United States and western Europe, this large-scale activity was more or less professionalized during the 1970s, when volunteer mothers were trained to keep an eye on the medical and psychosocial condition of children as part of preventionist programs. In some cases, playgroups and locals authorities explicitly opened playgroups for underprivileged children to offer them an educational environment that was not available at home.

Professional daycare facilities modeled after the French *crèches* differed in aim from the playgroups. The crèches offered daylong care to enable mothers to combine a career with having children. Despite the fact that feminist organizations strongly supported professional daycare in the 1970s, its development was not very fast in most western countries. There were blunt economic reasons for this, especially in the second half of the decade when governmental budgets were cut as a result of the recession. But a second reason was as influential as the financial one: professional daycare had become controversial, particularly for preschoolers. The opposing views were largely drawn from psychology. Psychoanalysts used the concept of "maternal deprivation" to point out the harmful effects of early separation; other psychologists concluded that infants generally profited from daycare.[53] Generally, public opinion followed the psychoanalytic line of reasoning thus emphasizing the traditional maternal role. In most countries it took almost two decades for emancipatory arguments in favor of daycare to gain political weight. But by that time, a new argument had appeared in the discussion: women were needed desperately in the labor market.

From the second half of the 1970s onward, the psychosocial view of child-rearing was increasingly challenged by a biomedical perspective, whose emphasis on constitutional factors in development in fact limited the claims of the "nurture" position. If, for example, temperament and the acquisition of language were determined by inborn factors it would be less easy to optimize individual potential through adjustment of the environment. The biomedical perspective derived its credibility largely from the successes in prenatal diagnosis, for example with respect to genetic diseases. It often led to a medicalization of developmental issues, in particular in popular accounts. The case of hyperactivity neatly illustrates this development. By the end of the 1970s, the diagnostic category ADHD (attention deficit hyperactivity disorder) came to replace "hyperactivity" as a label for an unruly child. Thus the child's behavior was medicalized, with a biological defect being identified as the cause of hyperactivity, rather than, for example, social overstimulation or confusing family relations. The medical diagnosis of ADHD also had consequences for treatment. The drug Ritalin repaired the biological deficit, so that the young patient could function again in ordinary circumstances.[54]

5.3 Role insecurity and generational conflict

Family relationships were not immune to the social changes of the 1960s and 1970s. Feminism deliberately extended politics from the public domain into the private sphere. The idea of "sexual politics" was targeted at the powerful position of the husband in the traditional family, and the dependent position of his wife. In 1963, the American feminist Betty Friedan indicted the confinement of women exclusively to motherhood. She painted a sad picture of middle-class mothers who lived like suburban widows in their comfortable houses on the outskirts of town. "Our culture does not permit women to accept or gratify their basic needs to grow and fulfil their potentialities as human beings."[55] American and European feminists translated Friedan's analysis into political claims for female self-determination. They generally saw participation in the labor force as the chosen instrument for emancipation. This required daycare facilities for their children as well as a redistribution of domestic duties between husband and wife. Feminist sexual politics were also concerned with the emancipation of children. For example, they propagated, toys, children's books, and educational materials that were non-sexist, in order to counter the stereotypes about men and women. The equal division of productive and reproductive labor between father and mother was seen as the most important contribution to non-sexist education. This kind of modeling would result, it was argued, in less traditional gender identities in the next generation. Actual practice soon tempered feminist optimism about reconstructing gender roles. It transpired that it was not that easy for most women and men to practice a non-traditional gender role.[56]

Family relations were also put under strain by the rapid expansion of the youth movement in the 1960s and 1970s. Adolescent rebellion became a defining characteristic of the new "youth culture," and thus many youngsters took issue with the rules and customs of their parents. Many commentators explained the conflicts between parents and children by reference to the so-called "generation gap": parents simply were too old to understand the attitudes of their offspring. Erikson's concept of "identity crisis" was employed by himself and many other social scientists to explain the roots of the protest movements. Young people felt lost, Erikson argued, and they tried to compensate for their insecurities by a strong commitment to radical politics. It was only a small step for political conservatives to pathologize adolescent protest: psychology had after all shown that the rebels were motivated by personal reasons rather than political ones.[57]

The public manifestations of the youth movement showed a complex mixture of politics and a new lifestyle. Long hair, for example, came to symbolize radical democratic politics, and political protest songs reached the top of the pop music charts. In due course, rebellion became a market. Leisure industries supplied adolescents with a range of items to sustain their subculture.

5.4   Conclusion

By 1970, the balance of power between the governors and the governed had changed as a result of the political upheaval. These changes were manifested in the universities, in schools, and at work, and also in family life. Family organization developed as diverse structures. Families where both mother and father held a job outside the home came to outnumber traditional families. A variety of child-rearing styles evolved. Some parents may have continued the familiar authoritarian relationship, but most engaged in "reasoning with their child." This democratic approach was a direct spin-off from radical humanism in politics. It granted autonomy to children: they were assumed to be the principal agents in their own lives and thus held accountable for their actions. The argumentative turn in bringing up children also generated doubt in parents; many became insecure, being able to rely neither on familiar patterns of child-rearing, nor on the authority of experts, nor on their own authority in family disputes. If in need, parents could take advantage of a number of resources provided by the welfare state, or consult one of the many child-rearing manuals that had appeared in the wake of Spock's commercial success.

6   Conclusion

In this chapter, we have explored the gradual advance of psychological practices relating to child-rearing and education and the more general "psychologization" of childhood in which these practices were embedded. We started with a sketch of the emergence of childhood as a separate stage of life, a process which started in the late middle ages and was confirmed at the end of the nineteenth century by the ban on child labor and the introduction of compulsory education. This process was linked a gradual increase in advice and social interventionism regarding education and child-rearing, especially during the nineteenth century. These developments were characterized by an enormous upsurge in literature proffering advice to parents; the rise of formal education as a socially controlled supplement to parental child-rearing; and the emergence of various institutions for children who, in one way or another, needed special attention.

In the second section, we discussed the introduction of psychological perspectives on childhood and new models of intervention, based on the "new psychology": the child study movement, the rise of educational psychology and a psychologically oriented pedagogy, and the emergence of psychological practices, which were geared toward assisting parents and teachers with regard to "difficult" children. The third and fourth sections discussed the prolongation of childhood and the expansion of psychological perspectives and practices concerning children in the middle years of the twentieth century (1920–1960). We considered the psychologization of parental advice literature, the rise of child guidance clinics and other institutions to help and advise parents in their duties, and the growing prominence of psychological notions and instruments in educational practice. The fifth section provided a tentative sketch of more recent developments, indicating that the psychologization of childhood has by no means come to an end. On the contrary, if anything, recent decades show a steady production of new problems and new modes of intervention, varying from minimal brain dysfunction and ADHD to the complexities of gender-role education, the prevention of bullying at school, and the effects of violent television shows and computer games on children's moral development.

We began with the popular Swedish writer Ellen Key, who in 1900 heralded the beginning of the "century of the child." Based on the developments discussed in this chapter, we may conclude that this prophecy has to a great extent come true. Moreover, we have tried to document how the growing emphasis on childhood has gone hand in hand with a rise to prominence of the psychologically informed child expert. It is important to note how these developments have been mutually reinforcing. On the one hand, notions about the importance of childhood as a separate phase in life and the vulnerability of children created a demand from parents and educators for advice. On the other hand, experts did more than simply cater for these demands. Their very work reinforced notions about the vulnerability of children, thus fueling new worries and new forms of parental insecurity.

The problematic relationship between expertise and parental competence has not gone unnoticed. From the 1970s onwards, a number of critics have taken issue with the growing influence of psychological expertise on child-rearing and education. A notable example is the American historian Lasch. In *Haven in a heartless world* (1977) and *The culture of narcissism* (1978), Lasch vehemently attacked psychological experts, characterizing their work as a "colonization of the family," tending to leave parents with a sense of insecurity and helplessness and thus producing problems in child-rearing rather than helping to solve them. Our history partly supports Lasch's thesis, as witnessed by the reception of the work of the Watsons. To some degree, we may even extend it: apart from fostering rather intangible feelings of parental insecurity, experts have in a very real sense contributed to defining "new" forms of abnormality, such as "feeble-mindedness" and ADHD. Nevertheless, as we hope that we have demonstrated, simply putting the blame on psychology and its practitioners does not do justice to the complexities of the historical process. If psychology left its mark, it could only do so by elaborating on concepts of childhood which were already prevalent. Thus, this chapter corroborates our perspective on the relation between social developments and the rise of psychology as a two-way street, carrying various forms of traffic.

PRINCIPAL SOURCES AND FURTHER READING

H. Cunningham (1995), *Children and childhood in Western society since 1500* (London: Addison Wesley Longman) is an authoritative resource for (social-)historical details throughout this chapter. With regard to family life see: M. Mitteraurer and R. Sieder (1982), *The European family: patriarchy to partnership from the Middle Ages to the present* (Oxford: Blackwell). The development of education is covered in M. J. Maynes (1985), *Schooling in Western Europe* (Albany: State University of New York Press). See for the United States: L. A. Cremin (1980–1988), *American education, vol. II: the national experience, 1783–1876* and *vol. III: the metropolitan experience, 1876–1980* (New York: Harper and Row).

A short, but illuminating review of subsequent paradigms of child-rearing advice is J. Newson and E. Newson (1974), Cultural aspects of childrearing in the English-speaking world, in M. P. M. Richards, ed., *The integration of a child into a social world* (London: Cambridge University Press), pp. 53–83. For the child study movement and its antecedents see A. W. Siegel and S. H. White (1982), The child study movement: early growth and development of the symbolized child, in H. W. Reese, ed., *Advances in child development and behavior, vol. 17* (New York: Academic Press), pp. 233–86. A recent study on the development of the educational sciences in the US is E. Condliffe Lagemann (2000), *An elusive science. The troubling history of education research* (Chicago: University of Chicago Press). Respecting the "feeble-minded" and the rise of intelligence testing, see L. Zenderland (1998), *Measuring minds. Henry Herbert Goddard and the origins of American intelligence testing* (Cambridge: Cambridge University Press). On the broader ramifications of intelligence testing for American education, see P. D. Chapman (1988), *School as sorters. Lewis M. Terman, applied psychology, and the intelligence testing movement, 1890–1930* (New York: New York University Press).

NOTES

1   I. Weijers (2000), Punishment and upbringing: Considerations for an educative justification of punishment. *Journal of Moral Education, 29,* 61–73.

2   W. Hall (1991), Pediatrics and child development: A parallel history. In F. S. Kessel et al., eds., *Contemporary constructions of the child* (Hillsdale: Erlbaum), pp. 209–25; R. R. Sears (1975), Your ancients revisited: a history of child development, in E. M.

Hetherington, ed., *Review of child development research, vol. 5* (Chicago: University of Chicago Press), pp. 1–73.

3 See for the United States: D. C. Charles (1987), The emergence of educational psychology, in J. A. Glover and R. R. Ronning, eds., *Historical foundations of educational psychology* (New York: Plenum Press), p. 20.

4 H. de Raaf (1911/1889), *De Beginselen der Zielkunde op eene aanschouwelijke wijze ten dienste van het onderwijs verklaard* [The principles of psychology explained and clarified for the benefit of education] (Tiel: Mijs), p. 4.

5 A. de Regt (1984), *Arbeidersgezinnen en beschavingsarbeid* [Working class families and the civilizing offensive] (Amsterdam: Boom), pp. 152–4.

6 Cunningham, *Children and childhood*, p. 147.

7 C. Darwin (1877), A biographical sketch of an infant, *Mind*, 2, 286–94; H. Taine (1876), Note sur l'acquisition du language chez les enfants et dans l'espèce humaine, *Revue Philosophique*, 1, 3–23.

8 S. H. White (1990), Child study at Clark University: 1894–1904, *Journal of the History of the Behavioral Sciences*, 26, 131–51; L. Zenderland (1988), Education, evangelism, and the origins of clinical psychology: the child-study legacy, *Journal of the History of the Behavioral Sciences*, 24, 152–66.

9 D. Depaepe (1998), *De pedagogisering achterna* [Following pedagogization] (Leuven: Acco), p. 136; Zenderland, *Measuring minds*, p. 92.

10 N. Rose (1990), *Governing the soul* (London: Routledge), p. 149.

11 For a broad overview of the reform movement see H. Röhrs and V. Lenhart, eds. (1995), *Progressive education across the continents* (Frankfurt am Main: Lang). For the US, see L. A. Cremin (1961), *The transformation of the school. Progressivism in American education 1876–1957* (New York: Knopf).

12 M. Levine and A. Levine (1970), *A social history of helping services. Clinic, court, school, and community* (New York: Appleton-Century-Crofts).

13 P. McReynolds (1997), *Lightner Witmer. His life and times.* (Washington, DC: American Psychological Association); the quote is on p. 76. See also: Levine and Levine, *A social history of helping services*, pp. 49–72; D. S. Napoli (1981), *Architects of adjustment. The history of the psychological profession in the United States* (Port Washington, NY: Kennikat Press), pp. 16–17.

14 J. Trent (1994), *Inventing the feeble mind: a history of mental retardation in the United States* (Berkeley; University of California Press); I. Weijers (2000), Educational initiatives in mental retardation in nineteenth-century Holland, *History of Education Quarterly*, 40, 460–76.

15 For a description of the development of the Binet scales, see T. H. Wolf (1973), *Alfred Binet* (Chicago: Chicago University Press).

16 Zenderland, *Measuring minds*, pp. 143–301; Trent, *Inventing the feeble mind*, pp. 131–83.

17 Figures from: S. Contratto (1984), Mother, social sculptor and trustee of faith, in M. Lewin, ed., *In the shadow of the past: psychology portrays the sexes* (New York: Columbia University Press), pp. 226–56; For "domestic science" see S. Schlossman (1976), Before Home Start: notes toward a history of parent education in America 1897–1929, *Harvard Educational Review*, 46, 436–467. D. Beddoe (1989), *Back to home and duty. Women between the wars, 1918–1939* (London: Pandora) discusses the public reaction to the "flappers."

18 W. Kessen (1993), Avoiding the emptiness: the full infant, *Theory & Psychology*, 3, 415–29. C. E. Vincent (1951), Trends in infant care ideas, *Child Development*, 22, 199–209.

19   D. Cohen (1979), *J. B. Watson. The founder of behaviorism. A biography* (London: Routledge), pp. 209–17.

20   S. Shields and V. Koster (1989), Emotional stereotyping of parents in child rearing manuals, 1915–1980, *Social Psychology Quarterly, 52*, 44–55.

21   As quoted in Newson and Newson, Cultural aspects of childrearing, p. 60.

22   B. Harris (1979), Whatever happened to Little Albert? *American Psychologist, 34,* 151–60; B. Harris (1984), "Give me a dozen healthy infants . . ." John B. Watson's popular advice on child-rearing, women and the family, in Lewin, ed., *In the shadow of the past: psychology portrays the sexes* (New York: Columbia University Press), pp. 126–55.

23   The quotes are taken from Newson and Newson, Cultural aspects of childrearing. The first one is on p. 62, the King quote is on p. 60.

24   As quoted in N. Rose (1985), *The psychological complex. Psychology, politics and society in England, 1869–1939* (London: Routledge), p. 198.

25   As quoted in Newson and Newson, Cultural aspects of childrearing, p. 64.

26   For the British clinics, see Rose, *The psychological complex*, p. 201; for the Netherlands, see F. Gerards (1979), Preventie voor jeugdigen in de ambulante ggz [Prevention for youth in ambulant mental health care], *Maandblad Geestelijke Volksgezondheid, 34,* 608–25. And for Germany, see R. Maikowski, P. Mattes, and G. Rott (1976), *Psychologie und ihre Praxis. Geschichte und Funktion in der BRD* [Psychology and its practice. History and function in the German Federal Republic] (Frankfurt-am-Main: Fischer), pp. 49–60.

27   D. Riley (1983), *War in the nursery* (London: Virago), pp. 97–8.

28   J. Lewis (1986), Anxieties about the family and the relationship between parents, children and the state in twentieth century England, in M. Richards and P. Light, eds., *Children of social worlds* (Cambridge: Polity Press), pp. 31–55.

29   I. Bretherton (1992), The origins of attachment theory: John Bowlby and Mary Ainsworth, *Developmental Psychology, 28,* 759–75.

30   Lewis, Anxieties about the family; Rose, *Governing the soul*, pp. 202–3.

31   A. M. Sulman (1973), The humanization of the American child: Benjamin Spock as a popularizer of psychoanalytic thought. *Journal of the History of the Behavioral Sciences, 9,* 258–65.

32   M. Wolfenstein (1951), The emergence of fun morality, *Journal of Social Issues, 7,* 15–25.

33   See R. B. Cairns (1983), The emergence of developmental psychology, in P. H. Mussen, ed., *Handbook of child psychology, vol. 1* (New York: Wiley), pp. 41–103, in particular pp. 86–7 for the postwar decade.

34   M. Schubeius (1990), *Und das psychologische Laboratorium muss der Ausgangspunkt pädagogischer Arbeiten werden!* [The psychological laboratory must become the base for pedagogical practice] (Frankfurt-am-Main: Peter Lang).

35   M. Walsh (1999), Quiz biz, *Education Week on the Web, 18,* June 16.

36   A. Binet and T. Simon (1908), Le développement de l'intelligence chez les enfants, *l'Année Psychologique, 14,* 1–94; quote p. 83, translation PvD/JJ.

37   For the early testing movement in general, see M. M. Sokal, ed., 1987, *Psychological testing and American society 1890–1930* (New Brunswick/London: Rutgers University Press).

38   L. M. Terman (1916), *The measurement of intelligence* (Boston: Houghton Mifflin), p. 11. For a historical and critical analysis of these claims, see D. L. Eckberg (1979), *Intelligence and race* (New York: Praeger).

39   F. Samelson (1979), Putting psychology on the map, in A. R. Buss, ed., *Psychology in social context* (New York: Irvington), pp. 103–68, quote on p. 107.

40 Chapman, *School as sorters*, p. 1.

41 For the UK, see A. Wooldridge (1994), *Measuring the mind: education and psychology in England, 1860–1990* (Cambridge: Cambridge University Press); for Germany, see Schubeius, *Und das psychologische Laboratorium* and R. Schmid (1977), *Intelligenz- und Leistungsmessung. Geschichte und Funktion psychologischer Tests* [The measurement of intelligence and achievement. History and function of psychological tests] (Frankfurt: Campus); for France, see W. H. Schneider (1992), After Binet: French intelligence testing, 1900–1950, *Journal of the History of the Behavioural Sciences*, *28*, 111–32.

42 For early uses of the term "school psychology" and its antecedents, see T. K. Fagan (1992), Compulsory schooling, child study, clinical psychology, and special education. Origins of school psychology, *American Psychologist*, *47*, 236–43. A short but useful overview of developments after the Second World War is T. Oakland (1993), A brief history of international school psychology, *Journal of School Psychology*, *31*, 109–22.

43 N. E. Cutts, ed. (1955), *School psychologists at mid-century* (Washington, DC: American Psychological Association), p. 3.

44 See for Skinner's influence on education, R. Glaser (1978), The contributions of B. F. Skinner to education and some counterinfluences, in P. Suppes, ed., *Impact of research on education: some case studies* (Washington, DC: National Academy of Education), pp. 199–266.

45 See L. J. Cronbach and P. Suppes (1969), *Research for tomorrow's schools: Disciplined inquiry for education* (London: Macmillan), pp. 202–12.

46 See for a provocative account, N. Lemann (1999), *The big test. The secret history of the American meritocracy* (New York: Farrar, Straus and Giroux).

47 See E. Zigler and J. Valentine, eds. (1979), *Project Head Start, a legacy of the War on Poverty* (New York: The Free Press), and A. C. Ornstein (1982), The education of the disadvantaged: a 20-year review, *Educational Research*, *24*, 197–211.

48 See for the United States, A. K. Wigdor and W. R. Garner, eds. (1982), *Ability testing: uses, consequences and controversies, part II* (Washington, DC: National Academy Press), pp. 173–285; for England, see Wooldridge, *Measuring the mind*, pp. 330–8.

49 A. R. Jensen (1969), How much can we boost IQ and scholastic achievement? *Harvard Educational Review*, *39*, 1–123. See for a sample of critical contributions to the debate, N. J. Block and G. Dworkin, eds. (1976), *The IQ-controversy* (New York: Pantheon). For a historical analysis of the debate, J. Harwood (1978), Heredity, environment, and the legitimation of social policy, in B. Barnes and S. Shapin, eds., *Natural order. Historical studies of scientific culture* (London: Sage), pp. 231–51.

50 F. Samelson (1992), Rescuing the reputation of Sir Cyril Burt, *Journal of the History of the Behavioral Sciences*, *28*, 221–33.

51 R. J. Herrnstein and C. Murray (1994), *The bell curve. Intelligence and class structure in American life* (New York: Free Press). See for critical reactions, B. Devlin et al., eds. (1997), *Intelligence, genes, and success. Scientists respond to The Bell Curve* (New York: Springer), and C. S. Fischer et al. (1996), *Inequality by design. Cracking the Bell Curve myth* (Princeton: Princeton University Press).

52 S. A. Mednick and A. E. Baert, eds. (1981), *Prospective longitudinal research: an empirical basis for the primary prevention of psychosocial disorders* (Oxford: Oxford University Press). This compendium reports about seventy studies in many different countries.

53 E. Singer (1993), Shared care for children, *Theory & Psychology*, *3*, 429–49. S. Scarr (1998), American child care today, *American Psychologist*, *53*, 95–108.

54 R. J. DeGrandpre (1999), *Ritalin nation: rapid fire culture and the transformation of human consciousness* (New York: W. W. Norton).

55   B. Friedan (1963), *The feminine mystique* (Baltimore: Penguin Books), p. 69. K. Millett (1969), *Sexual politics* (New York: Doubleday).

56   An important and influential example was N. Chodorow (1978), *The reproduction of mothering* (Berkeley, CA: University of California Press).

57   E. H. Erikson (1968), *Identity, youth and crisis* (New York: Norton). See also E. Herman (1995), *The romance of American psychology. Political culture in the age of experts* (Berkeley: University of California Press), p. 293.

3 Madness and mental health

Ruud Abma

Introduction

In this chapter, our focus is on the mental health field. Looking back from the twenty-first century, one is struck by the enormous quantitative growth of the mental health domain – institutions, professionals, and clients. In the 1890s, only a very small number of individuals could reasonably have been called psychotherapists. By 1990, a minimum of one-third of the US population had used psychotherapy at some point in their lives as an appropriate means for treating a broad array of physical, psychological, and behavioral problems and disorders. By even the most stringent criteria, a minimum of 100,000 fully qualified, highly trained psychotherapists are available to serve the mental health needs of the US today. Using a broader definition, there may be as many as 250,000 psychotherapists and counselors available.[1]

Secondly, the mental health field has expanded in a qualitative way: the array of treatment possibilities has broadened from custodial care and "moral treatment" in the nineteenth century to a wide variety of psychological and pharmacological approaches in recent decades. Correspondingly, the number of disciplines involved has expanded as well, often in a vehement struggle for supremacy. Nowadays, the mental health field includes not only psychiatrists and psychoanalysts but also clinical psychologists of various persuasions, social workers, and pastoral counselors, to which has been added most recently a new wave of physicians who adhere to a neurological and physiological stance.

This expansion of the mental health field is related in a rather complicated way to cultural and social issues, as well as to developments within psychiatry and psychology. On the one hand, it is a reflection of broader cultural developments, such as those we have encountered in earlier chapters, specifically, individualization, the rise of social management, and "psychologization." On the other hand, mental health practices also contributed to individualization by developing therapies specially aimed at treating individual disorders. As we will see, mental health professionals have from the start been active at the social level, as is demonstrated by the mental health movement, the community mental health centers and, more generally, the involvement of psychiatrists and psychologists in social management practices.

In this chapter, a chronological account is combined with a shifting thematic emphasis. Section 1 focuses on the nineteenth-century asylums, "moral treatment" and the early development of psychiatry. Section 2 shows how the treatment of "nervousness" and other Victorian illnesses in the late nineteenth century gave birth to psychoanalysis and ambulant mental health care. Sections 3 and 4 portray the expansion of the mental health services in the mid-twentieth century, highlighting the crucial importance of the First and Second World Wars: the prevention on a mass scale of mental disorders required new, psychological forms of social management. In the process, psychoanalysis was transformed into a dynamic psychology of adjustment, which was complemented by new forms of treatment that fitted both policy and community demands. With the advent of the counterculture during the 1960s (section 5), adjustment as a principle was replaced by self-realization, while at the same time anti-psychiatry heavily criticized the pretensions and practices of psychiatry. This paved the way for a massive proliferation of psychotherapy. Section 6 sketches the most recent developments: the rationalization of both the mental health system and the processes of diagnosis and treatment, the return of biological psychiatry, and the demise of psychoanalysis as a therapeutic framework.

1   Early history: asylums (*c.* 1800–1900)

The deviant kinds of behavior we nowadays associate with mental disorders have been reported since antiquity, as is shown for instance, by the way melancholia was described by Aristotle. However, it was only from the late eighteenth century onward that insanity became a medical issue.

1.1   *Alienation*

In pre-modern times no sophisticated system of treatment for deviant behavior existed. During the middle ages, people considered "insane" were usually not confined to special institutions, but were cared for by the family and the community. Only in cases where lunatics were considered dangerous because of their wild and aggressive behavior were they temporarily locked up in separate houses, like the famous *dolhuysjes* in the Netherlands. The first known asylum for more permanent care was founded in Valencia in 1409, followed by a dozen institutions in Spain and many more in other European countries (see figure 22). These asylums, mostly run by the Catholic church, had purely custodial functions.

From the seventeenth century onward, many agricultural workers in European countries drifted to the big cities to find work. City authorities found it difficult to maintain social order. Large institutions were founded, such as the *Hôpital Général* (General Hospital) in Paris in 1656, to confine jobless people who were not able or willing to conform to standards of rationality and productivity. The creed was that normal people act reasonably, respect the social order, and accept the productive economic ideal. Those who did not fit this pattern were considered "alienated." In the *Hôpital Général*, treatment consisted of a rigid daily schedule, with forced labor and

Figure 22   *Career of a madman*, engraving (1735) by William Hogarth, depicting the asylum for the insane at Bedlam in London. Notice the visiting ladies; before the nineteenth century, it was not uncommon to "exhibit" psychiatric patients to the general public. Source: Psychology Pictures.

religious excercises. The goal of all this was "re-education," whereby the regime forced the "immoral" poor to internalize the dominant moral norms.

1.2   "Moral treatment"

In the course of the eighteenth century doctors in various European countries, influenced by Enlightenment ideas, became convinced that madness was a disease and also that it could be cured. In England, William Battie published his *Treatise on Madness* (1758), which announced the beginning of psychiatry both as a science and a therapeutic practice. A few decades later, physicians such as William Tuke in England, Philippe Pinel (see figure 23) in France, Johann Reil in Germany, and Vincenzio Chiarugi in Italy, developed theories about the possible organic causes of madness. In the same vein, the American physician Benjamin Rush wrote in 1812: "The cause of madness is seated primarily in the blood-vessels of the brain, and it depends upon the same kind of morbid and irregular action that continues other arterial diseases."[2]

Figure 23   *Pinel et les aliénés de Bicêtre* ("Pinel and the insane of the Bicêtre"). This painting by Charles Müller depicted what would become known as the first psychiatric revolution, as the mentally ill were liberated from their chains. On Pinel's left, with the notebook, is his pupil and later successor, Esquirol. Courtesy Bibliothèque de l'Académie national de Médecine, Paris. Photo: J. L. Charmet.

These biological ideas about the causes of madness had hardly any practical value for treatment purposes. It is therefore no surprise that the first therapeutical endeavors were based on social or psychological principles rather than medical ones. The cure that was developed consisted of an intensive and detailed disciplinary system aiming at re-instilling morality in the mental life of the patients. To this end, the mentally ill were confined to separate institutions in the country, specializing in "moral treatment" (see figure 24). The first of these was the Retreat in York, founded in 1796 by William Tuke. In France, Philippe Pinel in his *Traité médico-philosophique sur l'aliénation mentale ou manie* ("Medico-philosophical treatise on mental alienation or mania") (1801) emphasized the psychological kernel of moral treatment: a patient was to be subjected to the imposing authority of a single man, "who, by his physical and moral qualities, is apt to exercise on him an irresistible empire and to change the vicious chain of ideas."[3] In other words, moral treatment consisted of a deliberate system of persuasion and influence, centered around the moral authority of the doctor, and located in a well-organized institution.

The moral treatment regime was popularized most eloquently by Pinel's pupil J. E. D. Esquirol. In 1816, he wrote:

> The patient with mania, restrained by the harmony, order and rules of the house, will get his impulsiveness better in hand and yield less to eccentric acts. . . . The calm that the psychiatric patients enjoy, far from the tumult and the noise, and the mental rest conferred by removal from their business and domestic problems, is very favorable to their recovery. Subject to an orderly life, to discipline, to a well calibrated regimen, they are obliged to reflect upon the change in their life.[4]

The European example was followed in the United States. The first American Retreat was founded by Eli Todd in 1824. While the Retreats in the US mainly served well-off citizens, the mentally ill and retarded from the lower social classes were

Figure 24 Meerenberg, a "modern" Dutch psychiatric hospital founded in 1849. Throughout the western world, institutions like this were built in the nineteenth century to replace the older asylums in the cities. The idealized engraving reflects the emphasis on quietude and leisure as prerequisites for restoring the balance of the mind. Source: Psychology Pictures.

usually housed together with criminals in prisons and almshouses (although a few state hospitals for the insane were established from the late 1820s onward). Alarmed by the pitiful condition of lunatics in prisons and almshouses, the philanthropist teacher Dorothy Dix started a crusade in the 1840s, campaigning for confinement of the mentally ill in separate institutions and for improvement in the quality of the state hospitals (see figure 25).

By the middle of the nineteenth century, moral treatment was employed at a number of mental hospitals amid enthusiastic reports of high discharge and recovery rates. Because of the non-medical nature of moral treatment, medical supremacy in the field was challenged by other professionals. Philosophers, jurists, and clergymen claimed to be at least as good as physicians in the practice of moral treatment. However, moral treatment did not appear in the long run to be as effective as was first thought, and was largely abandoned as a therapy in the 1880s.

1.3 Psychiatry

Besides the practical work with mental patients in the asylums, there was much speculation about the causes of mental illness. From the beginning of psychiatry as a medical discipline, explanations alternated between psychogenic and organic per-

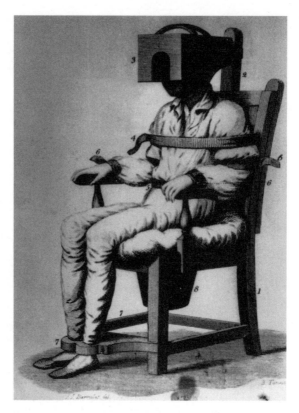

Figure 25 A "tranquillizing" chair, *c.* 1810. This instrument was developed by the American doctor Benjamin Rush, who held that physical restraint would compose the mind and dampen the passions. Patients remained locked up in the chair for as long as 12 to 24 hours. Despite the humane language of "moral treatment," instruments like these remained part and parcel of psychiatric life throughout the nineteenth century: physical restraint, rather than mental cure, was its dominant characteristic. Source: National Library of Medicine, Bethesda.

spectives on mental illness. During the first half of the nineteenth century, psychological interpretations dominated, especially in Germany. After 1850 however, the *Psychiker* (as they were called) had to give way to researchers with a more organic view on mental illness, the *Somatiker*.[5] The leading proponent of the latter was the Berlin psychiatrist Wilhelm Griesinger. In his 1845 textbook, *Die Pathologie und Therapie der psychischen Krankheite für Aerzte und Studierende* ("Pathology and therapy of mental illnesses for doctors and students"), he passionately defended a reductionist view of mental illness: "Geisteskrankheiten sind Gehirnkrankheiten" ("mental illnesses are diseases of the brain"). After the discovery of the microbe that produced syphilis, a disease which in many cases led to early dementia, Griesinger became convinced that organic causes would also be found for other kinds of mental illness. In France, the biological perspective was developed by Morel (who coined the term *dementia praecox* in 1860) and others, and in England by Maudsley.

However, German researchers were much more sophisticated than the French and the English, in that they concentrated from an early stage on systematic microscopic research into the brain. By 1911 there were 16 university clinics and 1400 psychiatrists in training in Germany.

No matter how enthusiastically the positive results in brain research were reported, for example in Griesinger's journal *Archiv für Psychiatrie und Nervenkrankheiten* (Archive for psychiatry and nervous diseases), the organic view had little to offer with regard to therapy. By the end of the nineteenth century, both the psychological and the biological positions were in crisis; there was still no acceptable theory about the origins of insanity. A way out was offered by the German psychiatrist Emil Kraepelin (1856–1926), who in successive editions of his textbook on *dementia praecox* presented an elaborate diagnostic system of various types of mental illnesses, based on decades of observations of patients in mental hospitals. Kraepelin's classification exerted a tremendous influence on subsequent psychiatric nosologies and on therapeutic attitudes.

1.4 Conclusion

During the "cult of curability" in the nineteenth century, asylums for the insane in western countries were transformed into therapeutic institutions, housing a steadily increasing number of patients. In the Netherlands, for instance, the number of inmates rose from 39 out of every 100,000 citizens in 1849 to 264 in 1928.[6] England's asylum population rose from 160 per 100,000 in 1859 to 370 per 100,000 in 1909.[7] This dramatic increase was partly constituted by the growing number of people diagnosed as suffering from neurosyphilis, alcohol misuse, and schizophrenia. Behind this, a major redistribution of illness (and care) was taking place that must be ascribed to the new form of social management that asylums offered. For instance, new patients in United States for the most part were European immigrants, 14 million of whom arrived between 1860 and 1900.[8]

Asylum treatment, however, did not correspond with developments in psychiatric theory. While the former largely remained psychological and social, the latter became increasingly biological. Still, the common ground of both treatment and theory was the tradition of the Enlightenment. Theoretically, the focus was on a rational, scientific explanation of insanity; there was strong optimism that the real causes of mental illness (as opposed to mythical or metaphysical beliefs) could be uncovered. On the practical level, progress was deemed possible by the development of new forms of individual treatment within the asylums.

Toward the end of the nineteenth century, the golden age of psychiatry had ended in disillusionment. On the therapeutic level, moral treatment had proved a clear failure. Patients hardly ever left the asylum cured, and if they were released they often soon returned – the "revolving door" is no recent phenomenon. On the theoretical level, progress had also been minimal, the repeated clash between biological and psychological explanations of insanity not resulting in a winning position for either. It is tempting to hail Kraepelin, the third element, as the winner, but his diagnostic system was descriptive rather than explanatory.

Although psychiatry in the early twentieth century was expanding rapidly, psychiatrists found their basic work of curing the insane almost impossible to accomplish. Moreover, in many countries, psychiatrists had gained a bad public reputation, because of the widely reported abuses within the institutions. Psychiatrists responded to their therapeutic failure by invading an adjacent area of pathology, that of "nervous disorders."

2   Nervous disorders (*c.* 1870–1920)

Alongside the development of institutions, therapies, and theories concerned with insanity proper, the late nineteenth century brought another type of mental illness to the fore: milder forms of mental disturbances, incidental rather than chronic, and characterized by such symptoms and complaints as fatigue, general weakness, mental instability, and collapse. "Nervous disorders" were introduced alongside madness as a new category of mental problems. This marked not only an expansion of the field nowadays called mental health, but also the appearance of neurologists as a new professional group.

2.1   Victorian illnesses

Symptoms of fatigue and weakness without any detectable physical origin had already been described in well-to-do circles in the seventeenth and eighteenth centuries. At the time, these illnesses were treated by a variety of therapies, such as mesmerism or "animal magnetism."

If various forms of emotional instability and strange behavior had a long history, they became much more prominent from the 1870s onward. This prominence was delineated (and enhanced) by the introduction of the novel disease-concept of *neurasthenia* ("weakness of the nerves"), exemplified in a book by the American physician George M. Beard, called *American nervousness* (1881). Neurasthenia was a useful concept because it carried the suggestion of a medical disease entity, while simultaneously avoiding the stigma of madness. Apart from identifying a new group of patients, it served as a vehicle for neurologists as a new category of medical specialists. From the mid-1800s onward, neurology had developed as a new medical specialization, claiming to offer valid results not just for nervous disorders, but for mental disorders in general. Neurologists denied that the asylum system had any therapeutic value. Instead they advocated treatment in private settings or in university clinics, using methods such as hypnosis or suggestion.

Like the psychiatrists half a century earlier, neurologists found it hard to make a firm connection between theory and treatment. For combating "Victorian illnesses," a host of commonsense prescriptions was offered, such as travel, rest, and moral exhortation. As America's first neurologist S. Weir Mitchell put it: "Let us bring in Dr. Diet and Dr. Quiet"; sanatoria and spas in Europe were ruled by the same philosophy. Private sanatoria for "nervous" patients both in Europe and in the United States had their heyday in the period between 1880 and 1920. The general theory behind these practices was that nervous disorders could be cured by some form of physical treatment. In the words of Mitchell: "You cure the body, and somehow find that the mind is also cured."[9]

A rival set of ideas concerning the causes of neurasthenia and hysteria, dating back to the eighteenth century, focused not on the nervous system but on mental functioning. In Europe, the roots of these illnesses were thought to be located in the private unconscious, in the form of uncontrollable uncivilized impulses; lifting repression through hypnosis or free association was considered the appropriate course of action. Hypnosis was especially used and developed by the famous French neurologist Jean Martin Charcot. Physicians flocked from all over Europe to see "the Master" in action at the Salpêtrière hospital (see figure 26). A few decades later, the new methods gained an audience in the United States also, via the *Journal of Medical Hypnosis, Suggestive therapy* and the popular *Suggestions*. When Charcot's successor at the Salpêtrière, Pierre Janet, visited the United States in 1905, he found a favorable climate for the psychological treatment of neuroses.

Regardless of the theoretical perspective, both neurologists and "mental healers" when dealing with patients implicitly counted on the same principle employed by asylum doctors in moral treatment, that is, the beneficial psychological influence of the authority of the physician. In the United States, the adoption of a psychological perspective was furthered by progressive groups within the Protestant Church. "Positive thinkers" such as Mary Baker Eddy had argued that minor physical

Figure 26 *The clinical lesson*, painting depicting French psychiatrist Charcot, demonstrating hysteria at the Salpêtrière in Paris, 1887. Source: Assistance Public Hôpitaux de Paris.

problems as well as a host of other personal problems would yield to the disciplined and liberated mind. The individual was to be architect of his or her fate, so it was said.

Of decisive importance was the "Emmanuel movement," led by the Reverend Elwood Worcester in the first decade of the twentieth century. Although accepting medical diagnoses, Worcester advocated using "the Christian religion as a healing power," aiming at the "alleviation and arrest of certain disorders of the nervous system which are now generally regarded as involving some weakness or defect of character." The list of potential clients included "nervous sufferers, victims of alcohol and other drugs, the unhappy, the sorrowful, would-be suicides, and other children of melancholy."[10] Religious enlightenment was the context in which psychotherapy in the United States evolved, most aptly illustrated by the bestseller, first published in 1908 and selling over 200,000 copies, *Religion and medicine: the moral control of nervous disorders* by Worcester, McComb, and Coriat.

In their practical work, clerics drew upon psychological ideas and methods, thereby creating an early form of pastoral-psychological work. In 1906, a collaboration between doctors and clerics was initiated with the founding of the Emmanuel Clinic for physical, mental, and spiritual help. Also, training courses (Worcester's "psychotherapy class") and conferences were devoted to "psychotherapy," thereby paving the way for a veritable psychotherapy movement that would last until the end of the First World War. As a result of this movement, after decades of desperately searching for a physical basis of hysteria and taking an explicit anti-psychological stance, neurologists increasingly saw themselves forced to recognize the importance of psychic causality.

2.2   Prevention

The introduction of the notion of neurasthenia had brought an apparently clear division between two types of mental disorder ("madness" and "nervousness"), reflected in a corresponding professional division between psychiatrists on the one hand, and neurologists and various other mental healers on the other. Psychiatrists, however, actively sought to bridge this divide, eager to improve upon their unfortunate record with regard to the asylums. To this end, they introduced a concept that would radically change the mental health field, that of prevention. Assuming that untreated neurosis would degenerate into psychosis, psychiatrists reasoned that moral treatment had failed because insanity reached a chronic state before psychiatrists saw it. Hence, in the name of prevention, they claimed jurisdiction over the diagnosis and treatment of neuroses.

Of course, these assertions implied making inroads into the field of activity of the neurologists. And although the neurologists had a higher status within medicine than psychiatrists, they could not avoid some form of cooperation with the former asylum doctors. Consequently, the boundaries between the two professional domains gradually became blurred. Eventually, psychiatrists and neurologists increasingly put aside rivalry and competition and combined forces as "specialists in nervous and mental disease."

The exodus of psychiatrists from the asylum also helped to create the new profession of psychiatric social work. The initiator was Adolf Meyer, who was born and medically trained in Switzerland and had emigrated to the United States in 1892. Meyer held the view that psychiatric disturbances in individuals were an expression of unhealthy living, of ineffective adaptions to the environment. While in charge of the New York Psychiatric Institute (1902–10), he developed the new assessment method of the psychiatric interview. This aimed at a description of personality development, and was complemented by home visits by social workers to patients' families, so that a more complete life history could be obtained and relatives could be involved in the treatment. Apart from individual therapy, social control was an issue here, as sexual perversion, rape and violent criminal behavior were seen as threats to the social order, and amenable to prophylactic measures within the mental health domain.

The cause of prevention was greatly furthered by the establishment of the National Committee for Mental Hygiene in 1909. The initiative came from a former patient, Clifford Wittingham Beers, who had suffered a mental breakdown at the age of 24, and had unsuccesfully attempted suicide. For a year he languished in a depression, then was committed to the Hartford Retreat. In 1902 his depression lifted and, apparently in a manic phase, he decided that he would launch a crusade for reform of the mental hospital, prompted by the abuses and cruelties he and his fellow patients had experienced. He ended up in a straitjacket in a padded cell, and afterwards was transferred to Connecticut State Hospital. Upon his release in 1903, he decided "to write a book about his experiences and to organize a movement that would help do away with existing evils in the care of the mentally ill and, whenever possible, to prevent mental illness itself."[11]

Contacting various authorities in the field of psychology and psychiatry, such as William James and Adolf Meyer, Beers managed to get support for his plans and in 1908, he founded the first mental hygiene society, in Connecticut, followed, in 1909, by the National Committee for Mental Hygiene. The official goal of this Committee was: "To work for the protection of the mental health of the public; to help raise the standard of care for those in danger of developing mental disorder or actually insane; to promote the study of mental disorders in all their forms and relations, and to disseminate knowledge concerning their causes, treatment, and prevention."[12]

The Committee initiated a publicity campaign, in which medical and philanthropic principles were combined with the goal of preventing mental illness and delinquency. Parents, teachers, social workers and policemen should be educated to become "mental hygiene observants," and with their activities support the work of professionals in the field, for instance within the Child Guidance Clinics (see chapter 2).

The changes within the mental hospitals and the activities of neurologists and psychiatrists outside hospitals took place within a broader context of social concern and intervention, which in the US was fueled by the Progressive Movement (see chapter 1). Various types of intervention were regrouped under the banner of "mental hygiene." The principle of prevention widened the field of mental health to include not just mentally ill and neurotic patients, but all individuals at risk: "Mental hygiene as a philosophy of prevention is an ideal and a guiding principle working wherever possible with the assets of life before the differentiation into the 'normal' and the 'pathological'," wrote Adolf Meyer in 1930.[13]

From here, it was but a small step to the complete medicalization of deviance. Especially in the United States, psychiatry during the first decades was transformed from a discipline concerned primarily with insanity to one equally concerned with normality. Psychiatry and social and pastoral work joined forces to promote the common goal of "adjustment" and assistance for all those who suffered from psychological malfunctioning.

2.3   Psychoanalysis

Meanwhile in Vienna, Sigmund Freud (1856–1939) had started to practice his own type of psychological therapy, which would change the course of psychiatry and mental health care in general. Educated as a neurologist, Freud had initially worked as a laboratory researcher, but financial pressures led him to start a private practice for patients with "nervous complaints." Inspired by the the work of Charcot and Janet, Freud began to experiment with hypnosis during the 1890s, in order to discover the causes of the otherwise inexplicable physical symptoms of his patients (mostly upper-class women from the city of Vienna) (see figure 27).

Figure 27   Sigmund Freud (1856–1939). More than anyone else, Freud left his mark on twentieth-century psychology. Source: Archives of the History of American Psychology, University of Akron.

Gradually, he realized that these symptoms were signs of psychosomatic rather than purely somatic disorders. He also became convinced that these neurotic symptoms had mental causes. This was the starting point for a whole new way of theorizing about mental illnesses: they stemmed from repressed thoughts, memories, and impulses, hidden in the unconscious. According to Freud, traumatic events from childhood were repressed, i.e. transferred to the unconscious part of the psyche. They did not totally disappear, however, but manifested themselves in dreams and neurotic symptoms.

In his treatment practice, Freud invited his patients to lie down and associate freely on what came into their minds, hoping in this way to gain access to the patient's unconscious. In essence, therefore, psychoanalysis was a "talking cure" (a term coined by one of his patients, Anna O.); rather than physical interventions, the examination of individual discourses (in which the analysis of dreams had a prominent position) would do what was needed.

Freud developed his theory hand in hand with his treatment techniques. The most fundamental trauma was supposed to be the child's awareness that it could not take the place of the same-sex parent. This universal desire and the impossibility of its fulfilment became known as the "Oedipus complex." By acting as a substitute parent, the doctor would induce the process of "transference," by which the patient subjected himself emotionally to the psychoanalyst, a procedure which was reminiscent of the way asylum and sanatorium doctors tried to exert moral authority over their patients, but much more sophisticated.

By 1908 there were enough people sufficiently interested in psychoanalysis to warrant convening an international meeting in Salzburg. Forty-two people attended, among them the Swiss psychiatrists Eugen Bleuler and Carl Gustav Jung. In the US, the psychologist G. Stanley Hall had learned about Freud's theory and, in 1908, began to give courses on psychoanalysis. In 1909, Hall invited Freud, Jung, and Ferenczi to visit Clark University (see figure 28). The same period in the United States also saw the beginning of analytic practice, the appearance of articles on psychoanalysis and translations of the papers of Freud and Breuer on hysteria. This reception was stimulated by the favorable climate engendered by the psychotherapy movement.

2.4   Conclusion

The later decades of the nineteenth century paved the way for the "second psychiatric revolution" (the first being the establishment of the therapeutic asylum by Tuke and Pinel). The misfortunes of both moral treatment and biological psychiatry forced psychiatrists to explore new avenues, all of which would contribute to the strengthening and expansion of the field of mental health. First of all, psychiatrists ventured out of the asylum and into the treatment of a different kind of pathology, that is, the nervous disorders. Second, both in Europe and the United States forms of psychological treatment – psychotherapy and psychoanalysis – were developed that would change the face of psychiatry permanently. In combination, both developments contributed to the establishment of the mental hygiene movement in the early 1900s.

Figure 28 Freud's visit to the United States, 1909. Seated are Freud (*left*), his fellow psychoanalyst Carl Gustav Jung (*right*), and their host Stanley Hall (*middle*). Source: Clark University Archives.

3   Mental hygiene (*c.* 1914–40)

Both clinical zeal and a desire for more effective social management led to a considerable expansion of the field of mental hygiene in the interwar period. This transformation was stimulated in a decisive way by the experiences of the First World War. For the first time, psychiatrists became directly involved in military activities. They were joined by the clinical psychologists, who had designed a new instrument to make psychodiagnosis more rational and objective: the psychological test. But in the eyes of the public during the 1920s and 1930s the real "new psychology" became psychoanalysis. At the same time, policy makers in the social field regarded psychoanalysis and its competitor at the time, behaviorism, as important pillars for their efforts to regulate both normal and deviant behavior.

3.1   *Shell shock*

From the beginning of the First World War in 1914, new technologies for destroying the enemy were exploited.[14] In addition to mass slaughter and physical injury, the use of these technologies also led to mental disorders, such as hysterical blindness, paralytic seizures, tremors, exhaustion, and total disorientation. In 1916, the British psychiatrist Myers introduced the concept of "shell shock" to describe these often persistent symptoms; they were initially attributed to the shell explosions, which were thought to produced minute cortical lesions which in turn caused the disorder. But since shell shock was found frequently in troops who had not been exposed to shelling, it was concluded that the disorders did not have physical causes but were to be seen as neurotic responses of individuals to traumatic situations.

At first, military psychiatrists stuck to traditional methods of countering the consequences of shell shock, derived partly from older military discipline ("biting the bullet") and partly from no less repressive psychiatric methods. Shell shock victims thus were subjected to military drill and exercise, electric shocks, isolation, cold showers, phantom operations and "suffocation therapy."

After a few years, the general frame of reference towards psychological problems in war gradually shifted from a disciplinarian to a psychiatric approach. This is demonstrated by the work of the Committee of Enquiry into Shell Shock in the UK; this body concluded that a more careful selection of soldiers and officers for emotional stability was necessary to prevent future problems in army personnel. The existing forms of care provided by army chaplains were also backed up by psychiatric and psychological expertise, and extended to the postwar private life of soldiers. Shell shock victims, when reunited with their families, were psychologically supported in their adaptation to normal life. Neuropsychiatric units were set up to take care of psychiatric problems at the front and to help demobilized soldiers to readjust to life at home. War neuroses also provided new material for observation and pointed to the relationship between psychic disorders and everyday living conditions.

3.2 Clinical psychology

The war also brought a new player into the mental health field: the clinical psychologist. In the first decade of the twentieth century, psychological intelligence tests had been developed, and these were much in use during the First World War. These tests introduced psychologists into the field of psychodiagnostics and clinical work in general, and contributed to public awareness of the uses of psychology.

At about the time that Freud developed psychoanalysis, Lightner Witmer, a psychologist at the University of Pennsylvania, had initiated a training program in a new field that he called "clinical psychology" (see also chapters 1 and 2). In 1896, Witmer had founded the first psychological clinic, and ten years later he began the publication of a professional journal, *The Psychological Clinic* (1907). Witmer's clinical method consisted of gathering together instructors, students, and those needing help, for the purpose of studying, doing research into, and treating mental disabilities and defects. In this decade only a few psychologists worked outside universities, and none of them engaged in actual treatment.

The number of university-related psychological clinics in the United States increased to a total of 19 in 1914. Naturally, the expansion of the new profession was anxiously watched by its competitors, the neurologists and psychiatrists. In the 1920s, opposition by psychiatrists to the diagnostic function of clinical psychologists

Figure 29   Rorschach testing, United States, *c.* 1930s. The introduction of the Rorschach and other so-called "projective techniques" helped to create a role for psychologists as diagnosticians in the clinical domain. Source: Archives of the History of American Psychology, University of Akron.

continued. There was also reluctance within psychology to pursue this course: in 1921, the APA reaffirmed that its objective was the advancement of psychology strictly as a science, and not as a profession. Nevertheless, a steadily increasing minority of clinicians was attempting to gain recognition within the organization (see figure 29). However, it would take a second world war for the acceptance of their specialty to come about.

3.3   Public interest in psychology

From the 1920s onward, psychological interpretations of human behavior attracted the interest of the lay public.[15] Within elite circles in the United States, there reigned a "cult of the self," a permanent search for hidden motives, which of course made Jazz Age Americans eagerly devour popular psychological literature, most of it in the psychoanalytical tradition. Especially influential was A. G. Tansley's *The new psychol-*

ogy and its relation to life (1920). This book was followed by a host of publications that enabled the public to learn about elements of Freud's psychological theory: the unconscious, repression, the sexual drives, and the psychological mechanisms and symbols by which drives were indirectly expressed in thought and behavior. Gradually, psychoanalysis was assimilated into popular thinking; much to the dismay of professional psychoanalysts, this was accompanied by all kinds of distortions and dilutions, and moreover was freely combined with glandular and behaviorist conceptions.

The acceptance of the "new psychology" went hand in hand with the promotion of mental hygiene. The National Committee for Mental Hygiene had been actively involved in the war effort, and this brought psychiatrists, social workers, and clinical psychologists into the limelight as professionals whose joint efforts contributed to public and individual mental health. The Child Guidance Clinics (see chapter 2), apart from their practical value in advising parents, were a highly visible symbol of mental health as a public issue. And it was Freudian psychology that forged the link between the various groups of professionals, as well as between professionals and the public.

Developments within American psychiatry were also significant: after the First World War it seemed undeniable that war neuroses had a psychological cause, and psychoanalysis became an irresistible force. Supported by local psychoanalytic societies, private psychoanalytic clinics were established during the 1910s, such as Chestnut Lodge (1910), the Austen Riggs (1919), and the Menninger Clinic (1919). These clinics would set an example for fashionable treatment of the "neuroses of the rich." One of the leading psychiatrists in the United States, Morton Prince, commented in 1929: "Freudian psychology has flooded the field like a full rising tide, and the rest of us were submerged like clams buried at low water."[16] During the late 1930s, when a whole generation of European psychoanalysts migrated to the United States, psychoanalysis became the leading theoretical orientation within psychiatry. The popularity of the so-called psychodynamic approach within psychiatry would last virtually unchallenged until the mid-1960s.

Among the European and American public, psychoanalysis popularized the importance of sexual desires and drives; sexual factors were supposed to be present in a variety of non-sexual phenomena. In his book *The psychopathology of everyday life* (1901), Freud had analyzed the dreams and slips of the tongue, for example, of normal people, demonstrating how unconscious processes influence the actions of us all, and not just the deviant feelings and behavior of neurotic patients. Although Freud's views were controversial, especially his idea that children should be seen as sexual beings, in their diluted form they had a deep influence on mental health policy and culture in general. One such influential notion was the idea that emotional relationships between parents and children have profound consequences for the quality of emotional life in adulthood. East coast intellectuals in the United States used psychoanalysis in their cultural struggle against New England puritanism, while on the other hand moral conservatives sought support in Freud to conquer the "internal wilderness" of mankind. As a result, psychoanalysis was americanized: its aim would no longer be "to transform misery into common everyday unhappiness"; it would be the pursuit of happiness itself.

The "new psychology," including both psychoanalysis and behaviorism, also had great potential for applied psychology as a means of social control, suggesting new ways in which the instincts, drives and wants of human beings might be regulated. Book titles from the mid-1920s, such as *Means of social control* and *Man the puppet: the art of controlling minds,* illustrated the confidence that knowledge of human motivation would be of considerable use to social policy makers. The implication of new developments within psychiatry and the mental hygiene movement was that this could be done most effectively by a program of individual treatment of large numbers of people. Psychoanalytic and behavioristic tenets, implying a certain plasticity of human nature, created the possibility of non-residential treatment, which in turn enhanced therapeutic optimism. As a result of all this, psychiatric medicine was freed of its dependence on disease and fired with a new ambition to intervene in the lives of the healthy. As early as 1932 W. A. White declared that (mental) health should be regarded as a positive concept (i.e. the absence of disease), not a negative one.

3.4   Conclusion

After the First World War, on both sides of the Atlantic, problems of adjustment, deviance and illness were increasingly subsumed under the banner of mental hygiene. In 1930 a first International Congress for Mental Hygiene was held in Washington, including many participants from European countries. Although no one really knew exactly what mental hygiene meant, its value as a leading concept was beyond doubt: it signified optimism within psychiatry, the belief that all forms of disorder, ranging from alcoholism, prostitution, juvenile delinquency, and child abuse to psychiatric illness, could be cured or managed by scientifically supported therapeutic interventions.

The psychoanalytic notion that adult problems had their origins in childhood psychological conflicts or trauma supported this optimism within the mental health field, and provided a common language for professionals from various backgrounds, including social workers and forensic experts. As the founder of the Dutch Child Guidance Movement, Eugenia Lekkerkerker, stated:

> Psychoanalysis had laid the foundation for an enormous expansion of the domain of mental health care, far beyond the original goal of taking care of the insane. In particular it gave the rationale for preventive activities, which are now also directed towards the "normal" person, who does not or not yet suffer from a pathological disorder.[17]

As they learned more and more about the endless variety of possible abnormalities on the psychological level, policy makers, professionals, and the public became increasingly concerned about managing abnormality. This concern fitted in well with the new framework that typified thinking in the mental health field: that of a continuum ranging from the normal to the pathological. It was also supported by new practices, as psychological tests offered the opportunity to measure each individual's position on the normal–pathological dimension, and a whole range of private and public institutions offered services for the prevention and cure of mental pathology. From this, a new psychology of adjustment emanated.

4 Adjustment (*c.* 1930–60)

The Second World War marked the onset of a range of new developments in the field of mental health. The war precipitated a growth in the number of professionals involved in diagnosis and therapy. To the general public, psychotherapy was still a little-known clinical activity in 1940, and in the US only 3 or 4 percent of the population had used mental health services; this figure rapidly climbed to 14 percent in 1957.[18] This expansion went hand in hand with a social reorientation of psychiatry, both in theoretical perspectives and in practical interventions, leading to the creation of community mental health care agencies. The war also enabled clinical psychologists to gain considerable ground within the field. Finally, the increased status of the US as a military, political, and economic power was paralleled by growing international prestige in mental health affairs, resulting in a leading position in this area also.

4.1 The Second World War

The ramifications of the Second World War went beyond the political and military spheres. Having learned from the First World War, military and civilian authorities in both the German and Allied forces were well aware of the strains that military engagement would put on servicemen and women. Therefore, in the course of recruitment, attention was paid to the physical and mental health of soldiers and officers, and a range of mental health services was provided to military personnel during wartime. For instance, the United States decided to provide military psychiatric services from the moment America joined the Allied forces. The number of psychiatrists available being far from sufficient, a crash course in the treatment of mental disorders was given to 2400 medical officers, a number equaling the total membership of the American Psychiatric Association in 1940.

Likewise, psychologists were called in to compensate for the shortage of psychiatrists in the services. This was not only from necessity, the broadmindedness of progressive psychiatrists such as William Menninger also playing a part. As a result, the number of psychologists involved in the military sphere increased dramatically, reaching up to 1700 at the end of the Second World War, with a significant number of these working in clinical capacities.[19] Apart from actual psychiatric and psychological treatment, much energy was devoted to the dissemination of psychological ideas and techniques among military personnel (see figure 30). Hundreds of thousands of copies of self-help books on emotional self-management, such as *Psychology for the fighting man* (1943), were distributed.

The war also accelerated a theoretical reorientation. Since psychological selection was part of recruitment procedures, mental breakdown could hardly be attributed to genetic or biological weakness. Consequently, when otherwise healthy officers and soldiers developed neurotic symptoms as a result of their involvement in war activities, this was seen as a normal response to an abnormal environment. The "environmental" interpretation of wartime breakdown pushed the general orientation of clinical professionals in decidedly social directions. Rather than inherent qualities of

Figure 30   A series of cartoons on the psychological impact of fear, used as part of a crash course in psychological adjustment for military trainees. Under normal circumstances, reason is in the driving seat, and fear and other emotions are under control (cartoon A); when unknown dangers appear, fear becomes uncontrollable (B, C); despair means fear takes over completely, with reason being knocked out (D); instead, a soldier may fight fear, and try to get reason back at the wheel again (E). Source: *War medicine, 1944*, p. 90.

individuals, mental health and illness came to be considered as conditions augmented or attenuated by social experiences; mental health required continuous adjustment to changing circumstances. This was a challenge to a new generation of psychiatrists: "The field of medicine must be recognized as inseparably linked to the social sciences and concerned with healthy adjustment of men, both individually and in groups."[20]

Adjustment, as an effective way of dealing with unhealthy circumstances, became the new target for clinical professionals. For instance, Carl Rogers, who was to become the most influential clinical psychologist of postwar America, defined clinical psychology as "the technique and art of applying psychological principles to problems of the individual person for purposes of bringing about a more satisfactory adjustment."[21] Behind the humane goal of individual well-being, social management issues were at stake: normal neuroses could and should be treated before reaching a point that threatened social stability.

As a consequence, it was felt that the popularization of mental health techniques should be included in social management strategies, which fundamentally changed the face of psychotherapy. Before the war, psychotherapy had been associated largely with the elite practice of psychoanalysis or with psychiatric techniques practiced in the institutional context of state hospitals. Now psychotherapists accepted that non-professionals could benefit from applying psychological knowledge and techniques to themselves, in order to prevent maladjustment, to assist in coping with problems, or to help in adequately presenting more serious disorders to a professional.

4.2 Community treatment

Considering the psychiatric endeavors during the war, it was only natural that measures were taken to provide adequate postwar care for returned servicemen. In the United States, the legal foundation for financial and non-material support was guaranteed by the Servicemen's Readjustment Act (also known as the "GI Bill"). The Veterans' Administration (VA) was instrumental in the actual organization of facilities. The number of psychiatric cases in the VA hospitals almost doubled between 1940 and 1948. In April 1946, around 60 percent of all VA patients were diagnosed as suffering from neuropsychiatric disorders of one kind or another.[22]

The GI Bill was followed by the National Mental Health Act of 1946, that in turn laid the foundation for the National Institute for Mental Health (NIMH). Here the shift in the emphasis of federal policy from mental illness to mental health, and a decidedly preventive and community-directed orientation, were realized and promoted. Also in 1946, a pressure group of "young Turks" with a background in military psychiatry, was formed within the American Psychiatric Association. Led by William Menninger, this "Group for the Advancement of Psychiatry" ("GAP") set out to push psychiatry in a social direction, as witnessed by their 1950 manifesto, *The social responsibility of psychiatry.*

Between 1955 and 1960 the federally funded Joint Commission on Mental Illness and Health carried out an extensive survey into mental health and illness in the US, and in its final report (*Action for mental health, 1960*) strongly advised that community mental health centers should be established throughout the country in the interests of social stability. This was legally enacted by the Kennedy administration in 1963. The reformist zeal of the postwar decades contributed to the increase of psychiatrists in the US, from 3000 during the Second World War to 17,000 in 1964.[23] During the same period, the psychiatric focus shifted from institutions to private practice; a majority of psychiatrists were working on an outpatient basis in 1964.

These changes were accompanied by rising public interest. From 1945 onward, citizens sought therapeutic assistance more insistently than ever before, and by 1960 mental illness had become a subject of great interest to the general public, to judge by the number of publications, investigations, debates, and newspaper articles devoted to it, and the popularity of the "pop psychology" TV show of Joyce Brothers. As a result, the idea of "psychotherapy for the normal" became widely accepted. The explicitly non-medical method of psychological counseling, developed in the 1940s by Carl Rogers, fitted in neatly with the new public demands.

Although the mental health industry in Europe did not expand as early and as rapidly as it did in the United States, by 1960 psychiatry and clinical psychology were well on their way to becoming established professions. In many west European countries too, a variety of outpatient services was established, importing both theories and techniques from the United States.

4.3   Psychologists on the march

Although clinical psychology had received increasing professional recognition by the late 1930s (mainly on the basis of expertise in testing), it still retained a distinctly subordinate position in the professional hierarchy, both within psychology and in its relation to psychiatry. Their enrolment in military mental health services had enhanced psychologists' status to the degree that in the postwar era they could both claim and have their share in diagnosis and even psychotherapy.

Being non-medical professionals, even clinically trained psychologists had been and still were excluded from psychoanalytical psychotherapy proper. (This state of affairs had led to vigorous debates both before and after the Second World War, to which even Freud himself had contributed in *The question of lay analysis*, in 1926.) A new kind of psychotherapy had to emerge before psychologists (with social workers, teachers, clergy, and other professionals in their wake) could enter therapeutic practice. Central to its development was the work of Carl Rogers, a former student of theology who, after turning to psychology, had made his career in the prewar years in the field of child guidance (see figure 31). His groundbreaking book *Counseling and psychotherapy* (1942) not only expressed great confidence in the therapeutic capacities of non-medical professionals, but also put considerable trust in the self-healing powers of the client (not "the patient"!), the effective therapist being no more than a facilitator of psychological change in the individual. In the same vein, Rogers' method brought about a decisive shift of emphasis, from an exclusive concern with the pathological to a focus on ordinary unhappiness and alienation.

Rogers' "client-centered" approach was partly inspired by philosophical theories from the European existentialist tradition, but on the other hand it gained respect by the adoption of empirical research methods to analyze the process of psychotherapy. The combination of professional innovation and scientific interest brought him sufficient prestige to become (in 1946) the first clinical psychologist to be elected as president of the APA. A few years later, Rogers was involved in the exploration of new ideas in clinical training at the Boulder Conference in 1949, the most important achievement of which was the introduction of the "scientist-practitioner" model.

At the same time that Rogerian counseling was making its way through the mental health institutions of the 1950s, the foundations were laid for "behavior therapy." Presupposing that all behavior was learned through reinforced stimulus–response associations, behaviorists claimed that this included behavior associated with mental illness, and that it could also be unlearned, given the appropriate methods. The first clinician to practice a form of behavior therapy was J. Wolpe, who was trained in South Africa as a medical doctor and psychoanalyst. Dissatisfied with the meager

Figure 31 Carl R. Rogers (1902–1986), father of counseling and non-directive psychotherapy, a new approach to psychological intervention, which considerably broadened the scope of psychology. Source: Carl R. Rogers Collection, Department of Special Collections, Davidson Library, University of California, Santa Barbara.

results of his analytical therapies, he ventured in the late 1940s into experimental psychology, searching for the means to create a more effective therapeutic method. After having moved to the United States in the mid-1950s, he wrote the book that would become a milestone in the development of behavior therapy: *Therapy by reciprocal inhibition* (1958).

In roughly the same period, a team at the Maudsley Hospital psychiatric clinic in London, led by psychologist H. J. Eysenck, had been studying the effectiveness of psychotherapy. They concluded that "the therapeutic effects of psychotherapy are small or non-existent, and do not in any demonstrable way add to the non-specific effects of routine medical treatment, or to such events as occur in the patients' everyday experience."[24] Inspired by Wolpe and by B. F. Skinner, who in 1954 had coined the term "behavior therapy," Eysenck and his team set out to expand and promote the new approach, opposing psychoanalysis with all the methods at their disposal. Apart from claiming a greater effectiveness for behavior therapy, the bottom line for Eysenck was always the scientific superiority of behaviorism: "we are concerned with the application of laboratory based scientific findings in the field of learning and conditioning, rather than with the use of Freudian principles."[25]

The rise of clinical psychology as a force within the therapeutic domain contributed to a growing acceptance within psychology as well. During the period 1957–60, of almost 3,100 psychology PhDs awarded in the US, one-third were in clinical psychology. The Clinical Division of the APA, the largest in the association, had 2,700 members, more than three times as many as the Experimental Division.[26]

4.4   The struggle of psychiatry

While psychotherapists of all varieties enlarged their territory within the domain of ambulant mental health care, psychiatrists in the mental hospitals were still trying to address the problems of patients who were a threat to themselves or their environment, the most difficult category being those with schizophrenia. Since the heyday of the asylum, they had not made much progress in curing this kind of patient; what they had to offer was mainly custodial care, which in large part meant some form of physical restraint.

In the course of the 1930s, when most institutional psychiatrists still favored a biological approach, attempts at curing schizophrenic patients had focused on physical treatment. Inspired by the belief that the grand mal convulsions of epilepsy were biologically antagonistic to schizophrenia, psychiatrists tried to induce these convulsions in schizophrenic patients by injecting insulin or administering electric shocks (electroconvulsive therapy or ECT). Apart from having considerable negative side-effects, these shock therapies appeared to cure some of the symptoms.

In the same period, a more extreme and irreversible form of medical intervention was introduced: the prefrontal lobotomy. This method of surgically severing portions of the brain was developed in 1935 by the Portuguese neurosurgeon Egas Moniz, who in 1949 won the Nobel Prize for his invention. In the United States, the neurologist Walter Freedman developed a simplified procedure, which enabled surgeons to operate on patients in a few minutes, using only local anesthetics. Since the effects on patients seemed beneficial, psychosurgery became a widely used method.

During the 1950s, shock treatment and psychosurgery were complemented with psychotropic drugs, after the first effective antipsychotic drug, chlorpromazine, was discovered in 1952.[27] Again, this innovation was a product of trial and error: there was no evidence-based biological theory that had led to the development of psychoactive drugs, nor did neurologists or biological psychiatrists of the time have a sound explanation for their effects. Not surprisingly, this produced both dissatisfaction and curiosity in medical researchers. Stimulated by the pharmacological industry, which had an obvious interest in more precise knowledge about the new psychiatric drugs, neurologists and biochemists set out to probe more deeply into the workings of the brain and the endocrine system.

New advances were also made with respect to diagnosis and classification, especially inspired by the earlier-mentioned Group for the Advancement of Psychiatry. Prompted by the massive number and variety of war neuroses observed during and after the Second World War, the GAP set out to create a descriptive system that was to include both psychotic and neurotic illnesses. The first edition of this *Diagnostic and statistical manual of mental disorders* (DSM) was published in 1952, listing 60 disorders, and, not surprisingly, heavily loaded with psychoanalytic concepts.[28]

4.5 Conclusion

Generally, the notion that Americans lived in a "psychological society" took hold rapidly in the 1950s and had become commonplace by the 1960s. The dividing line between serious theory and the simplifications of pop psychology became increasingly blurred. The rapid expansion of psychological services during this period resulted from two converging developments: the massive promotion of the concept of adjustment by politicians and clinicians on the one hand, and cultural changes resulting in an increasing preoccupation with the self on the other.

Although psychoanalysis (or rather psychodynamic psychiatry), especially in the US, had its heyday during this period, alternatives were on their way. Psychodynamic therapy was simply too time-consuming and complicated for the mass treatment of normal people with adjustment problems, and therefore ill-suited for the clinical work in the community mental health centers. The gap was filled by Rogers' client-centered approach which, together with other post-psychoanalytic therapies such as behavioral therapy, would eventually contribute to the decline of psychoanalysis in its classic form. Nevertheless, the proponents of these new therapies agreed with the psychoanalytic view that mental problems have psychological causes rather than biological ones, that they can be solved within the context of verbal, ambulant treatment, and finally that psychotherapy should be based on science, not morality. In other words, these alternatives used psychoanalysis as a stepping stone for their own invasion of the field of psychotherapy.

At the same time, the field of mental illness was expanded to include the psychological problems of people in general, such as sexual problems, difficulties in interpersonal relationships, and dissatisfaction with oneself. At the other end of the spectrum, psychiatrists in the institutions were struggling hard to find ways to relieve the symptoms of severe mental disorders. Their recourse to physical treatment methods, such as ECT and lobotomy, regardless of their effectiveness, contributed to the public aversion to asylums, especially since these physical therapies were frequently used as horror themes in books and movies.

5 Radicalism (*c.* 1960–80)

The 1960s and 1970s were a period of turmoil, both for society as a whole and for the field of mental health. On the one hand, western societies saw a continuous acceptance and growth of mental health care, and even the onset of an actual "personal growth" movement. On the other hand, radical groups contested fundamental assumptions of mainstream psychology and psychiatry. Institutional psychiatry, in particular, came under attack; mental hospitals were accused of being repressive institutions, which stigmatized the victims of social injustice. In the same vein, mental illness was designated as a myth that masked the reality of socially induced deviance and falsely justified the repressive power of the asylums. Alternative interpretations of mental illness, such as anti-psychiatry, joined forces with the anti-establishment battle of the counterculture, leading to a protest movement in almost all western countries, which aimed at the abolishment of mental institutions.

5.1 The counterculture

In many western countries, the 1960s were a period of youthful dissent. Since the coming of rock and roll, parents and social authorities had worried about the advent of a serious "generation gap" that would threaten cultural continuity and the maintenance of moral standards. From the mid-1960s onward, post-adolescents engaged in a left-wing political critique of various issues (racial segregation, university politics, and most vehemently, the war in Vietnam).

But the counterculture was not just about political consciousness: consciousness in general was explored, and psychiatry offered some of the means to do this. During the late 1950s, psychoactive drugs came to be used as a tool for the exploration of human consciousness. Harvard psychologist Timothy Leary, once an established director of psychological research, started to experiment with LSD, proclaiming that LSD was as essential to psychology as the microscope was to biology. In founding the "League for Spiritual Discovery" in 1966, Leary crossed over to the counterculture and provided the hippie movement with perhaps its most famous slogan, "turn on, tune in, drop out."

Authorities both within and outside psychiatry were quite ambivalent about the use of drugs. On the one hand, there was the legitimized prescription of drugs in the course of psychiatric treatment; within the counterculture, on the other hand, there was a voluntary and illegal use of drugs that was not only subject to legal punishment but also, as drug addiction, to psychiatric treatment.

While drug-induced consciousness-raising remained rather peripheral and temporary, other aspects of the counterculture would have a more profound and lasting effect, both within and outside the mental health domain. In the early 1970s, the critique of traditional forms of authority and hierarchy spread from targeting politics to a variety of cultural and professional institutions, including psychiatric hospitals. At the same time, the principle of self-realization became a widely accepted cultural norm, gradually replacing the earlier and more modest striving for "adjustment."

5.2 Anti-psychiatry

Seen in its historical context, the critical movement designated as "anti-psychiatry" seems a paradox. While ambulant psychiatric and psychological treatment blossomed, and new drugs were introduced that enabled psychiatric hospitals to leave behind crude ways of restraining psychiatric patients, the psychiatric hospital regime and the "medical model" of dealing with mental illness came under attack. In 1960 the psychiatrist Thomas Szasz published *The myth of mental illness*. He argued that most psychiatric disorders are expressive of problems in living, and are not due to diseases or chemical imbalances in the brain. Physical, surgical, or drug treatment was a fraud and concealed the real problem from both the practitioner and the public.

While Szasz opposed asylum psychiatry head-on, other professionals, both in the United States and the United Kingdom, were developing alternative treatments for psychotic and neurotic patients, such as group therapy and family therapy. Often it was found that individuals who were considered to be cured developed symptoms of mental illness after returning to their families, or, alternatively, another family member showed up for treatment. This "revolving door" problem inspired some therapists to invite the whole family for therapy sessions, focusing on the distorted communication patterns within the family. Or, as Jackson put it, family therapists "are much more concerned with influence, interaction, and interrelation between people, immediately observable in the present, than with individual, internal, imaginary, and infantile matters."[29]

In the UK, Ronald Laing, who during the 1950s had been experimenting with group and family therapy for schizophrenic patients, concluded that the medical approach to mental disturbances was a failure and instead designated society (and especially the family) as their cause. Laing saw a positive side to schizophrenia, which fitted in well with the countercultural imperative of "exploring the frontiers of the mind": it should be seen as a natural enlightened mental state that enabled ways of seeing that normal individuals could only reach by using psychedelic drugs.

Fueled by countercultural ideas and sociological analyses of mental institutions, labeling and deviance, the critiques voiced by professionals like Szasz and Laing evolved into a movement directed against the repressive practices within "total institutions" (Goffman) and the unjustified authority of the psychiatrist. In 1967, the British/South African psychiatrist David Cooper coined the term "anti-psychiatry," in his book *Psychiatry and antipsychiatry*. Critical publications in the same vein appeared in non-Anglo-Saxon countries, for instance *Bürger und Irre* ("Citizens and madness"), by Dörner in Germany, and *Wie is van hout* ("Who is made of wood"), by Foudraine in the Netherlands, the latter book selling over 200,000 copies. *Histoire de la folie* ("Madness and civilization"), published in 1961 by Michel Foucault, which was an early constructionist reinterpretation of the history of psychiatry, was hailed in retrospect as a predecessor of anti-psychiatry.

The anti-psychiatric sentiments were widely amplified in the media. As early as the 1940s, horrifying conditions within psychiatric hospitals had been presented to the public in books and movies such as Mary Jane Ward's *The snake pit* (1946 and 1948). Ken Kesey's novel *One flew over the cuckoo's nest* (1962) had subsequently pictured patients as defenseless victims of psychiatric power (see figure 32). When the novel was brought to the screen, in 1975, it was heralded as an anti-psychiatric statement. As historian John Reisman put it:

> The patient was portrayed as the victim of a system, a lunatic society that drove its more sensitive members to rebellion and then cast them into mental hospitals, where vindictive psychiatrists and nurses lay in wait.[30]

Anti-psychiatry thus turned the traditional rhetoric of the helping professions, based on benevolence and scholarship, upside down. Instead of leaders in the cause of humanitarian progress, psychiatrists were portrayed as servants of power who assisted in eliminating citizens displaying socially and politically deviant behavior.

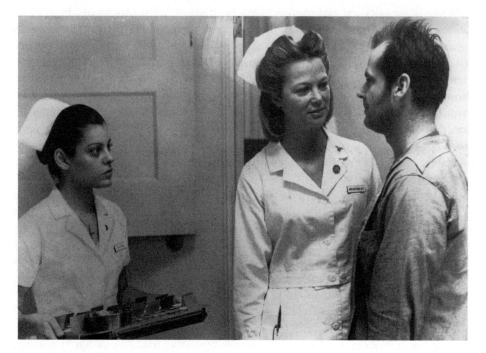

Figure 32   Jack Nicholson in *One flew over the cuckoo's nest* (1975). Based upon a novel by Ken Kesey, this movie drew attention once more to the arbitrary basis of psychiatric power, and its far-reaching consequences. Source: Kobal Collection, London.

The 1970s also saw vehement opposition to mainstream psychiatry and psychotherapy from the feminist movement. Women had always been a favorite target of psychiatry and psychoanalysis. They were considered to be the weaker sex, more neurotic or hysteric and prone to mental illness in general. Taken at face value, figures on hospitalization and use of mental health resources appeared to confirm this interpretation: over the ages and between countries, they consistently showed an over-representation of women. Also, as mothers, women were seen as the cause of mental problems (even schizophrenia) in their children. As early as the 1920s, Karen Horney had criticized Freud from within the psychoanalytic movement for the male bias in his theory. In the 1960s the feminist critique asserted that psychiatry should not label women as neurotic: "neurotic symptoms" in women were merely normal defenses against the oppression to which they were subject. Again, the critique was largely directed against psychoanalysis, probably because it was the dominant theoretical frame of reference. Neo-Freudians such as Erikson were attacked in Kate Millett's *Sexual politics* (1969). In general, feminist critique borrowed many tenets from anti-psychiatry, such as the abuse of power by medical professionals, the depoliticization of mental problems, the bias in professional concepts and theories, the conformism to the establishment, and the neglect of the subjective experience of individuals. Feminist psychologists such as Phyllis Chesler (*Women and madness*, 1972) criticized standard therapies, professionalism, and traditional concepts of mental health.

However, although both anti-psychiatry and feminism were critical of mainstream psychiatry and psychology, neither movement opposed psychology *per se*. In their search for an alternative approach to the interrelation between social and mental problems, both feminism and anti-psychiatry substantially contributed to an enlargement of the psychological domain, by providing it with a variety of new interpretations and therapies. This was exemplified in feminist theories that linked personal experience to social and political issues: "the personal is political." On the practical level, this credo gave rise to a host of self-help therapies; consciousness-raising groups helped women to see that their problems were not unique and should not be seen as a form of illness. Therapy thus became part of a process of growing political awareness, directed toward effective political action. While designed as a means to politicize personal experience, this strategy at the same time led to a psychologization of social issues.

5.3 A new psychological awareness

During the 1960s and 1970s, western societies saw a normalization of mental health care: the taboo on seeking help for mental problems largely disappeared, as can be seen from the rapidly growing number of patients, especially in ambulant mental health care. Between 1957 and 1976, the percentage of citizens in the US looking for help for mental problems rose from 14 percent to 26 percent.[31] The interest among the public in psychological issues was evidenced by the success of the monthly magazine *Psychology Today*, within a few years of its first publication in 1967, circulation totaled over one million copies. Especially among the younger intelligentsia, therapy almost became a way of life.

Generally, the public interest in psychology was welcomed by professionals. At the 1969 meeting of the APA on "Psychology and the Problems of Society," G. A. Miller in his presidential address depicted psychology as a means of promoting welfare. Because the demand for psychological services seemed practically limitless, Miller encouraged people to become their own psychologists. Self-help thus was not just a radical issue, it was part of the proto-professionalization process in citizens. As Herman put it:

> Psychological help was defined so broadly that everyone needed it. Neurotic emotional disturbance was gradually accepted as fact and product of modern existence rather than as the shameful secret it had been just a few decades earlier.[32]

Traditional authority, based on fixed norms and standards of conduct, was gradually replaced by a culture of growth and authenticity, and of democratic interpersonal relationships.

The dissemination of psychology, rather than being "more of the same," implied the introduction of new theories and therapies, fitting in with the changes in cultural values. The humanistic movement in psychology, headed by Carl Rogers and Abraham Maslow, sought ways to incorporate experiential knowledge into psychological science. They privileged the uniqueness of the individual and looked for ways to enhance psychological health, emphasizing personal growth, self-actualization, and the realization of one's potential.

In particular, Rogers' client-centered therapy was welcomed by the cultural critics of the 1960s as an avenue to a more democratic relationship between professional and client. Apart from client-centered therapy, a host of alternative therapies became fashionable for young middle-class progressives, such as Gestalt therapy, transactional analysis therapy, primal scream, and various group approaches, such as "encounter" and psychodrama. The therapeutic center Esalen in California became the meeting-point of self-actualizing therapy and counterculture, in the more general quest for "authentic interpersonal relationships."

The "friends of the new psychotherapies" were to be found within the middle classes, not just among "drop-outs," but also among social science and psychology students, social workers, psychiatric nurses, pastoral counselors and of course psychotherapists of a younger generation. In the quest for authenticity, talking about personal feelings and emotions became almost obligatory; in this respect, the humanistic rhetoric coincided with the basic principles of psychotherapy itself.

5.4   Conclusion

In this period, the social aspirations of the mental health professions were continued and radicalized. Humanistic brands of psychotherapy blossomed and were embraced by members of the hippie movement and protest movements such as women's liberation. Self-realization rather than adjustment became the new target in cultural and mental health politics. At the same time, psychiatry had to cope with both vehement opposition from anti-psychiatry and de-institutionalization policies within many western countries, favoring ambulant treatment over expensive hospital treatment. All in all, the 1960s and 1970s saw a significant enlargement and growing acceptance of mental health activities.

6   Rationalization (*c.* 1980–present)

The era of the humanistic psychotherapies and the anti-psychiatry movement had stretched the psychosocial aspects of mental health care and psychotherapy to their limits. This went hand in hand with a growing public demand for ambulant mental health services, a demand that included advice and help concerning life problems. "Therapy for the normal" thus became part and parcel of mental health care. This obviously created problems on the financial level. In many western countries psychotherapy had become part of publicly funded services during the 1970s, and the rising demand forced service providers to find ways to control costs. This called for a rationalization of both the mental health system and the psychotherapy process itself.

From the 1980s onward, in most countries, scattered public mental health services were reorganized into larger community centers, where intakes were centralized and therapeutic responsibilities were distributed among mental health workers according to the nature and gravity of the problems. The increasing complexity of the organizations was met by the introduction of managers, who were entrusted with guaranteeing both the cost-effectiveness and the quality of mental health care, and who more generally were supposed to negotiate government policies for the mental health domain. This found its most manifest expression in the introduction of the system of "managed care" in the United States, but various European countries witnessed similar developments."[33]

The urge to create an effective system of "managed care" converged with developments on the diagnostic and therapeutic levels. First of all, during the 1980s the third edition of the *Diagnostic and statistical manual of mental disorders* (DSM-III, 1980) was disseminated worldwide as the standard frame of reference for psychiatric diagnosis.[34] Psychoanalytic concepts, which had dominated the two previous editions, were replaced by a more neutral terminology. The list of disorders was also enlarged from 145 to 230, in order to include the many life problems that since the early 1970s had increasingly been presented to mental health professionals. Thus, the DSM-III categorized such everyday problems as shyness ("avoidance disorder"), stubbornness ("oppositional disorder"), tobacco smoking ("substance use disorder"), and significant deficiency in reading or arithmetic ("specific development disorder").

Although DSM-III, and its revised edition in 1987, helped to improve the reliability of psychiatric classification, it still reflected ignorance about the etiology of most disorders (especially schizophrenia and depression). In order to make progress on this level, psychiatry sought the help of biology and neurology. The identification of neural mechanisms involved in psychopathology had constituted a major leap forward in biological psychiatry. The discovery of the working of neurotransmitters and the visualization of differences between patients and "normal" people in brain activity led researchers to believe that psychological dysfunctions not only corresponded to impaired brain functions, but were also caused by them. Schizophrenia, for instance, was seen as the result of a disorder in the development of the brain. Brain-imaging techniques, such as "magnetic resonance imaging" (MRI) and "positron emission tomography" (PET), produced visible evidence of abnormalities in the brain that corresponded with specific mental disorders. Likewise, the new interdisciplinary science of psychoneuroimmunology was able to detect physiological correlates for mental states such as psychological stress. Although physiological researchers, well aware of the strains of modern social life, were wary of claiming a simple cause–effect relationship between biological and psychological phenomena, their efforts contributed to the rehabilitation of biology as a cornerstone of psychiatry and clinical psychology.

This rehabilitation was furthered by developments in pharmacology. Since the 1950s, several new generations of increasingly sophisticated drugs for the treatment of mental disorders had been produced and prescribed. During the 1990s, the public had proved as eager as policy makers and managers to adopt quick and easy solutions for psychological malfunctioning, and drug prescription and consumption expanded rapidly. Instead of engaging in time- and energy-consuming "talking cures" for symptoms of depression, patients welcomed new drugs such as Prozac as easy remedies for their ills.

Although drug therapy proved a much welcomed aid both for combating the discontents of civilization and for the social management of deviant behavior, it was by no means the only new development in treatment. From the array of post-psychoanalytic therapies, behavior therapy, after a period of steadily growing recognition during the 1970s, succeeded in becoming the most widely practiced approach in ambulant settings. In addition, the "token economy" technique derived from it has become the second favorite approach in institutional settings, next to drug treatment.

One undeniable advantage of behavior therapy is its wide range of applicability, both within and outside the clinical field. Moreover, it is not, unlike the psychodynamic therapies, limited to verbally gifted, introspective, intelligent, and educated members of western societies. Behavior therapy is rather straightforward and directive, and places a high value on routinized and experimentally evaluated procedures, which is obviously an asset in a period of increasing demand for mental health care. The adoption of concepts and techniques from cognitive psychology, cognitions cleverly being translated as "coverants" (i.e. covert operants), further contributed to the success of this form of therapy. As "cognitive behavioral therapy," as it is nowadays commonly known, it has developed into by far the most popular and widely used form of therapy.

Both drug therapy and behavior therapy boosted the new impetus toward rationalization within mental health care. On the one hand, they facilitated efficiency and cost-effectiveness by encouraging a standardized approach to mental problems, which was subsequently formalized by mental health managers in the form of protocols for diagnosis and treatment. On the other hand, they fitted in well with the demand of both researchers and policy makers for evidence-based therapies. Scientific respectability was further enhanced by the fourth edition of the DSM, issued in 1994. Since the previous revised edition, the DSM had been thoroughly redesigned to include the most recent developments in biological psychiatry, and to maximize both the reliability and validity of the classification system.

Unwittingly, the subjectivism and radicalism of the 1960s and 1970s seem to have reinforced in the following decades rationalistic and objectivistic approaches to mental illness in both psychology and psychiatry, as witnessed by the success stories of (cognitive) behavior therapy, biological psychiatry, diagnostic classification systems and, last but not least, more cost-effective and standardized approaches to treatment. Although most of these approaches date back to at least the 1950s, they flourished only from the 1980s onward. Together they succeeded not only in countering the psychosocial trend, but also in defeating the most powerful approach in the mental health domain, that of Freudian psychodynamic psychiatry.

This is not to say that the "rationalist" approaches concurred in all aspects. For instance, in its rise to prominence, behavior therapy fundamentally defied the medical model of both psychodynamic and biological psychiatry. Psychiatric patients weren't ill, they just suffered from "maladaptive" or "socially deviant" behavior. Feelings of unhappiness, depression or nervousness were the results of this maladaptation, not their cause.

7   Conclusion

In less than a century, the mental health perspective has come to pervade almost every aspect of western culture and modern life. Originally restricted to the problems of the seriously mental deranged, psychiatry has enlarged its jurisdiction to include virtually all aspects of individual behavior, as well as a whole range of social and cultural phenomena. In the process, psychiatrists gained the company of a whole range of other "mental health" professionals, prominent among them psychotherapists and clinical psychologists. And the end of this process seems nowhere in sight: year by year, the list of mental problems and disorders seems to become longer, and epidemiological studies suggest that the present use of mental health facilities reflects just a fraction of the "hidden demand" of all those suffering from problems.[35]

How can one account for this growing prominence of the mental health perspective? Undoubtedly, large-scale social and cultural developments such as individualization and secularization have been important factors. With the loosening of social structures, the increase in social mobility, and the disappearance of much of the authority of traditional moral leaders, we have lost many of the long-established reference points by which to orient our lives. Consequently, we are increasingly faced with the task of "turning inward," finding new points of reference and new guidelines through introspection, guided by the conceptual tools provided to us by the mental health paradigm, and seeking help from professionals when necessary.

However, these grand explanatory schemes should not blind us to some of the more specific backgrounds of the mental health "revolution." One of these is undoubtedly the theoretical framework which guided the mental health movement for much of the twentieth century, that of psychoanalysis. Freud's creation first enlarged the domain and jurisdiction of psychiatry, in fact saving it from unending confinement to the asylum. Second, it provided the public with the means for a new self-understanding: "the unconscious," "trauma," and many other psychoanalytic concepts became household words in the first half of the twentieth century. Whereas traditional psychiatry, as a branch of medicine, for the most part remained esoteric, psychoanalysis and most post-Freudian therapies took pride in informing and educating the public about the interpretation and treatment of mental illness. In the process, the dichotomy between mental health and illness lost its "all-or-nothing" character: health and illness became two poles of a continuum, with an infinite number of gradations in between.

Perhaps the most significant and pervasive aspect of the mental health perspective is the replacement of moral and ethical categories by psychological ones. In this respect, there is a striking continuity between the first psychiatric revolution and the developments in the century that lies behind us. If Pinel introduced a new perspective on "madness" as being an illness rather than a sign of moral derangement and a curse of God, so psychoanalysis and other mental health paradigms have in the twentieth century "secularized" and psychologized our view on a host of other phenomena formerly considered primarily from a moral point of view, from varieties of sexual behavior to delinquency, and from marital problems to juvenile unruliness.

Psychological tests, diagnostic catalogues such as the DSM, standardized forms of treatment and, lately, the reappearance of biological interpretations of mental disorders have solidified this new, psychological perspective, giving it an appearance of scientific objectivity and factuality. Together, they tend to create the impression that mental health problems are discrete disease entities, with a universal validity, residing within the individual and objectively diagnosable. In the process, they have established the position of psychologists, psychiatrists and other "psy-experts," lending them an authority over virtually every aspect of our lives. However, this scientification and objectivation of mental problems should not blind us to their historical and cultural specificity. Historically, the expansion of the mental health domain not only reflects scientific progress and better understanding of mental phenomena, but at least as much the increased strains and problems of modern western society. And from a transcultural perspective, the alleged objectivity of mental health nomenclature should not blind us to the culturally specific nature, expression and interpretation of many of the phenomena we consider as "mental disorders."

PRINCIPAL SOURCES AND FURTHER READING

A major source for this chapter, covering developments within psychiatry both in Europe and the United States is E. Shorter (1997), *A history of psychiatry. From the era of the asylum to the age of Prozac* (New York: Wiley). See also M. S. Micale and R. Porter, eds. (1994), *Discovering the history of psychiatry* (New York and Oxford: Oxford University Press), and M. Gijswijt-Hofstra and R. Porter, eds. (1998) *Cultures of psychiatry and mental health care in postwar Britain and the Netherlands* (Amsterdam/New York: Rodopi). For the United States, see also F. Castel, R. Castel, and A. Lovell (1982), *The psychiatric society* (New York: Columbia University Press).

For clinical psychology comprehensive sources are J. M. Reisman (1991), *A history of clinical psychology* (2nd ed.) (New York: Hemisphere) and D. K. Routh (1994), *Clinical psychology since 1917. Science, practice and organization* (New York and London: Plenum Press). See for a contextual history of psychotherapy: P. Cushman (1992), Psychotherapy to 1992. A historically situated interpretation, in D. K. Freedheim, ed., *History of psychotherapy. A century of change* (Washington: American Psychological Association), pp. 21–64.

For neurasthenia and the early treatment of mental problems outside the asylum see: A. D. Abbott (1988), *The system of professions. An essay on the division of expert labor* (Chicago/London: University of Chicago Press), chapter 10; E. Brooks Holifield (1983), *A history of pastoral care in America. From salvation to self-realization* (Nashville: Abingdon). For a comparative historiography of neurasthenia and its treatment in the United States, Britain, Germany, and Holland, see M. Gijswijt-Hofstra and R. Porter, eds. (2001) *Cultures of neurasthenia. From Beard to the First World War* (Amsterdam/New York: Rodopi).

The history of psychoanalysis and Freud's work is extensively treated. See H. E. Ellenberger (1970), *The discovery of the unconscious. The history and evolution of dynamic psychiatry* (New York: Basic Books); P. Gay (1988), *Freud. A life for our time* (New York: Norton).

Useful additional sources regarding the post-Second World War history of American clinical psychology are E. Herman (1995), *The romance of American psychology. Political culture in the age of experts* (Berkeley: University of California Press) and J. Capshew (1999), *Psychologists on the march. Science, practice, and professional identity in America, 1929–1969* (Cambridge, MA: Cambridge University Press).

For the vicissitudes of female patients in both early and recent psychiatry and psychotherapy, see E. Showalter (1985), *The female malady. Women, madness and English culture, 1830–1980* (New York: Pantheon).

NOTES

1 See G. Vandenbos, N. N. Cummings, and P. H. Deleon (1992), A century of psychotherapy. Economic and environmental influences, in Freedheim, *History of psychotherapy*, pp. 65–102 (p. 97).

2 Shorter, *A history of psychiatry*, p. 15.

3 P. Vandermeersch (1994), "Les mythes d'origine" in the history of psychiatry, in Micale and Porter, *Discovering the history of psychology*, pp. 219–31 (p. 222).

4 Shorter, *A history of psychiatry*, p. 19

5 See Vandermeersch, "Les mythes d'origine."

6 J. M. W. Binneveld et al. (1982) *Een psychiatrisch verleden. Uit de geschiedenis van de psychiatrie* [A psychiatric past. From the history of psychiatry.] (Baarn: Ambo), p. 21.

7 Shorter, *A history of psychiatry*, pp. 46–7

8 Castel, *The psychiatric society*, pp. 15–6, 48–9.

9 E. Caplan (1998), Popularizing American psychotherapy. The Emmanuel Movement, 1906–1910, *History of Psychology*, 1, 289–314 (quote p. 291).

10 Abbott, *The system of professions*, p. 301.

11 Reisman, *A history of clinical psychology*, p. 48.

12 Castel, *The psychiatric society*, p. 325.

13 Castel, *The psychiatric society*, p. 36.

14 See: J. M. W. Binneveld (1997), *From shell shock to combat stress. A comparative history of military psychiatry* (Amsterdam: Amsterdam University Press), chapter 6; M. Stone (1985), Shell shock and the psychologists, in W. F. Bynum, R. Porter, and M. Sheperd, eds., *The anatomy of madness. Essays in the history of psychiatry, vol. II: Institutions and society* (London/New York: Tavistock), pp. 242–71.

15 See J. C. Burnham (1988), *Paths into American culture. Psychology, medicine, and morals* (Philadelphia: Temple University Press), chapter 5.

16 Castel, *The psychiatric society*, p. 30.

17 R. Abma (2001), De patient [The patient], in J. Jansz and P. van Drunen, *Met zachte hand. Opkomst en verbreiding van het psychologisch perspectief* [The gentle force. Genesis and dissemination of the psychological perspective], 3rd ed. (Leusden: De Tijdstroom), p. 123.

18 Vandenbos et al., A century of psychotherapy, pp. 74–5.

19 Estimates of clinical psychologists involved range from 250 to 450. See: Capshew, *Psychologists on the march*, p. 172; D. S. Napoli (1981), *Architects of adjustment. The history of the psychological profession in the United States* (Port Washington, NY: Kennikat Press), p. 102.

20 W. Menninger, *Psychiatry in a troubled world*, quoted in Herman, *The romance of American psychology*, p. 119.

21 Capshew, *Psychologists on the march*, p. 135.

22 Herman, *The romance of American psychology*, pp. 242–3.

23 Castel, *The psychiatric society*, p. 60.

24 H. J. Eysenck (1966), *The effects of psychotherapy* (New York: International Science), pp. 39–40.

25 H. J. Eysenck (1964), *Experiments in behaviour therapy* (New York: Macmillan), p. 1.

26 Reisman, *A history of clinical psychology*, p. 295; Capshew, *Psychologists on the march*, p. 244.

27 E. M. Tansey (1998), "They used to call it psychiatry." Aspects of the development and impact of psychopharmacology, in Gijswijt-Hofstra and Porter, *Cultures of psychiatry*, pp. 79–102; also Binneveld, *Shell shock*, chapter 5.

28 See S. A. Kirk and H. Kutchins (1992), *The selling of DSM. The rhetoric of science in psychiatry* (New York: Aldine).

29 D. D. Jackson and J. H. Weakland (1969), Conjoint family therapy. Some considerations on theory, technique and results, in D. D. Jackson, ed., *Therapy, communication and change* (Palo Alto: Science and Behavior Books), p. 229.

30 Reisman, *A history of clinical psychology*, p. 310.

31 Herman, *The romance of American psychology*, p. 262.

32 Herman, *The romance of American psychology*, p. 311.

33 See D. Ingleby (1998), The view from the North Sea, in Gijswijt-Hofstra and Porter, *Cultures of psychiatry*, pp. 294–314.

34 Kirk and Kutchins, *The selling of DSM*; Reisman, *A history of clinical psychology*, chapter 11.

35 *The World Health report 2001. Mental health: new understanding, new hope* (Geneva: World Health Organization).

4 Work and organization

Peter van Drunen, Pieter J. van Strien, and Eric Haas

Introduction

"There are many factories that have scores of scientifically trained chemists or physicists at work, but who would consider it an unproductive luxury to appoint a scientifically schooled experimental psychologist to their staff." Thus complained the German-American pioneer of practical psychology, Hugo Münsterberg, in his book *Psychology and industrial efficiency* (1913).[1] On their part, psychologists did not take much interest in work as a possible field of expertise either, according to Münsterberg. At a time when pedagogical and medical psychology were already well underway, economic life, commerce, and industry were "surprisingly neglected."

Münsterberg's assessment served as a starting point for an ambitious outline of the prospects and possible usefulness of industrial psychology. In this respect, it clearly served rhetorical purposes. Nevertheless, it was by and large correct: while industrialization was one of the main factors in the rise of practical psychology in the late nineteenth and early twentieth century, work itself was not one of the first areas of human activity to be explored by psychologists. This lagging behind, however, was soon to be eliminated. Starting with Münsterberg's manifesto and spurred by the First World War and subsequent economic developments, from the 1920s onward the workplace would become a burgeoning field of psychological interventions. Far from being considered an "unproductive luxury," psychologists would find their place in economic life, both within the personnel departments of large companies and as well-paid consultants. Moreover, the vocabularies and technologies they introduced would permeate working life, and leave their mark on our everyday conceptions of what "work" is about.

This chapter starts with a brief historical sketch, focusing on the the Industrial Revolution, the nineteenth-century transformation which provided the background for the rise of systematic management practices (section 1). In section 2, we discuss the rise of a movement which set the scene for psychologists: scientific management. Section 3 deals with the advent of psychologists into the workplace, with particular attention to their most substantial early contribution, that of personnel selection. Section 4 discusses two subsequent enlargements of the psychological domain:

"human relations" and "the humanization of work." Finally, in section 5 we discuss a recent development, which in many ways appears to be the crowning glory of psychology's expansion in the domain of work and organizational life, that of human resource management.

1   Early history (before *c.* 1880)

"Work" is no recent invention. Nevertheless, it was only from the late eighteenth century onward that the subjects now associated with the psychology of work and organization began to attract serious attention. This was primarily the result of the vast changes in the nature of work which were brought about by the Industrial Revolution. As in other areas, the nineteenth century saw the first coordinated efforts at management of workers' behavior, which created the intellectual and social climate for the subsequent introduction of psychological perspectives and practices.

1.1   Pre-industrial times (c. 1775)

Unlike education and other domains/aspects of social life, the realm of work does not have a long tradition of pre-psychological reflection and interventions; work did not hold a prominent place in the scheme of values of early western civilization. On the contrary: it was generally considered as lowly, an obstacle to a worthy life rather than a means to achieve it. The citizens of Athens and the other Greek city-states, for example, were supposed to free themselves from it (i.e., leave it to slaves), in order to participate fully in democracy and lead a worthwhile and meaningful life.

With the advent of Christian theology and philosophy work was accorded a somewhat higher status, as is evident from the famous dictum *ora et labora* – "pray and work." In daily life, the medieval guilds with their elaborate systems of training and occupational hierarchies were an early example of systems which incorporated elements of what would nowadays be called "personnel psychology." Unlike the educational realm, however, these institutions did not generate more or less systematic "practice knowledge" and guidelines.

Of course, there were exceptions, especially in the military domain.[2] Theories about leadership and the organization of large armies date back at least as far as Alexander the Great. And as early as the late sixteenth century, intricate schemes were devised for coordinating the behavior of soldiers in combat, not only at an organizational level but also at that of minute movements of individuals. So, for instance, the Dutch general Maurits of Orange devised detailed schemes for the use of various weapons, in order to obtain maximum coordination and thus ensure continuous firepower. The use of the musket, for instance, was broken down into no fewer than 32 different movements, each carefully timed, and subsequently incorporated into an elaborate drilling program (see figure 33).

Figure 33 Military drill, *c.* 1700. Six illustrations from a Dutch handbook on the use of the musket. Source: Psychology Pictures.

It was only in the sixteenth and seventeenth centuries that work was accorded a more significant place in western culture, due to various developments. The advent of merchant capitalism went hand in hand with the emergence of the bourgeoisie as a new social class, providing a growing counterforce against the aristocracy. This was reflected in cultural and religious changes. With the rise of Protestantism, especially in its Calvinist variety, work became one of the key values of life. A Christian was supposed to lead a frugal life, using work to make the best of his talents, and forfeiting leisure, luxury, and sensual pleasure. Thus a new attitude toward work developed, commonly known as the "protestant ethic," and various forms of work, especially trade and commerce, were revalued. Formerly considered unsuitable for true gentlemen, they were increasingly seen as respectable activities, which could hold the key for improving one's social position.

Up till the end of the eighteenth century, this "new morality" was restricted to a small segment of society, the representatives of the new mercantilist-commercial bourgeoisie. This changed with the onset of the Industrial Revolution in England in the late eighteenth century.

1.2 The Industrial Revolution

Starting in the 1770s in England, and spreading across the European continent and the United States in the first half of the nineteenth century, the Industrial Revolution gave "work" a new meaning, both as an abstract idea and in everyday practice. In the ideological realm, this found its expression in a treatise which would for more than a century provide the philosophical underpinning and legitimation of industrialization and capitalism: *An Inquiry into the Wealth of Nations* by the Scottish philosopher Adam Smith (1776). In Smith's account, the acquisition of wealth acquired a new status: although perhaps not morally laudable in its own right, in the grand scheme of things it secured the greatest wealth for the greatest number of people. Work, driven by selfish economic motives, thus became a key social value. Moreover, Smith provided the economic rationale for what would become one of the key characteristics of industrial work: the mechanization and division of labor. By dividing the production process into numerous separate acts, performed by different people, he argued, output could be increased to hitherto undreamed-of levels.

In the latter decades of the eighteenth century and the first of the nineteenth century, the processes Smith described gradually became visible in everyday life. Measured as the number of people employed, industry would long remain second to agriculture, even in England. However, where industrialization got underway, its consequences were far-reaching. Household industries and small-scale workshops gave way to a new organization of working life: the factory. This entailed a number of changes, requiring what according to some observers amounted to little short of a "new (working) man."[3]

First, the factory and other forms of large-scale enterprise (such as mining) entailed a radical division between work and other spheres of life. Previously an integral part of domestic life, work was now carried out in a separate place. Workers' discretion about their own use of time, characteristic in agriculture and household manufacture, was replaced by production schedules with the pace being set by machines, requiring regular hours of attendance and steady output.

Secondly, the nature of work itself changed. Formerly an area of individual activity, the division of labor transformed it into a collective effort. Hand-made manufacture was replaced by mass production; variation and the individual stamp of the craftsman gave way to standardization.

Thirdly, the factory brought about a dramatic change in domestic relations as well, especially with regard to the involvement of women and children. Traditionally, work had been primarily the domain of men, with children and women participating as far as their capacities and (for women) their household tasks permitted. Now, increasingly, children and women came to be seen as regular members of the labor force. In many industries, they were even favored over men, both for being cheaper and more docile, and because of specific qualities that men were supposed to lack, such as dexterity. For women, this meant an entrenchment of their "double burden," with both full-time industrial work, and the primary responsibility for domestic duties and bringing up children.

Understandably, workers did not take kindly to the changes forced upon them. Industrial work was notoriously unpopular and resistance to industrialization was great. This found its most forceful expression in periodic anti-industrial revolts, such as those of the Luddites in England and the "saboteurs" in France (allegedly named after the *sabots* (boots) with which they tried to destroy the machines). Less conspicuous, but far more endemic, was the silent resistance of workers, trying to hold on to their old working habits and thus frustrating employers' attempts to coerce them into the routines required by industrial production. Within industry, this resulted in new management practices, to bring the workforce into line with the requirements of industrial life (see section 1.3). Alongside this, the new realities of working life also generated interest from other quarters (section 1.4).

1.3   Early industrial management

The demands of industrial production and workers' resistance to them created the need for new management practices. Some enlightened industrialists even considered adequate management of the workforce to be one of the core elements of a successful business undertaking. As the Scottish entrepreneur Robert Owen put it:

> Experience has . . . shown us the difference of the results between a mechanism which is neat, clean, well-arranged, and always in a high state of repair; and that which is allowed to be dirty, in disorder, without the means of preventing unnecessary friction. . . . If, then, due care as to the state of your inanimate machines can produce such beneficial results, what may not be expected if you devote equal attention to your vital machines [the human resource], which are far more wonderfully constructed?[4]

Most early industrialists took a less benevolent attitude. Workers were considered a nuisance rather than a resource, their unwillingness or incapacity to adapt to the codes of industrial life being a source of widespread exasperation and irritation among employers. Complaints about "faults of character" were almost universal, depicting workers as being "by nature" indolent, improvident, self-indulgent and volatile.[5] Perhaps most perplexing was their insensitivity to financial rewards: better payment tended to result in higher absence rates, rather than stimulating men to work harder.

In practice, two modes of intervention developed. The first was a crude, disciplinarian approach, aiming at regulating workers' behavior by strict rules, close supervision, and heavy penalties for transgressions. Some disciplinary functions were realized by the very nature of machine-bound work, which forced the "volatile" workers into a steady routine. Others could be enforced effectively by simple measures. So, for instance, it was customary in most factories to close the gates at the start of the working day, opening them only at the end of the day, thus preventing late arrival, early departure, and intermittent absences. All other activity was regulated by strict disciplinary codes. These were extensive lists of prohibited behavior, ranging from leaving the machine and insubordination to talking with fellow-workers, and were enforced by heavy fines and, especially in the case of children, by physical punishment. The severity of the codes and the crudity with which they were enforced only added to workers' distaste for factory life, making it little different, in their view, from prison or the workhouse for the poor.

The second mode of intervention was what some historians have called the "ethical" approach.[6] It aimed at changing workers' attitudes, thus adapting them to the requirements of industrial life. It concerned itself with behavior outside as well as inside the factory, with the attributes needed for industrial work, such as punctuality and "time thrift," as well as with more general habits such as drinking and swearing. In this "civilizing offensive" employers generally joined forces with the clergy or religious movements, such as the Quakers.

Compared with shop-floor discipline, the ethical approach tended to be somewhat more subtle and "humane," stressing "education" of the workforce rather than coercion. On the other hand, it was much more encompassing, permeating every aspect of workers' lives. The results were most clearly visible and effective in the "factory villages," where employers exerted almost full control over the behavior of the workers. Originally, these villages were a sheer necessity: especially in the countryside, the opening of mines and large-scale works was only possible if provisions were made for housing, schooling, and the like. As the century progressed, however, these villages gradually developed into an instrument of social management. This was for instance reflected in their layout; supervision was often facilitated by grouping the houses of the "common" workers around an overseer's cottage, giving at least the impression that no aspect of workers' behavior could escape managerial attention.

1.4   The labor problem

Alongside the extensive but rather crude forms of social management which developed within industry, the new realities of industrial work gave rise to a growing interest in the "labor problem" from other quarters.

PUBLIC CONCERN

Almost from its beginning, the Industrial Revolution aroused concern about the plight of the industrial worker. As early as the late 1790s, reports began to appear which sketched the dire conditions of life and work in industrial England. At first, these concerns were countered by the classical liberal view, that such conditions were the inevitable results of the economic development which was not be interfered with by mitigating governmental policy. As industrialization progressed, the call for governmental action grew louder, first in England, later on the European continent, and, toward the end of the nineteenth century, also in the US. Fueled by periodic unrest and, after the mid-century, also by the concerted efforts of labor unions and by middle-class fear of social revolution, this resulted in a gradual limitation of working hours, coupled with other means of governmental intervention, such as the establishment of labor inspectorates, and the development of "industrial medicine."

Within these interventionist policies, some issues received special attention. One of them, discussed earlier, was the growing concern over child labor, resulting in increasingly restrictive legislation, and the gradual introduction of compulsory education (see chapter 2). Another focus of special concern were female workers. Women were considered physically less equipped for the extremely long working hours and the harsh conditions of early industrial work. More persuasively, it was argued that this ran counter to their maternal and domestic responsibilities, which figured with increasing prominence in middle-class thought about the social role of women. Thus, as well as general regulation, all industrial societies witnessed specific and more restrictive legislation with respect to women. On the one hand, this provided some additional safeguards against extreme exploitation. On the other hand, it reinforced the middle-class notion of "separate spheres" for men and women, thus preparing the way for a gradual marginalization of women in the world of work. This in turn was reflected by lower wages, less security against dismissal, poorer career opportunities, and finally, in the twentieth century, it culminated in a social norm which saw work for married women as undesirable.[7]

SCIENCE

From the 1850s onward, there was also scientific interest in labor. Inspired by the nature of industrial work as well as the newly discovered thermodynamic laws of the conservation of energy, traditional moral conceptions of work gave way to a mechanical-energetic perspective.[8] Next to "idleness" for instance, traditionally considered to be the most important restriction on productive capacity, "fatigue" became an issue, i.e. the physiological limitations of the human body.

Particularly on the European continent (e.g. France, Italy, Germany), physiologists and other scientists engaged in extensive research to discover the laws of labor productivity and fatigue, making use of newly developed instruments such as chronophotography (developed in the 1870s by the French physiologist Marey, to record and analyze bodily movements) and the "ergograph" (developed by the Italian physiologist Mosso in 1884, to measure muscle fatigue; see figure 34). After

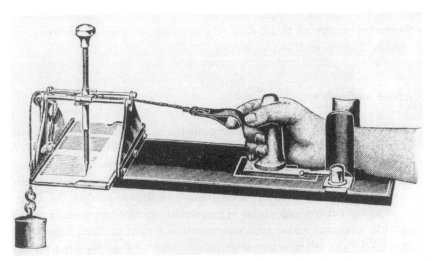

Figure 34 The "ergograph," an apparatus developed in 1884 by the Italian physiologist Mosso for the study of endurance and fatigue. Source: Psychology Pictures/Archives of Dutch Psychology.

1900, this new "science of labor" would become increasingly prominent in social debates on issues such as the optimal length of the working day, the difference between male and female workers, and the influence of fatigue as a cause of industrial accidents.

ORGANIZED LABOR AND SOCIALISM

Public concern and the call for governmental action was not restricted to the middle class. As the century progressed, workers themselves also began to play an important role. Anti-industrial revolts gave way to concerted action in the form of trade unionism and the socialist movement. The work of Karl Marx became an influential source of inspiration, providing a new concept of labor that stressed its psychological meaning: the ideal of work as self-fulfilment, combined with a vehement critique on the "dehumanization" of work under capitalist conditions, due to the alienation which resulted from the division of labor and capitalist organization of production in general.[9]

ATTITUDES TO WORK

If organized labor and socialism were critical of the changes brought about by the Industrial Revolution, at another level workers also adapted to the new possibilities it offered. With the changing economic and social landscape, an individual's occupation became to some degree a matter of personal choice. Especially in the United States, but to a lesser extent also in some European countries, guidelines for the choice of a suitable occupation began to appear along with success manuals, which both reflected and enhanced this new spirit.[10] Both members of the middle class and some workers began to consider themselves as "entrepreneurs of character," trying to make the best of their talents and interests. Advice was often sought, either from the moral guides of those days (the minister, teacher, or doctor), or from self-appointed experts such as phrenologists.

1.5   Conclusion

As in education, mental health, and other domains, the nineteenth century witnessed both the advent of new perspectives on work and workers' behavior and a massive extension of regulatory practices. Curiously enough, this did not result in the genesis of new forms of practical expertise, comparable to those in other fields (pedagogy, psychiatry, etc.). On the one hand, the emerging new science of work remained rather academic. On the other hand, social management practices remained rather crude, based on rules of thumb rather than new forms of expertise. Thus, while the Industrial Revolution indirectly stimulated the development of specific expertise in social science in other domains, expertise with respect to work itself was slow to develop. It was only in the 1880s that the management of workers became the subject of systematic theorizing. And it took another twenty years before a new field of expertise took shape, centered around a theory that would dominate the field until the Second World War: scientific management.

2 Scientific management (*c.* 1880–1920)

As industrialization progressed, the old methods of "shop management" were becoming ever more inadequate. This was partly due to the sheer increase of scale: with the expansion of markets and the introduction of mass production, factories became larger, employing thousands (and sometimes ten of thousands) rather than hundreds of workers. Growing technical complexity added to the problem, as did changes in ownership: increasingly, individual proprietorship gave way to shareholding, creating the need for more "objective" management and decision-making, based on rational policy-making rather than the intuition of a single entrepreneur.

Among the problems confronting industry, labor relations figured prominently. Labor legislation, trade unions, and other forms of organized labor placed increasing limits on the management of workers' behavior, especially in its older form of brute discipline. Even more perplexing to industrialists was the "silent resistance" of workers. In particular, "soldiering" was a much discussed problem; this was the concerted attempts of workers to keep production low, even to the point of violence against over-zealous co-workers.

All these problems first became visible in the United States, which in the last decades of the nineteenth century gradually replaced Great Britain as the leading industrial country of the world. They resulted in what business historian Alfred Chandler has called "the managerial revolution."[11] Characteristic of this development was a rationalization of company management, embodied by the genesis of the salaried manager. After 1900, this would result in the inception of "management" as a distinct discipline, with its own journals, training programs ("business schools," with the Master of Business Administration (MBA) title being introduced in 1902), and professional associations. In the early days, however, the new positions were predominantly filled by engineers, technically educated experts, who gradually extended their expertise to include other aspects of "shop management" as well. It was one of these, F. W. Taylor, who laid the basis for what would become the dominant paradigm for managing labor in the early decades of the twentieth century, that of scientific management.

2.1 "A mental revolution"

Frederick Winslow Taylor (1856–1915) was an almost prototypical self-made man. Starting his career in industry in 1876 as an apprentice machinist without any qualifications, he managed to become chief engineer of one of the bigger steel companies in the United States within six years, meanwhile also acquiring a degree in mechanical engineering. He produced numerous inventions, one of which (high speed steel) made him a fortune. This allowed him to retire in 1901 at the age of 45, and to devote the rest of his life to the development and promotion of a systematic theory of management, a cause which he considered to be long overdue. This culminated in two works, which brought him fame: *Shop management* (1903) and *The principles of scientific management* (1911).

Taylor modeled his management ideas on his experience in technical engineering. Just as the latter had improved efficiency by careful attention to the construction and design of machines, so modern management should focus on optimizing the efficiency of labor. Following others, Taylor's first contribution in this respect was an intricate payment scheme, designed to increase worker effort and productivity, the so-called differential piece-rate system. Soon after this was published, however, Taylor realized that financial incentives could only be effective if they were combined with managerial control over the work process. This was to become the cornerstone of scientific management.

Traditionally, industrial managers showed little interest in the specific details of the work process. By and large, it was left to the workers and foremen to execute their assigned tasks as they saw fit. Consequently, managers lacked information regarding the time needed to perform particular tasks, and so payment schemes were generally based on average output in the past. As such, Taylor argued, they not only suffered from the results of "soldiering," but also forfeited possibilities for enhancing productivity by optimizing work methods. If efficiency was to be raised substantially, managers should become more actively involved in designing optimal work methods, rather than leaving this to the discretion of the workers themselves. As Taylor put it: "The art of management [is] knowing exactly what you want your men to do, and then seeing that they do it in the best and cheapest way."[12]

In order to realize these objectives, Taylor proposed a series of innovations in industrial management, the most important of which were (a) a radical division between the planning and the execution of work, and (b) detailed study of the work process, to assess the most efficient way in which a task could be performed and the time it required. Both ideas rested on the assumption that there was "one best way of doing the job," and that centralized and careful planning was the key to enhancing productivity.

The most crucial aspect of planning, according to Taylor, was time study. Originally, this was approached in a rather crude and global manner, by simply taking the maximum output of a good worker as the standard of performance Subsequently, however, Taylor increasingly focused on the need for detailed time study, based on careful analysis of the separate movements a job entailed. So, for instance, work on lathes in the steel industry was broken down into no fewer than 47 separate movements, varying from "lifting work to shears" to "oiling up" and "cleaning machine." Overseers were introduced, who would carefully record and time each of these movements, to arrive at a "scientific" assessment of the time a job required (see figure 35).

In hindsight, Taylor's ideas appear almost commonplace. Compared with the traditional organization of the nineteenth-century factory, however, they were little short of revolutionary. This was reflected in the dramatic increase in efficiency and output that Taylor reported, which was never less than 50 percent, and sometimes as much as 300 percent. As Taylor stressed, these results were not merely attributable to the technical innovations of his system. In the end, he asserted, what counted most was the "mental revolution" that it implied, with a new attitude among both

Figure 35   Time study. For many workers the well-dressed overseer with his stopwatch was the embodiment of Taylorism and increased control over their work. Source: Psychology Pictures/Archives of Dutch Psychology.

workers and industrialists, based on cooperation and mutual benefit rather than opposition and incompatibility of interests. According to Taylor, scientific management was a means to reconcile the apparently opposing interests of workers in high wages and of employers in low labor cost; by cooperating, both parties would profit from enhanced productivity.

According to Taylor, the key to cooperation was a carefully designed bonus system, which ensured that workers got their share of the benefits of increased productivity. He repeatedly emphasized that the bonus for workers who outperformed the "scientifically" determined norms of production should be ample, ranging up to extra payment of 60 percent (but no more, lest they should become "shiftless, extravagant and dissipated").[13] On the one hand, he warned employers against cutting back on these bonuses, or raising norms of production when workers exceeded these norms, and on the other hand, he urged workers not to oppose his system; Taylorism could only work if both parties changed their attitudes from conflict to cooperation. In this respect, he was especially critical of trade unions, who in his view symbolized the "old mentality" of opposing interests and would be obsolete under the new system.

Apart from a change from conflict to cooperation, Taylor's system implied another dramatic shift: a radical individualization of performance. Traditionally, groups of men ("gangs"), rather than individuals, were the unit of production, and piece rates and bonus systems were based on the collective performance of these groups. Considering this an insurmountable obstacle to efficiency, Taylor emphasized the importance of individualized measurement of performance as a necessary prerequisite for successful introduction of his system. As he put it: "When workmen are herded into gangs, each man . . . becomes far less efficient than when his personal ambition is stimulated. . . . Personal ambition always has been and will remain a more powerful incentive to exertion than a desire for the general welfare."[14] As well as material gains, he claimed, workers stood to benefit from his system in other respects: "they live rather better, begin to save money, become more sober, and work more steadily."[15]

2.2 Reception and impact

Scientific management found a quick reception; within a few years, Taylor acquired the status of a "business guru." Both for engineers and for the new professional group of managers, his theory provided a clear-cut and easy to grasp formula, which enhanced their professional status and identity. Following in the tracks of Taylor himself, many "efficiency experts" began to offer their services as consultants to industry and other kinds of enterprise. Some adhered strictly to the rules laid out by Taylor, others went their own way. Next to those of Taylor himself, the ideas of Frank and Lilian Gilbreth became especially widely known. Based on Taylor's original conception of time study, the Gilbreths (he an engineer, she a psychologist) in the early 1900s introduced the more encompassing and refined methlodology of "motion study." The central idea was to maximize performance through detailed analysis of the motions required followed by redesigning the worksite so as to eliminate every unnecessary movement (see figure 36). To this end, the stopwatch was supplemented by the newly invented "high tech" equipment of the day, such as the "cyclograph"; this was a motion recorder, which provided a visual trace of the movement of the worker, thus making it possible to define the "perfect" (i.e., most economic) movement and to detect "erratic" motions.

American industry proved fertile soil for these new ideas. In the first decades of the twentieth century, "efficiency" became its almost universal slogan. As early as 1912, more than fifty branches of industry were reported to have introduced Taylorist schemes, and an inventory undertaken five years later by one of Taylor's numer-

Figure 36 A motion study of bricklaying, 1909. (a) The traditional method of providing the bricklayer with material. (b) The "new" method, developed to reduce any unneccessary motions and optimize efficiency. Source: F. B. Gilbreth, *Motion study* (New York: Van Nostrand, 1911).

ous disciples recorded more than 150 firms which had adopted scientific management.[16] Other countries quickly followed; as early as 1906, German and French
engineers started to copy Taylorist methods, and by 1915 his major works had
been translated into nine languages, including Japanese and Russian as well as French
and German.[17]

Workers' reactions to Taylorism were less sympathetic, varying from skepticism to
downright hostility. In spite of Taylor's warnings, many employers could not resist
cutting back on bonuses and raising productivity norms. Moreover, trade unions
resisted the enhanced managerial control over workers' behavior, and the break up
of solidarity among workers implied by Taylor's individualized measurement of performance and payment scheme. As one labor leader put it, Taylorism was not so much
a science of management as a science of exhaustion.[18]

With worker opposition building up as rapidly as enthusiasm among entrepreneurs, Taylorism became a source of fierce industrial battle. In 1911, attempts to
introduce time study at the Watertown Arsenal in Massachusetts resulted in a massive
strike, which led the American Congress to establish a committee which was to investigate the social consequences of scientific management. Similar collisions occurred
in subsequent years in Europe, for instance at the Renault automobile factory in
France.

But if workers were occasionally successful in their fight against Taylorism, they
could not stop its general advance. After the First World War, Taylorism became generally accepted among industrialists, both in the United States and in Europe, and
resistance among workers gradually waned. In the process, scientific management lost
much of its specificity as a separate "theory" or "school." What remained was the
general idea of detailed monitoring and control of production processes and workers'
behavior, which would become part and parcel of twentieth-century management.

2.3   Conclusion

If the field of labor had in the nineteenth century lagged somewhat behind with
respect to the development of social management, Taylorism brought it back in line
again. Overall, Taylor's ideas perfectly reflected the general idea of social management as outlined in earlier chapters of this book: a concerted attempt to control
human behavior, inspired by motives of social order and efficiency as well as by a
humanitarian ethos, proceeding by monitoring behavior in increasing detail, combined with an individualizing approach, and performed by a new class of behavioral
experts.

The almost paradigmatic nature of Taylorism as a model practice of social management was not lost on contemporary observers. From 1910 onward, scientific
management would increasingly serve as a source of inspiration for social reformers.
Its key notion of "efficiency" became the leading principle of the Progressive Movement in the United States, and the starting point for ambitious programs to monitor
and evaluate achievements in such varied fields as education and public administration.

If Taylorism had any weakness, it was its rather rudimentary scientific foundation.
Especially with respect to the behavior, motives, and mental life of workers, Taylor's

ideas were exclusively based on practical experience, rather than being connected to developments in psychology or any of the related sciences. However, they paved the way for other groups of experts to come to the fore, especially industrial psychologists.

3   "Psychotechnics" and selection (*c.* 1910–1960)

While expertise about the management of workers' behavior was relatively late to develop, the same holds for the entrance of psychology onto the scene. With psychological practices in other fields already well underway, it was only after 1910 that the psychology of work began to take shape. The First World War dramatically accelerated its development, with psychologists in both camps seizing the opportunity to show their usefulness. From the early 1920s onward, work became one of the leading fields of psychological practice, with personnel selection and vocational guidance as its main spearheads.

3.1   Overture

After 1900, psychologists hesitantly entered the field of industry and commerce, an early example being Walter Dill Scott, an American psychologist who started work on the psychology of advertising in 1902. It was only after 1910, however, that activities in this field really gained momentum. Of decisive importance was the work of the German-American psychologist, mentioned earlier, Hugo Münsterberg (1863–1916).[19] A former student of Wundt, Münsterberg emigrated in the late 1890s to the United States, where he became director of the psychological laboratory of Harvard University. Following a series of lectures in Berlin on the possibilities of applied psychology, in 1912 he published a book outlining the potential industrial and commercial uses of psychology; this was *Psychologie und Wirtschaftsleben* (1912), translated into English in 1913 under the telling title *Psychology and industrial efficiency.*

In his attempt to carve out a niche of expertise for psychologists within industry, Münsterberg cleverly built on the success of scientific management. On the one hand, he applauded Taylor for his attempt to place management on a scientific basis. On the other hand, he argued that Taylor fell short of his own ambitions in ignoring psychology, the science that could legitimately claim human behavior as its subject.

In his book, Münsterberg listed a wide range of topics which would profit from psychological expertise, ranging from the study of fatigue to advertising. It was however his work on personnel selection that attracted particular attention. In accordance with a Wundtian approach to psychology, Münsterberg conceived suitability for a job in terms of distinct elementary functions. In the case of telephone operators, he identified fourteen separate functions (attention, memory, speed, accuracy, etc.) needed for their tasks, and used eight different tests to measure them (the so-called "analytic approach"). In his tests for motormen for the Boston Street Railways and for navigating officers on large steamers, however, he considered one factor, reaction time, as the crucial attribute for success (the "synthetic approach"). For testing this aptitude he designed an ingenious apparatus, in which the traffic situation was simulated.[20]

Münsterberg's work appealed to the imagination of both psychologists and industrialists. Taylor's work had revealed the wide differences in achievement between individual workers. Moreover, the attempt to match the man (and, occasionally, the woman) to the job fitted in nicely with the quest for efficiency. And finally, Münsterberg's experiments were well chosen, involving complex tasks, which revealed wide differences in ability, and possibly having wide ramifications for public safety as well as industrial efficiency.

But perhaps most importantly, the idea of matching individuals with particular occupations corresponded well with the general transformation toward a society in which individual aptitude and achievement were considered the proper basis for one's role, rather than the traditional model of sons following in the steps of their fathers (and, sometimes, daughters their mothers). This was reflected in the evolution of the parallel field of vocational guidance, which together with personnel selection would become one of the cornerstones of psychological activity in working life. By emphasizing motives of both efficiency and social justice, Münsterberg and others managed to link their professional enterprise to two of the most popular social themes of the day.

Within a few years, industrial psychology gained recognition as one of the core disciplines of practical psychology. The rapid adoption of the notion of "psychotechnics" demonstrated both Münsterberg's influence and the development of the field. This term, originally used by Münsterberg and others to denote applied psychology in all its diverse manifestations, quickly became almost exclusively associated with industrial psychology, and more specifically with personnel selection.

3.2   *The opportunities of war*

For the early advocates of industrial psychology, the extension of their program to military matters was but a small step. Here, almost from the start, they had an audience which was eager to learn about the possibilities of the new science. In Germany, for instance, as early as 1911 articles began to appear which stressed the potential use of psychological knowledge for the analysis of military tasks, such as shooting.[21] This interest was partly rooted in a long-standing tradition of military application of medical expertise for the selection of personnel. It also stemmed in part from the specific problems raised by the introduction of new technologies: with the trucks, the airplanes, telegraphy, and new forms of artillery came the question of how to select the men who were to operate these expensive, vulnerable, and strategically important new machines. As one historian has put it: in earlier wars men had to be given arms, but now the question was how the new armaments should be manned.[22]

Almost as soon as the war began, psychologists in the combatant countries became involved – more often than not at their own initiative. In England, for instance, they participated in studies of the problem of fatigue in munitions factories. In the attempt to increase production hours of work had been extended to the point where, due to fatigue and associated health problems, there was a falling-off rather than a rise in output. A government-funded body, the Health of Munition Workers' Committee, was established to investigate the problem, and to this end it enlisted the aid of psychologists.[23]

Of the various European countries, Germany proved by far the most responsive. As early as 1915, a *Prüfstelle* (testing station) for the examination of lorry-drivers was founded in Prussia, an example which was quickly followed in other parts of the country. Similar undertakings for other specific functions followed, for personnel such as telegraphists, sound rangers, and aviators. Following the example of Münsterberg, most testing procedures used a combination of traditional laboratory apparatus and new instruments, specifically geared to the tasks under investigation. Soon, the military use of psychology overshadowed other fields of practical psychology. Thus, for instance, it is estimated that the total number of lorry drivers who were examined in Germany was well in excess of 10,000 (see figure 37).[24]

Impressive as these figures might have been, they were dwarfed by the scale of activity in the United States. As soon as that country had declared war on Germany, the American Psychological Association (APA) established no fewer than twelve committees to investigate the potential contributions of psychologists to the war effort. Most of these came to nothing. Two of them, however, resulted in programs that would decisively influence the development of psychological practices (see figure 38).[25]

The first program, already briefly mentioned in earlier chapters, entailed the psychological examination of recruits, specifically to weed out those unfit for service because of insufficient mental capacity. This led to the development of a new kind of instrument, the group intelligence test. Within months, two such tests were constructed: the Army Alpha, for recruits with an adequate command of written English; and the non-verbal, allegedly "culture-free" Army Beta, for people who were illiterate and immigrants who could not read English. Before the war was over, more than 1.7 million men had been examined using these tests.

A second program, headed by Walter Dill Scott, involved the psychological examination of candidates for specific military functions, such as potential artillerymen, aircraft pilots, and officers. Scott devised a number of skills tests related to technical functions; in subsequent years these would become part and parcel of industrial psychology. Another innovation was his Rating Scale for Selecting Captains: a questionnaire intended to gauge the non-cognitive aspects of leadership, such as character, ambition, tact, and loyalty. Though less publicized than the intelligence testing program, Scott's program was at least as impressive, with more than 3.5 million men being investigated before the war was over.

As well as being the first successful mass application of psychological expertise, the testing programs also had broader cultural and political effects. In other chapters, we have already discussed the impact of the intelligence testing program on ideas about social merit, fueling public campaigns for sterilization of the so-called "feeble-minded" and restriction of immigration of allegedly intellectually backward "races." With regard to occupational aptitude, its influence was manifested in changed conceptions of military fitness, stressing intelligence rather than formerly valued qualities such as "character" and "morale."[26]

(a)

(b)

Figure 37 First World War testing practices: Europe. (a) A test station for lorry drivers, Germany. (b) Testing the emotional stability of pilots, France. Sources: (a) Institute for the History of Psychology, Passau; (b) Psychology Pictures/Archives of Dutch Psychology.

(a)

(b)

Figure 38 First World War testing practices: United States. (a) Group intelligence testing of recruits, United States. (b) Examination of professional skills. Source: National Archives, Washington DC (111-SC-386 and 111-SC-385).

3.3 Expansion

Both in the United States and Europe, the wartime contribution of psychologists served as a launching pad for industrial psychology.

In the US, Scott used his wartime experience and reputation to found the first successful psychological consultancy firm (1919). A few years later (1921), the pioneer of mental testing, James McKeen Cattell, founded the Psychological Corporation, whose purpose was to provide psychological services to industry, the community, and the public. In the following years it grew to become a multimillion-dollar business. Popular books, such as Henry Link's *Employment psychology* (1920) and Watts' *Introduction to the psychological problems of industry* (1921), acquainted both the general public and business leaders with the promises and successes of the new discipline. In Britain, the National Institute of Industrial Psychology (NIIP) was founded in 1921 by Charles S. Myers; this institute would become the mainstay of developments in industrial psychology in interwar Britain.[27]

Developments on the European continent were even more impressive. If industrial psychology in the United States and Britain would always take second place to educational and, later, clinical psychology, on the Continent the domain of work developed into the most significant area of practical psychology in the interwar years. Among German industrialists in particular, *Psychotechnik* became the management theme of the day, often in combination with scientific management. Almost all large enterprises boasted their own "psychotechnical laboratory," furnished with the latest psychological "high tech" equipment. The gospel, spelled out in handbooks and newly created psychotechnical journals, quickly spread to other countries, such as the Netherlands, France, Spain, Switzerland, and even Russia. This proliferation was both reflected and enhanced by the International Association of Psychotechnics. Founded in 1920, the Association would until the early 1950s play an important role as an international platform for industrial psychology.[28]

Although there were several attempts to broaden the field of industrial psychology to other activities, such as ergonomics, personnel selection was to remain by far the most prominent application until the Second World War. Inspired by the slogan "the right man in the right place," it promised efficiency, social justice, and human well-being. These motives were reflected in the complementary field of vocational guidance, which also boomed after the First World War.[29]

3.4 New conceptions

Although psychologists played an important role in the development of "scientific" personnel selection and vocational guidance, it was by no means exclusively their domain. Both fields were characterized by fierce boundary disputes with other disciplines, especially in Germany and other continental European countries. These were accompanied by debate about appropriate methodology in both fields.

Originally, German psychotechnics was the affair of engineers as much as psychologists. Its program had been formulated by the psychologist Hugo Münsterberg, but the movement owed at least as much of its success to a professor of engineering and industrial sciences, Georg Schlesinger. As early as 1912, he had begun to experiment with personnel selection techniques, and in 1918 he created an Institut für industrielle Psychotechnik (Institute for industrial psychotechnics) at the Technical University of Berlin. He hired Walther Moede, one of Wundt's former students, to give short courses for engineers on selection procedures and other aspects of personnel management. With dozens of engineers attending these courses every year, this was to be the seedbed of the dissemination of psychotechnics within German industry.[30]

Testing procedures initially reflected this predominance of engineers. Great stress was put on the importance of exact measurement, preferably by means of sophisticated apparatus, specifically designed for the purpose. Gradually, the laboratory apparatus used by Münsterberg and other pioneers was replaced by new inventions, mostly types of "miniaturized task" devices.

Originally pleased about the attention paid to their discipline, psychologists gradually became dismayed by both the predominance of engineers and the "inflation of apparatus," as they called it. Within academic psychology, the methodology of natural science had gradually lost its supremacy since the First World War. A *Geisteswissenschaftliche* (humanistic) approach gained prominence, which promised a deeper understanding of man as an "organic whole." This was reflected in a new outlook on personnel selection and vocational guidance. The role model of the engineer, which had inspired the pioneers of psychotechnics, gave way to that of the diagnostician, who saw separate phenomena as indicators of a deeper, underlying pattern in the way that medical practitioners viewed the symptoms of their patients. This was reflected in a blossoming of character typologies, which served as a conceptual framework for "diagnosing" the mental make-up of job applicants.

From the late 1920s onwards, this new model gradually became the dominant paradigm within personnel selection and vocational guidance.[31] On the one hand, it reinforced psychologists' claims for jurisdiction, effectively outmaneuvering engineers and other "charlatans." Perhaps more importantly, it also led to a change of focus in both areas. Attention shifted from separate functions such as reaction speed and memory to the person as a whole, with personality characteristics considered to be at least as important as skills (see figure 39). Sometimes, the old instruments were preserved but used in another way, with observation of the candidate becoming as important as exact measurement of separate attributes. However, especially from the 1930s, new types of assessment tools took over, such as graphology and newly developed projective techniques such as the Rorschach inkblot test.

As well as its use in civil society, the new approach also deeply influenced military selection, especially in Germany.[32] From the late 1920s onward, the German army

---

→

Figure 39   Changing expert-models and methods, from (a) the psychologist as an engineer, concentrating on exact measurement, to (b) the psychologist as a quasi-medical diagnostician, concentrating on behavior observation. Source: Psychology Pictures/Archives of Dutch Psychology.

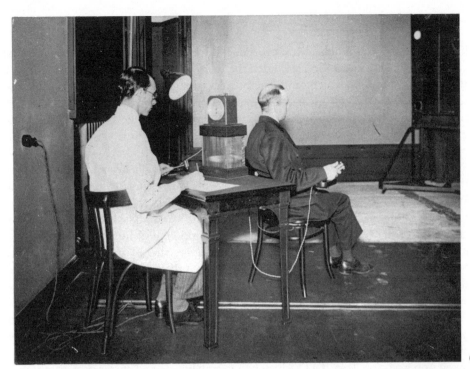

(a)

(b)

had begun to experiment with procedures for the assessment of steadiness of character in candidate officers. Under the Nazi regime, this was extended into a three-day program, in which candidate officers, alongside more traditional tests, had to perform complex individual and group tasks, such as building a bridge and participation in a leaderless group discussion. Their behavior, body posture and facial expressions in stressful situations and during electric shocks were observed, and interpreted in terms of character.

American and English industrial psychology had originally been rather immune to this "personalistic" shift in personnel selection. This changed during the Second World War and its aftermath. Like its predecessor, this war gave industrial psychology a new impetus. On the one hand, it again saw standardized mass selection procedures. On the other hand, it stimulated methodological innovation. With some modifications, the German program was in 1942 adopted by the British War Office Selection Board, and subsequently, in 1949, by the Office of Strategic Services (OSS), the precursor of the present CIA, in the USA for the selection of potential secret agents. The OSS program would form the basis for what would become known as the assessment center method (ACM), an all-round, in-depth investigation of both personality characteristics and specific skills and competencies. Together with psychoanalytically inspired projective techniques, such as the Rorschach test and the Thematic Apperception Test (TAT) which had meanwhile gained currency, it contributed to the introduction of a more "clinical," personality-oriented approach to selection in the United States and England in the late 1940s and early 1950s. In contrast to Europe, the popularity of this approach in the English-speaking world was rather short-lived. As early as the mid-1950s, psychologists started to question its validity and reliability. To this was added a growing public concern about the "invasion of privacy" that this approach entailed. Rather than resulting in a backlash against testing, these criticisms led to a change of methods, and from the late 1950s onward, clinical procedures gradually gave way to empirically corroborated, "objective" devices such as personality questionnaires.[33]

3.5   Conclusion

As with other fields, the psychology of work did not spring from nowhere. To a large extent its path had been prepared by scientific management. On the one hand, Taylor's brainchild had convinced industrialists of the usefulness of expert knowledge with respect to personnel management. On the other hand, it had left for psychologists the clearly defined niche of personnel selection. If employers were initially somewhat reluctant to use industrial psychology, its wartime achievements helped to overcome their doubts.

Apart from these specific conditions, the main theme of psychology ("the right man in the right place") corresponded well with the move toward a society in which individual aptitude and achievement were considered the proper determinants for one's place in society. This was reflected in the evolution of the parallel field of vocational guidance, which together with personnel selection would become one of the cornerstones of the involvement of psychologists in working life.

Thus, practical psychology both reflected and enhanced growing social mobility and a "democratization" of life chances. However, its innovative role in this respect should not be overestimated. Some preconceptions about inborn or socially conditioned differences in ability remained firmly in place, for instance concerning gender and ethnic differences with regard to occupational suitability, or, especially in Europe, the relevance of social background. In other words, the meritocratic ethos was far less pervasive than suggested by the rhetoric of psychologists. Not only were psychologists reluctant to challenge social preconceptions about differences between men and women, whites and non-whites, but in many cases they explicitly endorsed them, as evidenced in theories about gender differences in vocational aptitude. It was only in the late 1960s that these preconceptions and theories would be challenged.

4   Work in its social context (*c.* 1920–1980)

In the preceding section, we discussed the introduction of a more widely ranging approach to personnel selection, focusing on "the whole person" rather than isolated attributes. This change of perspective coincided with a similar shift within the realm of organizational theory and practices. Here, the rationalistic perspective of Taylorism, relying exclusively on detailed analysis of tasks and financial rewards, gave way to a more encompassing, psychological perspective, which stressed the social dynamics of the workplace: the human relations paradigm.

4.1   Origins: the Hawthorne studies

Although Taylorism was undoubtedly the dominant paradigm in social management in the workplace in the early decades of the twentieth century, it did not reign exclusively. Parallel to the inception of scientific management, and largely independent of it, there also developed a tradition of more socially oriented personnel work.[34]

Just as Taylorism was the continuation of early nineteenth-century disciplinary practices, so personnel management evolved from the earlier "ethical approach" to the workforce (see above, section 1.3). As time progressed, this approach had gradually been extended and professionalized. At the turn of the century, many large companies started to experiment with all kinds of "personnel work," varying from isolated provisions, such as pension plans, housing facilities, and recreational and educational facilities, to attempts at creating a veritable "factory community," with the combined goals of creating goodwill among the workers, improving conditions of living, and extending supervision to include the behavior of workers in their "free" time as well as during working hours.

Although widely practiced, until the 1920s personnel work remained a rather peripheral phenomenon. First, it did not seem to relate directly to the production process, the "core business" of industrial enterprise. And second, it lacked a coherent perspective and theoretical foundation. Typically, it was relegated to female social workers, and considered to be a form of "enlightened charity" rather than an integrated element of company policy. This was to change from the mid-1920s onward, following a series of experiments at a large plant belonging to the western Electric Company in the United States: the Hawthorne studies.[35]

In the history of organization theory, the Hawthorne studies count as one of the most dramatic examples of experimental research leading to a fundamental shift in perspective. The studies were begun from a Taylorist mechanical perspective. Inspired by wartime experiments in British munitions factories (see section 3.2), they were intended to examine the effects of rest pauses, length of working hours, and various levels of illumination on productivity. The results were perplexing, especially with respect to the effects of illumination. Contrary to expectation, a decrease of light in the test room, even to moonlight conditions, in some cases resulted in increased production. To comprehend these results, the mechanical paradigm had to be set aside in favor of a social perspective. The increase in production was attributed to the special attention the workers received during the experiments, a phenomenon since known as the "Hawthorne effect" (see figure 40). Social factors, the experiments suggested, were more important than physical ones.

To corroborate and further develop the new perspective, the assistance of Elton Mayo, a professor at Harvard Business School, was requested. Under his supervision,

Figure 40   The Hawthorne experiments, relay assembly testroom. The extra attention the workers received proved to be more decisive for production rates than physical circumstances – a phenomenon since known as the "Hawthorne effect." Source: F. J. Roethlisberger and W. J. Dickson (1949), *Management and the worker* (Cambridge: Harvard University Press).

interviews and observations of work groups were conducted over a period of several years. Observations in a "bank wiring room," in which a group of men produced telephone apparatus, showed the existence of informal groups, with a status hierarchy of their own alongside the formal hierarchy.

This also shed a new light on the problem of "soldiering," which Taylor had sought to overcome by increased managerial control over the work process and by individualized payment schemes. From the new perspective, this problem was conceptualized as a social-psychological phenomenon: the existence of a group norm about what constituted "a fair day's work." Rather than the Taylorist solutions, Mayo and his co-workers focused on a psychological approach. Worker resistance, they demonstrated, could be overcome by giving them the opportunity to air their dissatisfactions, creating the impression that they were taken seriously. As the dictum had it "just as contented cows produce more milk, happy workers produce more goods."

The details and "lessons" of the Hawthorne studies would not become public until 1939, when they were summed up in a famous monograph by two of Mayo's co-workers, *Management and the worker*.[36] Together with earlier publications by Mayo himself, this study is considered to be the starting point of a new approach to the management of worker behavior, which after the war quickly gained acceptance: the human relations movement. As with the move to a more holistic approach in personnel selection, this change in organizational perspective resulted in a shift in professional boundaries: Taylorist engineers gave way to organizational sociologists and psychologists, who would become the main advocates of the new approach.

4.2   The human relations movement

During the Second World War the western allies consulted psychologists not only about personnel selection and human factors engineering, but also on problems of motivation and morale, leadership and cooperation in groups, and on the effects of propaganda and "psychological warfare." A notable example of a social science perspective was that provided by *The American soldier*, by S. A. Stouffer and associates (1949), a multivolume work containing numerous studies which showed the key role of primary group relations in maintaining morale and efficiency.

The study of group phenomena received another impetus from Kurt Lewin's field theory and his use of groups to bring about attitude changes. In his prewar experiments with various types of leadership in youth groups, a democratic style of leadership had appeared to lead to a more favorable group climate than an authoritarian one. During the war he showed that changes in habits could be better effected by letting people make commitments in front of a group, than by only persuading them at an individual level. His further studies of group dynamics were to influence the direction taken by the emerging interest in leadership and participation in decision-making.

Perhaps the most famous Lewin-inspired study was an investigation at the Harwood textile factory on "overcoming resistance to change," conducted by Coch and French (1948). The designs of the garments produced were often changed, and so the seamstresses were frequently confronted with changes in the production line. The misgivings to which this led caused a larger decrease in the daily output than could reasonably be expected. In the experiment that was conducted subsequently, three groups were formed, with various levels of participation. The group in which all members of the group participated in designing a new production schedule adapted most rapidly to the new situation. A group in which participation took place by delegation needed more time, but in both groups, after an initial dip, output stabilized at a higher level than before. The third group, that served as a control group, got instructions by superior order as before. This led to such negative feelings that the group had to be disbanded.

Leadership style was also investigated under the banner of human relations. Drawing on Lewin's experiments with youth groups, the effect on productivity of democratic versus autocratic leadership was examined further. The relationship appeared to be not linear, but to depend on the character of the task situation. This led to the concept of two complementary dimensions of supervisory behavior: instrumental versus social. Questionnaires were devised to measure the actual or desired style of leadership in particular situations.

At the Research Center for Group Dynamics, in Michigan, this led to the obvious next step of managerial and leadership training which was directed toward increasing an individual's awareness of the social processes occurring within groups and organizations. A related strand in this development were the sensitivity or "T-group" training courses run by the National Training Laboratories, the first of which were held at Bethel, Maine in 1947. The philosophy guiding the training was that changing individuals and their interpersonal behavior would lead automatically to organizational change. However, in the course of time this philosophy turned out to be too optimistic, and it was found that organizational change could only be realized by more task-related intervention techniques.

After the war, the new approach quickly found its way to Europe as well. The continent was faced with numerous problems: the restoration of a peacetime economy, rebuilding the towns and cities which had been devastated by the ravages of war, reconstruction of the industrial infrastructure, and, last but not least, restoring the "sunken morale" of the populace. To "prevent further economic, social and political deterioration" the United States launched the Marshall Aid Program (1948), and created an organization – the OECD (Organization for Economic and Cultural Development) – to administer it. As part of the program European productivity teams visited the US, and this naturally led to an orientation toward American management methods.

In many west European countries there was a feeling among the postwar leaders that, next to financial and economic support, and enhancement of industrial productivity, there was a need for more fundamental change, leading to a new sense of community and more democratic social relations, which would prevent a re-emergence of totalitarianism. Ideals like this focused attention on the motivation of workers and on styles of leadership. Supported by Marshall Aid funds, questionnaires were constructed to gauge the morale of the workers on the shop floor, and, under the general title of Training Within Industry (TWI), in several European countries courses were organized which aimed to promote a new and less authoritarian super-visory style.

4.3 Humanization of work

By the mid-1960s, a welfare state was well established in most advanced industrial nations. Their populations had achieved a hitherto unknown level of prosperity. Grad-ually, the social harmony of the late 1940s and 1950s gave way to social unrest and proposals for more radical social reform. There was a call for democratic rights that went further than casting one's vote every few years. Industrial psychologists were depicted as "servants of power,"[37] and many of them now felt that they should put their knowledge not only at the service of management, but at that of the whole "client system." Some even wished to serve solely the interests of the workers. As well as more traditional methods of development, action research, in which all parties involved had a say, became a favorite method of organizational change.

The social man of the human relations movement now became the self-actualizer; workers should experience their work as a challenge and a source of personal fulfil-ment. Herzberg's "motivator hygiene" theory, which was influenced by Maslow's hierarchy of motives, became immensely popular. Overcoming workers' alienation, humanizing work, and democracy on the shop floor, became the new missions of work and organizational psychologists. This reflected the growing interest in the quality of life in general, and the quality of working life in particular, that began to gather momentum during this period, and which became an international movement for the quality of working life in the early 1970s.[38] This movement drew not only on the American experiments described in the previous section, but also tied in with pio-neering investigations conducted in the 1950s and 1960s by the Tavistock Institute of Human Relations in London. The most well-known of these was a study on the human effects of technological change in a Durham coalmine, which introduced the concepts of "self-regulating work groups" and organizations as "open, socio-technical systems."

The socio-technical paradigm was to stimulate worldwide research and experi-ments in job-enlargement, job-enrichment, and organizational design in the follow-ing decades. For example, an extensive program of work restructuring was undertaken at Philips Industries in the Netherlands using the socio-technical para-digm (see figure 41), while in the Swedish automobile works of Saab-Scania, and subsequently those of Volvo, the assembly lines were replaced by production teams.

Industrial democracy was another major issue. In Norway it led to a series of "experiments in industrial democracy" under the auspices of the Oslo Work Research Institute. Dissatisfied with limited forms of participation which left significant decision-making untouched, some researchers even advocated full worker demo-cracy, modeled after socialist examples such as the Yugoslavian model of "self-government." In the course of time, however, high ideals and abstract blueprints made way for practical experimentation, monitored by interdisciplinary research teams, as was the case, for example, in the international project for the study of indus-trial democracy, IDE (1981).

(a)

(b)

Figure 41 Job enrichment and the humanization of work: redesign of the conveyor-belt system (a) into self-regulating groups (b), at Philips Electronics, the Netherlands, *c.* 1970. Source: Philips Company Archives.

4.4   Conclusion

In combination with the personalizing trend in personnel selection, the successive paradigms of "human relations" and "humanization of work" extended the management of work far beyond the original, somewhat limited framework of Taylorism and classical psychotechnics. Technical rationalization was extended to include social factors too, as represented by the term "sociotechnics." Alongside detailed planning of work and optimization of payment schemes, issues such as the social climate and workers' attitudes became prominent new areas of intervention.

The increasing psychologization was reflected in the extension of the professional domain of industrial psychology. Originally almost exclusively confined to personnel selection, psychologists' expertise and professional roles were broadened to include organizational issues also. Indicative of the process were the successive changes of name, from "psychotechnics" to "industrial psychology" (the favored term in the postwar decades), and from that to the "psychology of work and organization" (the current name, introduced in the early 1970s). Besides organizational psychology, some psychologists also ventured into the more technical and science-oriented domain of ergonomics, often in close cooperation with engineers.

Although this is far more difficult to assess, the ways in which workers themselves experienced work and its importance probably also changed.[39] Perhaps the new paradigms of "human relations" and "humanization" were not so much discoveries of eternal psychological truths (as their proponents tended to suggest) as reflections of the changing attitudes of workers. With the "command society" giving way to the "negotiating society," democratic leadership styles became more important. And with increasing prosperity, the importance of economic motivators decreased, in favor of "intrinsic" motivation. In any case, changes in industrial psychology were reflected in its counterpart of vocational guidance. Here, exploration of interests gradually became more important than assessment of skills and competencies. Moreover, the balance between professional expertise and self-discovery gradually shifted, as exemplified by the inception of "counseling" techniques, in which the psychologist helped to explore clients' own ideas, rather than exclusively relying on tests and professional expertise.[40]

Democratically and humanistically inspired as the new projects were, they also had an obvious drawback. Their relation with the primary economic goals of commercial enterprise was not always altogether clear. More often than not, they were considered to be luxuries. This became clear during the worldwide economic recession of the late 1970s and early 1980s. The ensuing reorganizations, downsizings and dismissals put a damper on the high expectations of the previous period. Interestingly enough, these very circumstances also led to the development of a new paradigm, which reigns to this very day: human resource management.

5   Human resource management (*c.* 1985–present)

Although not altogether new, it was only in the last decades of the twentieth century that the concept of "human resources" gained wide currency.[41]

The central idea of human resource management (or HRM, as it is generally called) is a revaluation of the importance of the human factor for organizations: according to its proponents, people are to be valued as an organizational asset, a resource, rather than a matter of costs and necessity. As such, they are of vital importance to the prospects and viability of organizations, even more so than other assets such as advanced technology or access to markets. As the rhetoric has it: factories can be built, technologies bought, markets developed, but it requires serious and sustained effort to build and sustain that other vital ingredient of success, "human capital."

Launched in the mid 1980s by American management theorists, the notion of human resources spread rapidly in the 1990s, capturing the hearts and minds of senior management as well as representatives of traditional "personnel departments" and psychological consultancies. Indicative of the persuasive power of HRM was the alacrity with which societies, journals, company departments, and external consultancies in the fields of personnel management and personnel psychology changed their names to incorporate the new acronym.

It is matter of debate whether HRM is not to a large extent a matter of old wine in new bottles. Nevertheless, of itself, its popularity does suggest that "the human factor" has risen to an even greater prominence in the world of work than it already enjoyed. Many leading companies, within traditional industry as well as the "service economy," have indeed developed new policies regarding the management of their personnel. Perhaps the most important catchword in this respect is "integration." On the one hand, HRM should be an integral part of general business policy, rather than a separate activity relegated to personnel departments. On the other hand, "integration" refers to the coordination of various aspects of personnel management. Thus, for instance, personnel selection is no longer considered an isolated activity but part of an "HRM cycle" which includes recruitment, training, development, and also assessment of performance.

At the level of professional "tools" and instruments, one of the most significant developments was the revival of the assessment center method.[42] As we saw in section 3.4, this method was originally devised for the selection of military officers and secret agents (see figure 42). In the 1950s and 1960s, it fell into disrepute as a result of methodological concerns over the objectivity, reliability, and validity of the procedures used. However, from the 1970s onward the assessment center made an impressive comeback. To a great extent, this reflected a growing unease of both employers and testees about traditional psychological tests, which might have been scientifically valid, but did not appear to bear directly on the principal concern, i.e. actual performance at work. From this perspective, assessment centers appeared to be far superior, because they concentrated on "real-life" tasks. In this respect, they resembled the "miniaturized tasks" of the early psychotechnicians, albeit the simulations were now of higher, managerial responsibilities, rather than technical crafts. Also the use of assessment has changed as a result of the "modern" human resource paradigm. Rather than a candidate's suitability for a specific job, it tends to be geared to his overall prospects. In this respect, the expected outcome is not only advice with respect to hiring, but also concerning specific strengths and weaknesses, or "developmental prospects," and "topics in need of extra attention."

Figure 42 The military origins of the assessment center method: Burma Town Test for American pilots, 1944. Source: Archives of the History of American Psychology, University of Akron.

Perhaps even more important than these developments in the domain of aptitude and performance is a renewed interest in motivation or, as it is nowadays commonly termed, "commitment." This includes dedication to one's own job as well as loyalty to the goals (or "mission") of the organization at large. The renewed popularity of the theme was partly inspired by analyses of Japanese success, in which the almost family-like bonds between workers and corporations were highlighted as one of the decisive factors. With it came a growing awareness that true commitment could not be bought or brought about by intensified supervision or more detailed instructions and procedures. Rather, organizations needed to look for new ways to encourage workers to identify with their work, in relation to the goals set out for themselves, their immediate colleagues and the organization at large. This tendency found its most striking expression in the notion of a "psychological contract," which in HRM theory is considered to be more important than the traditional legal agreement.[43]

With respect to motivation, a wide array of new topics and techniques have developed, both "soft" and "hard." On the one hand, there is a renewed interest in the function of material rewards, as exemplified by performance-related pay, profit sharing and share schemes. On the other hand, a host of new techniques regarding leadership, group building and individual supervision and coaching have been introduced, with the dual aim of instilling in workers a sense of purposefulness regarding their own work and a sense of being valued and cared for, by their co-workers and supervisors as well as by the company at large. Finally, there is a growing attention to "values" as key factors in the "fit" between organization and employee.

Almost as a matter of course, the advance of HRM and related theories have also given new impetus to notions of individualization. It is not only that collective agreements tend to give way to individual contracts (either legal or "psychological"), individualized paying schemes and renewed emphasis on individual performance. There is also a growing emphasis on individual differences with respect to "what makes people tick": motivation, work objectives, and preferred working conditions. Partly, this is a reflection of the growing diversity of the workforce, and specifically the influx of women. Traditional personnel policies were primarily geared toward the prototype of the white male worker, looking for secure, full-time employment, possibly combined with career perspectives promising higher status and financial rewards. In the course of the 1980s and 1990s, this model increasingly came under siege, not only because female workers and people with different cultural backgrounds gained a more prominent place, but also because, especially in the higher echelons, the importance of these traditional values became less self-evident for male workers. This process has been reflected in new models of personnel management, which stress the need to tailor arrangements to the needs and wishes of individual workers.

With the introduction of the HRM concept, personnel and organizational psychology have risen to a new level of prominence within working life. Its main tenets are reflected in everyday activity, the self-concept of workers, and changing perspectives within vocational choice and career guidance. To be sure, the shelves of popular bookstores still abound with books on various aspects of the "how to get ahead" theme. Alongside these, however, there is an increasing body of literature addressing the wider theme of the place and importance of work within one's "life project." An important impetus was the growing participation of women in the workforce, for whom the central question was not just how to make a career, but how to combine working life with other activities, their role as mothers and primary caregivers of their children.[44] From the 1990s onwards, traditional career motives began to appear less self-evident for men as well, especially among the well-qualified. This tendency is reflected (and, once more, reinforced) in popular models of career guidance and counseling, which increasingly take general values and "life goals" as their starting point, rather than occupational aspirations.

6   Conclusion

At the beginning of the nineteenth century, industrialist Robert Owen urged his fellow entrepreneurs to pay more attention to the "human resources" of their enterprise. A century later, psychologist Hugo Münsterberg argued for the inclusion of scientific experts to manage the problems of human work. Now, at the dawn of another century, we can conclude that both objectives have been realized. "Human resource management" is generally accepted as one of the key factors of business success, and psychologists and other social experts play an important role in personnel management and organizational planning and development.

The growing recognition of "the human factor," and expertise pertaining to it, is reflected in general culture and everyday life. Of course, economic factors are still relevant with respect to work, from the point of view of both employers and individual workers. Alongside that, however, the traditional moral perspectives on work have given way to a thoroughly psychologized outlook; the "Protestant ethic" has been replaced by the "psychological ethic." Work is considered to be an important factor in our psychological as well as economic well-being, and both organized business and individual workers, almost as a matter of course, seek psychological expertise to realize their goals in this area.

Not surprisingly, this individualization and psychologization of work is heralded by its proponents as sheer and unqualified cultural progress, benefiting workers and employers alike. This optimism, however, may be counterbalanced with at least two observations. First, one is left to wonder to what extent these changes are tied to a climate of economic prosperity and optimism, and what might happen to "psychological contracts" and "life projects" when recession sets in. Secondly, and more fundamentally, some observers have questioned the impact of changing conceptions of work on social cohesion in general. A prominent example is Richard Sennett, who argued in 1998 that the temporalization of working conditions has also resulted in an erosion of other cultural ties and commitments.[45]

If these observations are to some extent speculative, there is one area of the "psychologization of work" which provides more substantive ground for doubts with respect to the wholesomeness of recent developments: the staggering rise of "burn out" and other work-related mental problems. This has given rise to a whole new and rapidly expanding domain of psychological expertise relating to work, known as "occupational health psychology." While on the one hand they are another demonstration of psychologization as a general cultural trend, these developments also suggest that the changes in working life which have been induced at least partly by psychologists and other "psy" experts are not self-evidently beneficial.

PRINCIPAL SOURCES AND FURTHER READING

Comprehensive, up-to-date literature on the topics discussed in this chapter are scarce. For a brief introduction into the history of work, see M. Kranzberg and J. Gies (1975), *By the sweat of thy brow* (New York: Putnam). A general introduction to the history of management thought is D. A. Wren (1972; 4th ed. 1994), *The evolution of management thought* (New York; Ronald Press).

Concerning the early industrial revolution and its consequences for the management of workers' behavior see S. Pollard (1965), *The genesis of modern management. A study of the industrial revolution in Great Britain* (London: Arnold). A useful introduction to late nineteenth-century developments and the rise of scientific management is D. Nelson (1975), *Managers and workers. Origins of the new factory system in the United States 1880–1920* (Madison: University of Wisconsin Press).

W. Hollway (1991), *Work psychology and organisational behaviour* (London: Sage) is a good introduction to the history of psychological practices within this field. Another broad overview is S. Shimmin and P. J. van Strien (1998), History of the psychology of work and organization, in P. J. D. Drenth, H. Thierry, and C. J. de Wolff, eds., *Handbook of work and organizational psychology, vol. I* (Chichester: Wiley), pp. 71–99. For an American perspective, see R. A. Katzell and J. T. Austen (1992), From then to now: The development of industrial-organizational psychology in the United States, *Journal of Applied Psychology, 77*, 803–35.

NOTES

1 H. Münsterberg (1973, 1913), *Psychology and industrial efficiency* (Easton: Hive), pp. 306–7.

2 See J. A. van Doorn (1975), *The soldier and social change: comparative studies in the history and sociology of the military* (London: Sage).

3 H. Eckert, *L'orientation profesionnelle en Allemagne et en France* [Vocational guidance in Germany and France] (Paris: l'Harmattan), p. 57.

4 Quoted after Wren, *Evolution of management thought*, p. 66.

5 Pollard, *Genesis of modern management*, pp. 194–7.

6 Pollard, *Genesis of modern management*, p. 193; Wren, *Evolution*, p. 52.

7 D. Simonton (1998), *A history of European women's work. 1700 to the present* (London: Routledge).

8 A. Rabinbach (1990), *The human motor. Energy, fatigue, and the origins of modernity* (New York: Basic Books).

9 See L. Kolakowski (1981), *Main currents of Marxism, vol. I: the founders* (Oxford: Oxford University Press).

10 See for the United States, J. Hilkey (1997), *Character is capital. Success manuals and manhood in Gilded Age America* (Chapel Hill: North Carolina Press).

11 A. D. Chandler (1977), *The visible hand. The managerial revolution in American business* (Cambridge: Belknap Press).

12 F. W. Taylor (1971/1903), *Shop management* (Westport: Greenwood Press), p. 21.

13 Taylor, *Shop management*, p. 27.

14 Taylor, *Shop management*, p. 37.

15 Taylor, *Shop management*, p. 56.

16 Nelson, *Managers and workers*, p. 69.

17 See for the international reception of Taylorism: J. A. Merkle (1980), *Management and ideology. The legacy of the international scientific management movement* (Berkeley: University of California Press); J.-C. Spender and H. J. Kijne, eds. (1996), *Scientific management. Frederick Winslow Taylor's gift to the world?* (Boston: Kluwer), chs. 5–7.

18 Quoted after R. Smith (1997), *The Fontana History of the Human Sciences* (London: Fontana), p. 608.

19 M. Hale (1980), *Human science and social order. Hugo Münsterberg and the origins of applied psychology* (Philadelphia: Temple University Press).

20 See P. J. van Strien (1999), Early applied psychology between essentialism and pragmatism, *History of Psychology, 1*, 205–34.

21 H. Gundlach (1996), Faktor Mensch im Krieg. Der Eintritt der Psychologie und Psychotechnik in den Krieg [The human factor in the war. The genesis of psychology and psychotechnics in the war], *Berichte zur Wissenschaftsgeschichte, 19*, 131–43.

22 Gundlach, Faktor Mensch im Krieg, p. 135.

23 Hollway, *Work psychology*, p. 55.

24 Gundlach, Faktor Mensch im Krieg.

25 See various contributions in M. M. Sokal, ed. (1987), *Psychological testing and American society, 1890–1930* (New Brunswick: Rutgers University Press).

26 J. Carson (1993), Army Alpha, Army brass, and the search for army intelligence, *Isis, 84*, 278–309.

27 C. T. Frisby (1970), The development of industrial psychology at the NIIP, *Occupational Psychology, 44*, 35–50.

28 H. Gundlach, An outline of the history of the IAAP, in: H. Gundlach, ed., *Applied psychology, vol. I: The first congress, Geneva 1920* (London: Routledge), pp. 1–24.

29 F. J. Keller and M. S. Viteles (1937), *Vocational guidance throughout the world. A comparative survey* (London: Cape).

30 See P. Hinrichs (1981), *Um die Seele des Arbeiters* [For the soul of the worker] (Köln: Pahl-Rugenstein): B. Wilpert. (1990), How European is work and organisational psychology?, in: P. J. D. Drenth, J. A. Sergeant and R. J. Takens, eds., *European perspectives in psychology, vol. III* (Chichester: Wiley), pp. 3–20.

31 U. Geuter (1992), *The professionalization of psychology in Nazi Germany* (Cambridge: Cambridge University Press), pp. 143–59. For the Netherlands, T. Dehue (1995), *Changing the rules. Psychology in the Netherlands, 1900–1985* (Cambridge: Cambridge University Press), chs. 2 and 3.

32 U. Geuter (1992), *Professionalization of psychology*, ch. 3.

33 See M. Hale (1982), History of employment testing, in A. K. Wigdor and W. R. Garner, eds., *Ability testing. Uses, consequences, and controversies* (Washington, DC: National Academy Press), pp. 3–38.

34 See Nelson, *Managers and workers*, ch. 6; R. Gillespie (1991), *Manufacturing knowledge. A history of the Hawthorne experiments* (Cambridge: Cambridge University Press).

35 See Gillespie, *Manufacturing knowledge*, for a detailed description and analysis of the Hawthorne experiments.

36 F. J. Roethlisberger and W. Dickson (1939), *Management and the worker* (Cambridge, MA: Harvard University Press).

37 L. Baritz (1960), *The servants of power. A history of the use of social science in American industry* (Westport: Greenwood Press).

38 See N. Rose (1990), *Governing the soul* (London: Routledge), ch. 10.

39 See C. Z. Stearns and P. N. Stearns (1986), *Anger. The struggle for emotional control in America's history* (Chicago: University of Chicago Press).

40 See for example E. G. Williamson (1965), *Vocational counseling. Some historical, philosophical, and theoretical perspectives* (New York: McGraw-Hill).

41 See for an overview and critical appraisal of the human resource paradigm, K. Sisson and John Storey (2000), *The realities of human resource management. Managing the employment relationship* (Buckingham: Open University Press). A popular and representative introduction to the field and its relation to psychology is W. D. Cascio (1998, 5th ed.), *Applied psychology in human resource management* (Englewood Cliffs: Prentice Hall).

42 D. W. MacKinnon (1977), From selecting spies to selecting managers – the OSS assessment program, in: J. L. Moses and W. C. Byham, eds., *Applying the assessment center method* (New York: Pergamon Press), pp. 13–31.

43　See for example N. Anderson and R. Schalk (1998), The psychological contract in retrospect and prospect, *Journal of Organizational Behavior, 19*, 637–47.

44　See A. Hochschild (1992), *The second shift: working parents and the revolution at home* (London: Piatkus Publishers), and C. L. Cooper and S. Lewis (1993), *The work place revolution. Managing today's dual career families* (London: Kogan Page).

45　R. Sennett (1998), *The corrosion of character. The personal consequences of work in the new capitalism* (New York: Norton).

5   Culture and ethnicity

Paul Voestermans and Jeroen Jansz

> The conquest of the earth which mostly means the taking it away from those
> who have a different complexion or slightly flatter noses than ourselves, is
> not a pretty thing when you look into it too much.
> **Joseph Conrad,** *Heart of Darkness (1899)*

Introduction

On 22 February 1802 on the island of Marie near Tasmania an expedition of five
explorers, among them Pétit and Péron, two members of the French Société des
Observateurs de l'Homme (Society for the Observation of Man), ran into fourteen
armed Aboriginals. The two groups managed to indicate their friendly intentions to
each other. The Aboriginals became somewhat excited about the white strangers and
wanted to see what these men were like, preferably under their clothing. After much
deliberation their curiosity was satisfied: Michael, the cabin boy, got out of his clothes.
The ship's log, which was discovered in 1890, contained an official statement telling
that the naked boy:

> suddenly displayed such a striking proof of his virility that all of them exclaimed loudly
> in surprise.... Such a state of force and vigour ... surprised them greatly, and they gave
> the impression of applauding that state, like people for whom it is out of the ordinary.
> Several showed with a kind of contempt their own soft and flabby organs, they bran-
> dished themselves with an expression of regret and desire that seemed to indicate that
> they did not experience it as often as us.[1]

At the time of the expedition (see figure 43), the image of "savages" (a word
derived from Latin "the people of the woods") was dominated by Montaigne's idea
of the *bon sauvage*. Not yet corrupted by civilization, they lived a free and happy life,
with a strong and vigorous constitution.[2] It seems that Péron was not entirely convinced that the native people were so strong. On the contrary, on comparing the
island's inhabitants with western individuals, he concluded they were weaker. This
bold claim was corroborated by measuring their muscular strength by means of an
instrument called a dynamometer.

Figure 43   The "savages" of the island of Marie, as represented by the artist Lesueur, who was part of the scientific expedition. Source: Collection Musée de l'Homme, Paris.

Concerning the virility of the indigenous people, Péron speculated that their sexual desire might be periodic, which could be seen as an indication of their intimate link with the animal kingdom. For Péron the *bon sauvage* was a fantasy. According to him it would be more accurate to focus on the childlike, or even animal-like, nature of the native people. By intention and on the surface, Péron's report lent scientific support to continuance of the "civilizing" mission; unintentionally and covertly it fanned the fire of prejudice.

This chapter discusses the ways in which psychological concepts, theories, and instruments were used to conceptualize the nature and characteristics of non-western peoples, in particular the "others" in the colonies. The first section discusses the earliest studies of the mentality and behavior of the "other" in the historical context of the emergence of colonialism. As will become apparent, these studies were intimately linked with attempts to "civilize" the colonial subjects. The second section of the chapter focuses on the emergence of the nature–nurture debate around 1900. It sketches both the early forms of a nativist, racist* psychology in the school of thought

---

*   The concept of race is, of course, highly problematic. In this chapter we use "race" as a historical term. Concerning "racism," we follow Graham Richards in differentiating between "racism" and "racialism." Both racism and racialism took the existence of races for granted. Racism included hostile and derogatory attitudes and practices with regard to people of another "race." Racialism limited itself to no more than accounting for differences between people in terms of the biological features of race. G. Richards (1997), *"Race," racism and psychology. Towards a reflexive history* (London: Routledge), pp. xi–xii.

of Galton and the opposing culturalist perspective which followed Boas. The third section documents the gradual shift from racist psychologies to studies of prejudice. The latter came to dominate social psychology after the Second World War, although the hereditary, and often racist view remained on the agenda, as the final section of the chapter about the emerging multicultural society will show.

1 Early history (*c.* 1500–1900)

1.1 Colonizers and colonial subjects

The letter which Amerigo Vespucci wrote to the court of Spain in 1505, titled *Mundus Novus,* about what now is called Brazil, can be seen as a remarkable beginning of information and misinformation about overseas peoples. It described vividly the inhabitants of *las Indias* or the New World, mixing direct observations with moralizing interpretation. It informed the readers, for example, how local women were used for sexual gratification: "When they had the opportunity of having intercourse with Christians they were driven on by excessive lasciviousness and threw all decency to the winds." Thus, in one breath, as it were, the whole burden was attributed to the native people: they were greedy and lascivious, while the Christians, as users and usurpers, seemed to escape that verdict.[3]

Mundus Novus was an early expression of the mission that the western world thought it must undertake. In this letter, as in many other texts, it was argued that the natives' behavior required the severe hand of a ruler. Colonial rule was inspired by Christian ideals. From the Bible, religious leaders regarded the native peoples as the accursed descendants of Ham.[4] Conversion was attempted in nearly all cases and its lack of success contributed in fact to the interpretation of the nature and behavior of the people in terms of inferiority; in other words, they were lazy, stupid and corrupt.[5]

During the seventeenth century, international trade grew enormously. Colonial powers such as Great Britain and the Netherlands expanded their overseas territories, and the exploitation of colonial resources resulted in an unprecedented prosperity in the home countries. In due course, conquering the world for the rather mundane purpose of making money came to supplement the Christian ideal of saving the souls of the "savages." The changing stakes of commercial capitalism demanded greater exploitation of both natural and human resources. The colonial subjects were urged, if not forced, to do the hard and unpleasant work.[6]

The activity of the indigenous peoples of the colonies thus became an economic asset. Harsh forms of social management were imposed in order to turn local ways of life into productive activity. The effects of this kind of discipline were very diverse across the globe. In some colonies the inhabitants more or less accepted behavior regulation. But in many other distant lands local people opposed western control. In general, the colonizers came to realize that the natives were not all easy to manage. This generated a host of derogatory images of overseas peoples ranging from emphasizing their "beastly" cruelty to the degenerate nature of the "savage" races. These images underpinned oppressive practices such as slavery, and other outright cruelties.

This happened for example in Tasmania during the "black war" of the 1830s when white settlers hunted Aboriginals down as though they were animals, thus virtually extinguishing them.[7]

In the nineteenth century the perspective on the indigenous peoples changed, and so did the relations between usurpers and subjects. At home, the moral compass moved in the direction of a more secular and scientific account of human nature (see chapter 1). The maintenance of a dominant colonial position now required a more secular legitimation, rather than one founded on Christian principles. It resulted in a thorough reworking of the image of "the other," as part of a "civilizing offensive" that unfolded from the early 1800s onwards.

1.2   The "civilizing offensive": France and Britain

The imperial powers generally embraced the concepts of civilization and progress and linked them to the idea of supremacy. In fact, western colonizers worked from the premise that history thus far had given the white, Christian world an obligation to put the larger remaining parts of the globe to use. The earlier paradigm of salvation and exploitation was now supplemented with efforts to bring native peoples under the sway of "culture."[8] The dominant notion of culture was borrowed from Edward Burnett Tylor (1832–1917) who equated it with civilization. Tylor formulated the so-called "evolutionary" perspective on culture, which stated that in the end all peoples of the world would "evolve" to the same level of cultural complexity and sophistication. At a particular point in time, however, comparison would inevitably show that cultural evolution had resulted in a hierarchical order of cultural achievements, with African cultures at the bottom, and western civilization at the top. This emphasis on culture stimulated an interest in the "psychological" nature of the local inhabitants.[9]

The actual practices based on the Tylorian notion of culture were diverse; the "civilizing offensive" was far from monolithic.[10] Three nations played a crucial formative role in their separate implementations of the civilizing mission: the French, the British, and the Germans. The first two are discussed here, Germany is covered in the next section.

For the old colonial powers, Britain and France, "civilization" was much more than a concept, or idea, because there were important stakes involved. The control of their colonial subjects had to be anchored in the central moral values which dominated culture in the mother country. The French continued the Enlightenment tradition in which human development was understood as the unfolding of reason. Primitiveness was in French eyes an erring force that thwarted reason. It ought to be corrected with the help of solid, scientific research. To that end they borrowed craniometric methods from American scholars, measuring the shape of the skull in order to assess the mental capacity of native people.[11]

The British understood human nature not so much as a rational, independent source of progress, but as a motivating force that contributed to progress, once the appropriate economic and political measures were taken. Like the French, the British were convinced that primitiveness had to be corrected. A universal human spirit could supposedly be wrought from hard work and free trade. The utilitarian principle that comfort would in the long run hold sway over everyone was the basis for imposing an economic order and other institutions on the local inhabitants. This generally resulted in harsh and degrading regimes in the British colonies to ensure that the proper conditions for civilization were met.

The Anglo-Saxon inhabitants of North America based their view of primitive peoples on their experience with Negro slaves and the native population of so-called "Indians" (see figure 44). Despite the fact that the US constitution endorsed the view that all citizens were equal, many white American entrepreneurs employed slaves in the cotton and tobacco industry and took land from Native Americans. Slavery and exploitation were legitimized by denigrating the mental capacities of Negroes and Native Americans, thus depicting them as inferior to whites.

1.3 The theory of race and its counter-argument, the *Völkerpsychologie*, in Germany

RACE AND BIOLOGY

In the first half of the nineteenth century, the proponents of white, or western, superiority started to draw their arguments from biology. This "biologization" of cultural differences was to receive a new impulse in 1859, when Darwin's theory of evolution was published. Darwin shared the common notions of his days with respect to "the savages." He observed, for example, that an Aboriginal woman "uses very few abstract words, and cannot count above four" and therefore cannot "exert her self-consciousness, or reflect on the nature of her own existence." It seems that he did not think highly of Aboriginal women when he translated his observations into doubts about their ability to reflect. In general, he adopted a middle position with respect to racial ranking: he did not argue explicitly along racial lines, but he also avoided any notion of the influence of cultural forces.[12]

Darwin's followers were far more explicit and radical than their source of inspiration.[13] Many intellectuals used evolutionary thinking to draw a sharp distinction between the uncivilized races abroad and the inhabitants of the western home countries. Gradually, the conviction grew that darwinism was not merely a methodology and research orientation, but a model of the development of species, including the human one, based on inequality. Mechanisms such as "natural selection" and "the struggle for life" were held responsible for the existence of superior and inferior races across the globe. This implied a harsh verdict on "primitive" people: they were backward as a result of their low position on the evolutionary ladder.

The social implications of evolutionary thought were particularly addressed in the work of Herbert Spencer. In his "social darwinist" doctrine he invented the phrase "survival of the fittest" (see chapter 1), and directly translated it into judgments of racial superiority and inferiority. According to Spencer, the primitive brain could not deal with complexities and was therefore unfit for civilization. This did not mean, however, that primitive minds were inferior in all aspects. Their visual acuity and a number of other lower psychological functions were superior as a result of their

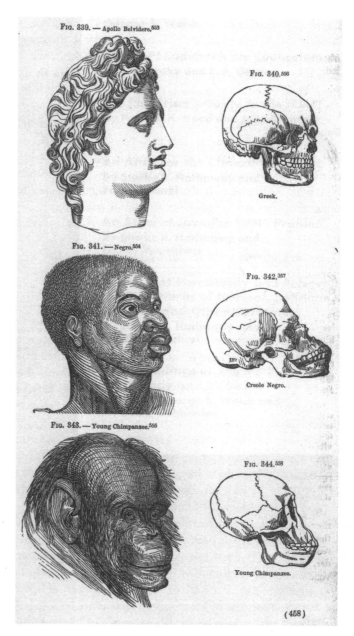

Figure 44 Typical illustration from a nineteenth-century textbook, suggesting that "negroes" are halfway between Caucasians and chimpanzees. Source: J. C. Nott and G. R. Gliddon (1868), *Indigenous races of the earth* (Philadelphia: Lippincott).

animal-like nature.[14] Spencer's idea of primitive superiority in natural functions would be echoed in later psychological research among indigenous people in the colonies.

As the nineteenth century progressed, biological arguments were used increasingly to underpin the idea of western racial superiority. White anatomy and physiology were set as the standard against which the outer appearances and way of life of other races were measured. Books about anatomy, the descent of man and biological development were illustrated with plates which showed Negroes occupying a place in between anthropoid apes and Caucasians. The racist understanding of ethnicity, with its emphasis on biologically determined inferiority, enabled the ranking of peoples around the globe on an evolutionary ladder of biological adaptation. The notion of culture was thus "biologized" as nothing other than the visible part of people's racial nature. Temperament, intellectual, physical and moral features were assessed within this racist frame, and it was often employed to justify the regime to which the indigenous peoples were subjected.

VOLKSGEIST AND VÖLKERPSYCHOLOGIE

Notwithstanding the hegemony of racist ideas in the nineteenth century, there were also intellectuals who doubted the hereditary inferiority of natives and savages. They launched a counter-argument to the biological claim of fixed mental characteristics of races or peoples. In 1851, the German scholar Moritz Lazarus coined the term *Völkerpsychologie* for the systematic, scientific study of the historical origins of ways of life. *Völkerpsychologie* rested on the Romantic idea of *Volksgeist*. The original formulation of *Volksgeist* by Herder was expanded by Herbart at the beginning of the century. Herbart understood this "spirit of a people" (or a nation) as a power that provides individual minds with shared content. He postulated mental forces that operate supposedly both at the individual and the social level. In the practical translation of these abstract ideas, Herbart embraced the German emphasis on education (or *Kultur*): through training or education individual minds became attuned to each another, thus contributing to the *Volksgeist* of a people. Herbart stressed the necessity of studying what he called "the dawn of mental life in natives and savages" because it would contribute to understanding what forces determined the *Geist* or spirit of a people.

Philology was an integral part of the emerging *Völkerpsychologie*, as shown by the name of the journal founded by Lazarus and Steinthal in 1860, the *Zeitschrift für Völkerpsychologie und Sprachwissenschaft* (Journal of *Völkerpsychologie* and Linguistics). Philologists studied the development of language communities. The German notion that Aryan culture had spread centuries ago from east to west encouraged conceptualization about the diffusion of culture in terms of discrete language communities. Nineteenth-century scholars generally assumed that Aryan culture had been superior and assessed the degree of similarity between the languages of their time and the Aryan one. They reported that the more favored races had a language of high standing; other races, in particular those of darker skin color, were relegated to the shadows.[15]

In the last decades of the century, the *Völkerpsychologie* flourished, leaving its mark on other disciplines. Thus, in psychology, Wundt's magnum opus *Völkerpsychologie* (the ten volumes were published between 1900 and 1920) was the culmination of a psychological approach to culture and language.[16] Anthropology, as practiced by scholars like Péron, but also later on by German scholars, was concerned largely with the habitat, racial features, and biological characteristics of a people. With the notion of *Volksgeist* available to them, psychology and anthropology were jointly able to redirect research into native peoples by including myth, language, and other elements of the alleged spirit of a people.

After the discovery in the 1890s of the Benin bronzes, many anthropologists and Völkerpsychologists made a case for the complexity of the so-called *Naturvölker*.[17] They severely criticized the common belief that Negroes were unfit for civilization, arguing that their capacity for language put them on a par with western people. However, such a judgment did not preclude the placement of Negroes in an inferior position. They were regarded as needing further education, and the study of the *Volksgeist* was put forward as a means to a better psychological understanding of how this education could be implemented. This accounts for the ambivalent stance of *Völkerpsychologie* on the issue of the worth of primitive peoples. On the one hand, the Völkerpsychologists were clearly at odds with racist and racialist thinkers because of the biological determinism of the latter two groups. On the other hand, there was much less disagreement with respect to the issue of ranking peoples. The Völkerpsychologists employed the notion of *Volk*, or people, rather than race. Yet they used this notion in a way similar to the use of race by others. A *Volk* was understood as a kind of fixed, and more or less discrete, entity which possessed a *Volksgeist*. However, *Volksgeister* came in various sorts. On the basis of the stage of the *Volksgeist*, cultural groups as well as nations could be ranked in the larger historic-evolutionary framework of civilizations. Western civilization was positioned at the top. Toward the lower end were the peoples whose *Volksgeist* was too backward, historically, for them to be able to improve their living conditions without support. So from the perspective of *Völkerpsychologie* also, there was much civilizing work to do. The "savages" (a term often at that time already between quotation marks or qualified by adding "so-called") still had a long way to go up the evolutionary ladder to full humanity. In this respect, the emphasis on culture and history did not turn out to be a viable alternative that could effectively establish a counter-force to biological racism. The cultures and histories of the so-called primitive peoples were as much a source of debasing and degrading comment as race was.[18]

Not all nineteenth-century anthropologists and Völkerpsychologists embraced the notion of white, or western, superiority, although criticism remained limited to a minority of isolated individuals. The idea of the "psychic unity" of mankind, for example, was put forward as a fundamental attack on racist claims. German scholars, such as Virchow and Waitz, argued against considering primitive peoples as animals. They claimed that the use of language demonstrated that every group had a general capacity for progress, no matter how primitive their way of life. If the conditions were right, each culture could evolve to a higher level, which would eventually show the equality between peoples.

1.4   *The Cambridge Torres Strait expedition*

The British psychologists who joined the anthropological Cambridge Torres Strait Expedition in 1898 took a more empirical approach, compared with the rather speculative *Völkerpsychologie*. Rivers and his students Myers and McDougall sailed overseas to investigate the primary psychological functions of the "primitives," comparing them with the functions of "civilized" Europeans.[19] Rivers and his students established a kind of field laboratory where they experimentally investigated psychophysical phenomena, such as visual and auditory acuity, reaction time, and weight discrimination (see figure 45). They reported that the primitive people outperformed the civilized ones in most perceptual tasks. This superiority was interpreted in Spencerian terms, that is, the senses used all the energy available, so there was nothing left for (abstract) reason.[20] In other words, the colonial subjects may have had excellent sensory perception, but their capacity for sound reasoning was definitely underdeveloped. These observations were commonly understood as a corroboration of white superiority: no one could outdo the civilized, white Europeans in their capacity for reasoning.

The Torres Strait studies elicited criticism almost immediately from fellow psychologists. Tichener, for example, seriously doubted the conditions of research, emphasizing an issue that later became known as the "equivalence problem" in cross-cultural comparison.[21] It was impossible to attribute the differences found

Figure 45   Cambridge Torres Strait expedition: psychologist Rivers examining the "visual acuity" of indigenous people at Mabuiag, 1898. Courtesy of the Cambridge University Museum of Archaeology and Anthropology, UMCAA.P.754.AXH1.

between western and the so-called exotic subjects to differences in culture, because the differences could very well have been caused by the inequivalence of the testing situation. In other words, the local people probably understood the laboratory procedures and equipment differently from the western participants back home in Cambridge. Whatever its weaknesses, Rivers' exotic psychology represented the anticipation, if not the foundation, of what would later be called cross-cultural psychology.[22]

1.5   Conclusion

The articulation of western superiority in biological terms at the end of the nineteenth century was to all intents the apotheosis of a development that had started at the end of the eighteenth. At that time the balance of power was to the advantage of the western world. Other great civilizations such as the Islamic world, China and India had become stagnant and had abandoned their expansionist strivings. The nineteenth-century western economy was much stronger; it enabled global domination by western civilization in the course of the century.

The opening and the closing of the nineteenth century were marked by two important expeditions to colonial territory. The academic and practical goals of the French *Societé* and the British Cambridge team were different and so were their political and cultural contexts, but they also had a lot in common. Both expeditions were equipped by colonial powers in order to gather detailed knowledge about the nature and habits of "the others" overseas. Both used psychological instruments, be it questionnaires for the assessment of mental features or a field laboratory for the quantification of psychophysical properties. The results of these empirical psychological investigations were interpreted in a racist mindset and employed to rank alien cultures and races below those of white, western civilization and race.

2   Nature versus nurture (*c.* 1880–1920)

In the last decades of the nineteenth century, European colonialism developed into global imperialism. The pre-eminent colonial power, Great Britain, expanded its empire well into Asia; other early colonial nations, such as the Netherlands, consolidated their position abroad. The speed of western expansion is starkly shown by the fact that by 1880 one-tenth of African territory was colonized; on the eve of the First World War only one-tenth was not colonized.[23] The United States of America emerged as a new colonial power, especially in the Pacific area. At home, the ethnic and racial composition of the American population changed rapidly. After the Civil War many former slaves migrated from the rural southern states to the cities in the North. In addition, immigrants from eastern and southern parts of Europe sought a better future in the American industrial areas. Their settlement incited fears among the white Anglo-Saxon Protestant elite, the "WASPs," who were afraid that intermarriages between their own creed and Jews and Catholics would undermine the quality of the Great American race.[24]

2.1   *Galton, hereditarian thought and practice*

Francis Galton was a key figure in the translation of ideas about heredity into practical interventions to protect the quality of what was considered superior "stock." He took great pains to show that it was possible to quantify racial psychological differences, rather than merely passing a value judgment. Although his trip to Syria, Egypt, and Namibia exemplified the standard sentiments of his time, which precluded any interest in the lifestyle of the people he visited, he tried to argue objectively in his *Hereditary genius* (1869) that certain features of native peoples were a barrier to social evolution. They lacked foresight, he said, and they also were impulsive and lazy, although they were capable of sudden hard work if they craved food. In his eugenic agenda, Galton tried to persuade his audience not to mix races, but to breed in the purest possible lineage.

Galton coined the use of the terms "nature" and "nurture" to stipulate the effects of heredity and environment respectively. Questions about the relative contribution of natural endowment and environmental stimulation soon resulted in a controversy which has never since left us: that of "nature versus nurture." Galton's conviction that nature was the determining factor was broadly shared among European intellectuals, fitting well into the scheme of the western civilizing offensive. As early as 1873 however, Alphonse De Candolle presented a rival hypothesis, stating that on the basis of available statistical data, various environmental variables influenced the rates at which different European countries brought forth important scientists. In *Inquiries into human faculty* (1883) Galton accepted De Candolle's alternative but he rescued his "nativism" by arguing that only individuals endowed with an innate taste for science would profit from environmental variables. It was in this debate with De Candolle that Galton seemed to open the door for an interaction between nature and nurture: "the interaction of nature and circumstances is very close, and it is impossible to separate them with precision," but he then continued by stating: "We know that the bulk of the respective provinces of nature and nurture are totally different." It is not clear what made Galton shun interaction and settle on a nativist position.[25]

Galton's publication set the tone for a debate, in which advocates of both perspectives tended to defend their own position, rather than attempt to develop more refined conceptions of the ways "nature" and "nurture" might interact. Neither the nativists nor the environmentalists came to realize that the deployment of innate capacities in a given environment involves a third element. In establishing an optimal "fit" between capacities and environment one has to take into account the given ways of managing the environmental resources.

In the 1880s, Virchow was one of the few scholars who advocated a compromise between nativism and environmentalism. He attacked the non-empirical and speculative status of the naturalist accounts of race, and argued "that the understanding and evolution of races and species had to be based on serious research into our cellular mutability, rather than nebulous theories on the ascent of Man."[26] Virchow also supported the idea of the inheritance of acquired characteristics. The environment could cause cellular variation which was not identical with the cellular structures the organism inherited from its parents. The assumption that acquired characteristics were transmitted to the next generation precluded the construction of so-called phylogenetic trees. According to Virchow, too much was unknown for it to be possible to construct a tree linking man's heritage to that of animals.

Virchow's critical inductivism was committed to hard facts, but failed to inspire viable empirical investigation. He did not succeed in persuading scholars from the nativist and environmentalist camps. By the end of the nineteenth century, anthropology had developed into a rather soft "science of race" which was less based on empirical procedures and more on political ideas of superiority and inferiority. Judgments about backward races became harsher and heralded ideas such as the "cleansing power" of "selection," the "healthy selfishness" of the "superior races," and the elimination of the "inferiors."[27]

2.2   *Psychology and race in the United States*

Through this rather simplified model of nature versus nurture, ideas about white superiority became the received wisdom in American, British, and German psychology. With the exception of a small minority, most authors explained the excellent qualities of the white, or Caucasian, or Nordic "race" on the basis of hereditary factors. In the United States, where many psychologists were involved in public debates about the consequences of immigration, a particularly influential axiom concerning the mental abilities of the non-white minorities was given currency, namely that non-white minorities were genetically inferior and unable to participate of their own accord in the blessings of civilization. Native Americans and black slaves became the cultural groups on whom this axiom was tested, so to speak, but its effect spread further than these groups. The ideas about mental abilities, inferiority, and aptness for civilization became part of the way the general public reacted to these minorities, since these notions fitted well with an existing negative attitude. They also determined much of the discussion among intellectuals, psychologists included, about other people around the globe.

The founding father of American psychology, G. Stanley Hall, for example, argued in his magnum opus *Adolescence* (1904) that the "primitive" races still were in what he called the adolescent phase of development. This was not a sign of innate inferiority, but of their lagging behind in the civilizing process. Hall thought it was the Christian duty of the white race to nurture the adolescent races in order to reach civilization. He propagated guidance and control of "the primitives" and thought that the segregation of Native Americans and Negroes was beneficial to their education.[28]

Even stronger views about the innate (mental) superiority of the "white race" were expressed by psychologists who affiliated with the eugenics movement. Goddard became the leading eugenics psychologist of his time. In a 1917 publication about immigration, for example, he reported that 40 percent of the new arrivals were mentally "unfit" by his diagnostic standards (see figure 46).[29] Such results and comparable ones from his fellow psychologists were embraced by the eugenics societies as underlining the necessity for restricting immigration. In defending those restrictions a typical psychological issue was raised, that of intelligence. This happened in the wake of the real breakthrough for psychology's account of innate intelligence, which

Figure 46 Psychological examination of immigrants on Ellis Island, 1917. Source: Archives of the History of American Psychology, University of Akron.

came in 1917 with the large-scale assessment of Army draftees (see chapter 3). The high scores of people of British descent, and the low scores of those of Polish ancestry and of "colored Americans" was interpreted by Yerkes, Goddard, and Terman in a straightforward manner. The scores reflected differences in innate levels of intelligence. Their 800-page report detailed the differentiation of intelligence according to race, region, and nation.[30]

The public at large became involved when the *New Republic* journalist Lippmann raised serious questions about the methodology of the testing operation. This resulted in a heated debate with Terman which filled several issues of the periodical.[31] Meanwhile, Brigham's *A study of American intelligence* (1923) popularized the results of the testing operation (see figure 47). He interpreted the results in an explicitly racist manner: "The intellectual superiority of our Nordic group over the Alpine, Mediterranean and Negro groups has been demonstrated. If a person is unwilling to accept the race hypothesis as developed here, he may go back to the original nationality groups, and he cannot deny the fact that differences exist" (p. 192). In addition, Brigham advocated drastic eugenic measures such as segregation of races, sterilization, and immigration restriction. In 1925, T. R. Garth reviewed systematically what the psychology of race had to offer. He concluded that the 73 psychological studies in his review seemed "to indicate the mental superiority of the white

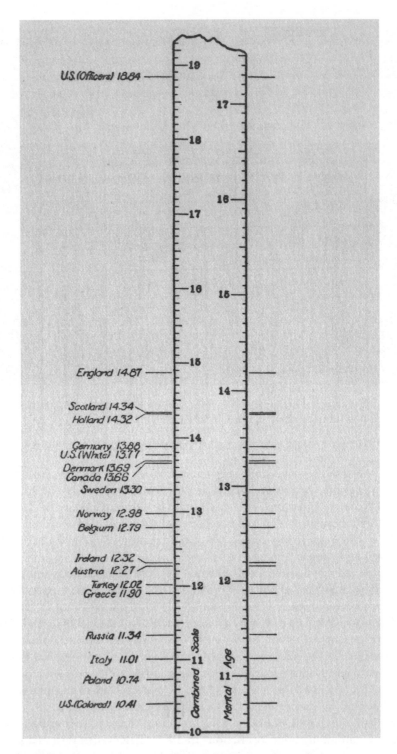

Figure 47 Differences in "native" intelligence between various ethnic groups, as presented in C. C. Brigham's *A study of American intelligence* (Princeton: Princeton University Press, 1922).

race."[32] Garth's conclusion corroborated the general position of American psychologists in the early 1920s. The majority defended a racist perspective on ethnic, regional, and national group differences, in particular with respect to intelligence, the key concept of psychology.[33]

2.3 Boas and plurality of culture

The psychologization of racial differences was also criticized, however, in particular by the anthropologist Franz Boas. His work initiated a research tradition which was relatively free from racism and entailed a more positive outlook on the lifestyle of "primitive" people. Franz Boas was born in Germany where he received his education in physics and geology. He was trained by Virchow and also by Bastian, who inspired him to supplement the emphasis on natural circumstances with one which considered history and culture.[34] Boas himself, however, had initially been convinced that Galtonian biometrics would lead to a "definite" solution of the problem of the effects of heredity and environment. Later, when he had moved to New York, he became one of the most articulate critics of nativist approaches. The evidence for racial "types," which had been obtained through anthropometrics and statistical analysis, proved to be inconclusive. Boas had already shown in 1901 that "the bulk of the two groups of races (African, Australian and Pacific versus Asian, American and European) have brains of the same capacities."[35] In studying the form of the head, Boas noticed that immigrant children who got better food and hygiene when in the US developed a head-shape which was more full-grown compared with that of children living in poor circumstances. This unexpected result led him to abandon anthropometry and focus on the relative contribution of environmental arrangements and natural endowment. In this line of work, Boas became one of the staunchest critics of white supremacist race theories.[36]

Boas introduced an anthropological notion of culture, which took issue with the prevailing Tylorian one (see above). He substituted Tylor's hierarchy by a flexible order in which the plurality of culture was emphasized. This open position stimulated a dynamic view of culture as a composite, that is to say, as something put together from people's elementary thoughts and from folkloristic components. Cultural differences could thus readily replace the racial ones, abandoning the idea of the "mental organization of different races of man as differing in fundamental points."[37]

2.4 Conclusion

In a formal, political sense the world was dominated by western imperialism on the eve of the First World War. The US was extensively involved in this imperialism, establishing western economic rule all over the globe. The debate in the US about intelligence and mental abilities set the scene for a further "construction" of non-western people in terms of inferior mental capacities and other negative traits. This made the attitudes of the colonial rulers harsher and they were less inclined to accept the way of life of the people they tried to control.

However, global domination was never complete. China and Japan, for example, were never conquered and even India and Africa, although colonized with great effort, resisted the introduction of the western way of life to a great extent. This was the case among minorities in the US itself as well, despite the effort to mold them into US citizens in the "melting pot" of mixing cultures. In fact, the domination of other people in terms of lifestyle and rational conduct was far more difficult to achieve than economic domination. Colonial subjects were forced to adopt western standards but that adoption remained skin-deep and bore the traces of coercion.

It was in this process of slowly trying to make people adopt a western way of living that new sciences like biology and psychology played a remarkable role. Around the issue of intelligence and genetic inferiority a discourse developed that flourished on the already existing economic exploitation. Psychology firmly fixed widespread beliefs about the fundamental inequality of races. The inhabitants of the colonies, immigrants, and former slaves suffered most when their white bosses and rulers translated these racist ideas into everyday practice.

However, the psychology of race was never uncontested. Gradually but slowly scholars who were convinced that language and reasoning were inherent qualities of human beings all over the world admitted that civilization was something that peoples from other cultures could achieve also, once they were duly educated. These culturalists, inside and outside psychology, were convinced that revealing the workings of their mind would do justice to so-called "primitives." It would be possible to understand properly the mental make-up of peoples who had for some reason lagged behind in cultural progress. Yet, in the interwar years the intellectual and political battle between those who adopted the culture perspective and adherents to the idea of the power of biological determinants had still to be fought in the context of imperial exploitation.

3   Between the wars (*c.* 1920–1940)

In the 1920s the balance in American psychology shifted gradually from nature to nurture. In emphasizing the environment, psychologists paved the way for a new perspective on why the integration of non-western people or the adoption of the western way of life was so difficult: it was not on account of inborn characteristics, but an inappropriate dynamic in the way the confrontation of cultures was carried out.[38]

In Europe, interwar psychology was dominated by racist views. British psychologists generally followed the American racist psychology of the 1910s, and Germany became the stage for a unique and sinister development when the Nazi typology of the *Übermensch* was translated into an unprecedented program of racist mass murder.

3.1   *Psychology and race in the United Kingdom and Germany*

In Great Britain, issues of race came onto the psychological agenda in the 1920s. The scale of British research was small and hardly comparable with that which had been done in American psychology before the First World War. Karl Pearson, who was Galton's fellow in establishing the field of psychometrics, founded the *Annals of Eugenics* in 1925. The very first volume opened with a lengthy article by Pearson and Moul about the characteristics of immigrant children.[39] The researchers concluded from their large survey that Russian and Jewish children were inferior to British children in many aspects, ranging from intelligence to personal hygiene. Pearson and Moul continued by advocating eugenic immigration restriction in order to safeguard the quality of the British race. Another important figure on the British scene was personality psychologist R. B. Cattell. He published his ideas about Nordic supremacy and anti-semitism in the 1930s, and translated his views into enthusiasm for segregation and the population policies that were developed in Nazi Germany.[40]

When German psychologists addressed "race," their style was speculative, rather than psychometric and experimental. The psychological themes connected directly to earlier ideas about "primitives" and differences between peoples. Carl G. Jung, for example, supplemented the all-too-common western view of the "primitives" in need of civilization with the notion that the "primitive" psyche had much in common with the psychoanalytic unconscious. He traveled to, among other countries, India, Kenya, and New Mexico, and came to understand the condition of the "savages" as ancestral to that of the civilized peoples.[41] Jung believed in white, Christian superiority, and felt personally embedded in the German collective unconscious. Although Jung did not express or support Nazi racism and anti-semitism in public, his racialist convictions may have played a role in his decision to stay in office after the nazification of the German Society of Psychotherapy in 1933.[42]

Under the Nazi regime racist ideas and practices were taken to their extremes. German biological anthropology already had a "therapeutic" agenda concerned with the improvement of the German *Volk* through interventions in the lives of individual couples. This resulted, under the aegis of Eugen Fischer, in the murderous Nazi biological policy with its encompassing eugenic program. Efforts to breed an Aryan super-race in the *Lebensborn* program were combined with the mass extermination of Jews and other groups considered to be inferior in the Nazi racial doctrine. The number of racist publications in psychology increased rapidly. Psychological accounts of, for example, the German *Übermensch* and its opposite *Der Gegentypus* (a term introduced by Jaensch) effectively became part of official Nazi politics.[43]

3.2   Criticism of racism in American psychology

While European psychology remained firmly entrenched in racist ideology, American psychology took an interesting turn in the 1930s. Psychologists became more concerned about the part played by environmental resources. In 1930, Thomas Garth published a sequel to his 1925 review of race psychology. He concluded that the so-called "racial difference hypothesis" was "no nearer being established than it was five years ago. In fact many psychologists seem practically ready for another, the hypothesis of racial equality."[44] Defending the hypothesis of racial equality meant that the observed mental differences between races were attributed to environmental rather than hereditary factors. Brigham was another important figure to recant on his earlier views. In 1930 he made a grave criticism of race psychology when he wrote: "Comparative studies of various national and racial groups may not be made with existing tests. . . . One of the most pretentious of these comparative racial studies – the writer's own – was without foundation."[45]

The debunking of the concept of race made space for those researchers who were already concerned with monitoring the encounter of cultures, and how to understand the causes of prejudice and what social science could contribute to combat it. For example, Dollard and his colleagues proposed the frustration–aggression hypothesis to explain white southerners' racism. They reasoned that the poor whites experienced serious economic reverses during the Great Slump of the 1930s. This frustration made them aggressive, which was abreacted on the black Americans in their immediate social context. The blacks came to function as "scapegoats" for the miseries of white people.[46]

3.3   Culture and personality

In American anthropology, Boas and his followers developed the "Culture and Personality" approach after the First World War. Focusing on the interface of individual and culture, it merged Boasian anthropology with psychoanalysis. Freud's work was considered helpful because of its emphasis on early infancy as the crucial determinant of the formation of cultural habits. Boasian anthropologists assumed that interaction with adults and the confrontation with societal structures, ranging from subsistence systems to institutionalized religious practices, would have far-reaching consequences for the individual's personal life. Klineberg, who was convinced "how deep down culture could go into the little movements of the hands," studied the bodily expressiveness and caring practices of the mothers in particular in black culture. Socializing practices that turned youngsters into competent men and women, making them fit for marriage and parenthood in line with customary practices, became the new focus.

On a global and more speculative level the Culture and Personality researchers attempted to describe whole cultures in terms of fundamental personality structures, or traits, derived from basic motives described in predominantly psychoanalytical terms. Ruth Benedict pioneered this project in 1934 when she wrote about the Pueblo Indians, the Dobu, and the Kwakiutl. She characterized each culture using Nietzsche's dichotomous account of the creative process, the Dionysian and Apollonian ways. For example, she labeled the conspicuous consumption that occurred in the Pueblo *potlatch* as Dionysian, and contrasted it with customs of Apollonian restrictiveness among the Kwakiutl. Benedict's work stimulated further interest in culture and personality. Several anthropologists followed her suggestion for linking institutional arrangements with basic personality features.[47]

The impact of the Culture and Personality approach exceeded its subject matter *per se*. A first general effect was the involvement of psychology in anthropological research. From now on both anthropologists and psychologists assumed that differences in cultural customs and traditions resulted in a particular type of person. In short, personality became culture writ small, and culture became personality writ large. A second effect was the creation of a new terminology in which the way of life of native peoples in the distant corners of the world could be understood better. Margaret Mead's work in the 1920s and 1930s was particularly influential in that regard. Her comparative study of the upbringing of children in New Guinea, and her lessons about environmental influences on sex and temperament in the "primitive societies," not only contributed to understanding of the indigenous ways of life, but also made the western world aware of its own cultural presuppositions (see figure 48).[48]

3.4 Conclusion

The interwar years in the United States were characterized by the countering of racist psychology. Many psychologists as well as social scientists came to believe that culture "crept into the hands and bodies" as it were of those who proved to be not easily integrated into the dominant way of life. This environmentalist line of reasoning replaced naturalist arguments in explanations of the "backwardness" of minority groups. The adoption of the nurture perspective moved on the waves of the political tide, as much as earlier racist thinking had. The passing of a new Immigration Restriction Law in 1924 was an important societal factor. The 1924 law installed a very restrictive regime at the United States borders based on admission quotas according to country of origin. This immigration policy changed the role of psychological race research. Before the 1924 law, psychological knowledge had been employed to substantiate inferiority claims and the propagation of eugenic measures. Now, psychology was needed to facilitate the "melting pot" of races and nationalities. The research was refocused on prejudice on the part of the dominant groups and on culturally induced tenaciousness with respect to already established practices on the part of immigrants or peoples in developing regions and countries. German psychology, by contrast, intensified racist ideas in the 1930s. The political climate fanned the fire of racist typologies in the service of exclusion and extermination.

4 The multicultural society (*c.* 1945–present)

Ideas about people from different races, nationalities, or ethnic groups changed radically in the postwar period as a result of three important historical developments. The first one was the acknowledgment of the Holocaust. The mass extermination in the name of Aryan supremacy resulted in a widespread distrust of racist theorizing and eugenics after the war. The Nazi horrors also led many to wonder in despair "how it had been possible." This disturbing question resulted in thousands of publications about the roots of Nazi evil.

The second postwar development was decolonialization. The colonies in Asia, the Middle East, and Africa claimed their political independence from the 1940s onwards. In the process, former colonial subjects of the British, French, and Dutch empires migrated to the motherlands. Thus metropolises became multicultural societies where people from different backgrounds needed to adjust to one another. Decolonialization placed race relations on the social agenda in many western countries, and it continued to inspire cross-cultural comparison of psychological attributes.

(a)   (b)   (c)

Figure 48 "Stimulation and frustration." Mother–child interaction in Balinese culture, as studied within the "Culture and Personality" paradigm. The mother stimulates the child (a) but is unresponsive to the child's reaction (b and c). Source: G. Bateson and M. Mead, *Balinese character. A photographic analysis* (New York: New York Academy Press, 2nd ed., 1962).

The third notable development was the burgeoning of the Civil Rights Movement in the United States. Despite the constitutional creed of civil equality, American society had been characterized by a strict social hierarchy in which non-whites were second-class citizens. The political struggle of the 1950s aimed at the emancipation of black Americans from their submerged position. The ideology of the melting pot in which all people could be molded into becoming US citizens by simply educating them to adopt white cultural standards showed the cracks of failure. Psychological expertise was mobilized in the well-orchestrated attacks on racism and segregation. The following section discusses the psychology of prejudice and race relations in the postwar period. The focus is on American research, because US psychologists pioneered in these fields, with European colleagues generally following in their wake.

4.1 The nature of prejudice

A first important line of research in American psychology concentrated on the roots of racial prejudice. Most psychologists considered prejudice a serious impairment of harmonious relations between people of different racial, national, and ethnic backgrounds. In 1950 *The authoritarian personality* was published by Theodore Adorno and his colleagues. The studies in this volume explained racial prejudice from a psychodynamic point of view. Authoritarian, patriarchal family relations produced a kind of rigidity in the deepest layers of personality. This authoritarian personality could not tolerate ambiguities, feared the non-familiar, and was thus prone to xenophobia. The research of Adorno and his team dated back to the 1930s when they studied the roots of anti-semitism in Frankfurt, Germany.[49] After their flight, the Jewish refugees concentrated on anti-semitism in the United States and concluded that such prejudice was rooted in a personality disorder which could result in disastrous actions under the "appropriate" social conditions.

American social psychologists followed up on the studies of prejudice that were done in the interwar years (see figure 49). After the war they generally embraced an eclectic approach in which learning theories were combined with some psychodynamic ideas. The major publication in this tradition was Gordon W. Allport's *The nature of prejudice* (1954), which emphasized the irrationality of prejudice, and the necessity to combat it in the quest for social harmony. In his environmentalist position statement Allport also proposed to abandon the use of the word "race" and use "ethnic" instead.[50]

A second line of research emerging in the 1950s focused on the psychological consequences for the individual of racism, prejudice, and oppression. Studies by black psychologists Kenneth and Mamie Clark, for example, documented the damaging consequences of segregation for children. Children from the ethnic majority suffered from feelings of guilt, and minority children had to cope with damaged self-esteem. This type of developmental research was highlighted in 1954 when the US Supreme Court quoted psychological research in the *Brown v. Board of Education* case, which ruled out segregation in schools. The impact of the Civil Rights Movement resulted in an almost permanent and ferocious public debate about racism and desegregation.

Figure 49   Drawing used in a famous study by Gordon Allport (1947). Although focused on the psychology of rumor, the study also illustrated the pervasiveness of prejudice. Participants were asked to describe the scene to someone else, who in turn described it to a third person, and so on. At the end, the razor had changed hands from the white man to the black man. Source: G. W. Allport and L. Postman, *The psychology of rumor* (New York: Russell & Russell).

"Self-esteem" and "ethnic identity" became household words in these exchanges, illustrating the far-reaching psychologization of political issues related to race and discrimination.[51]

A third line of research emerged in the 1960s when local and federal authorities established fact-finding commissions in response to the so-called "race riots" in American cities.[52] These experts produced accounts of which the Moynihan Report certainly was the most famous and controversial. The civil servant Daniel P. Moynihan headed a group of experts who published *The Negro family: the case for national action* in 1965. The report concluded that the life of the Negro-American was characterized by deep-seated structural distortions as a result of centuries of oppression. It also held that the present "tangle of pathology" would continue unless state intervention occurred. Although the Moynihan Report included research such as Clark's that had been applauded earlier by the emancipation movement, it was attacked for "blaming the victim."[53] Moynihan had taken the white middle-class family as a norm, the critics said, for instance in his conclusion that matriarchal black families were incomplete because they generally lacked a responsible and committed father.[54]

The reception of the Moynihan Report reflected a change in political context. By 1965, the Civil Rights Movement underlined the claims for political rights with forceful expressions of pride in black identities. In doing so, the definition of black culture was taken out of the hands of the "oppressive majority," as it was now called. Black pride was also reflected in American psychology. In 1968 the Association of Black Psychologists was established, with the abandonment of the "damaged Negro" stereotype among its principal political aims. In one of its key publications in 1972 the Association urged psychologists to "stop trying to compensate for the so-called short-comings of the black child and try to develop a theory that capitalizes on his strengths."[55] In fact, the Association embraced cultural relativism when it argued that psychology should recognize that the experience of a black child is both qualitatively and quantitatively different from what a white infant experiences. A responsible psychology, it was argued, must be sensitive to these experiential differences.

4.2 Cross-cultural comparison

After the war, research on the interface of personality and culture continued, particularly in anthropology. The "modal personality," a concept coined by Cora Dubois (1944), was an important approach. The modal personality of a culture was constructed on the basis of statistical data. Thus the Galtonian approach of measuring personality characteristics was combined with the basic tenets of the Boasian study of cultures. Inkeles and Levinson, for example, introduced the notion of "industrial man" in 1954 as a specification of the "modal personality" of the western world.[56] It was subsequently employed as an instrument to assess the progress of modernization in developing countries. Modal personality research also scrutinized the basic cultural orientations of American groups that remained in some ways in a disadvantaged position, such as African-Americans, Native Americans, and Latinos. This kind of research sensitized psychologists to a fairly benign form of cultural relativism which ended the generally monolithic view of culture endemic in US circles. Consequently, "culture" was understood by many researchers as an important psychological variable.

The statistical approach of modal personality research firmly established a trust in numbers as a basis for cross-cultural comparison. In particular, the research of Geert Hofstede, based on data from IBM companies all over the globe, became widely known and cited.[57] He elevated the level of analysis from individuals to nations and introduced a number of dimensions for cross-national comparison. Nations were typified as more or less feminine, that is to say more task-oriented or more relationship-oriented; more or less preoccupied with power, in the sense of being oriented toward equality or inequality; more or less individualized; and more or less achievement-oriented. His work was used, for example, to predict the success of introducing a welfare system, since relationship-oriented countries were more likely to adopt such a system than task-oriented ones. Hofstede's work was a direct offshoot of the increasing "Galtonization" of the behavioral sciences. Structural features of nations were "psychologized" by means of large surveys about psychological attributes of individuals and groups. The economic qualities of countries, particularly developing countries, came to be described in a jargon of traits and psychological states of their inhabitants. This kind of psychologization turned culture into something that could be used as a variable in extensive correlational designs. What had begun in the culture and personality approach as a deep-seated feature of behavioral patterns became a factor to be manipulated in large-scale investigations of economic feasibility.

4.3   Hereditarianism revisited

As we have seen, nativist explanations for racial differences were almost banned from public debate in the postwar decades. Public discussion about the hereditary basis of capacities re-emerged in 1969 when the American psychologist Arthur Jensen published his essay "How much can we boost IQ and scholastic achievement?" He concluded that Head Start and other compensatory programs were mostly a waste of money. IQ, he argued, was for about 80 percent determined by genetic factors, and so it was very difficult to compensate for any deficit by means of social intervention.[58] Jensen's pessimism was expressed in a racialist, if not racist, vein when he suggested that black children generally had a worse genetic endowment than white children. Comparable views were voiced by Hans Eysenck in Great Britain, who observed that "American Negroes on the average score something like 15 points of IQ below whites," and explained the difference in hereditary terms as he did the poor performance of black students in school.[59]

The most influential recent publication in the hereditarian tradition was *The bell curve* (1994) by Herrnstein and Murray. They presented a large amount of statistical data to relate cognitive capacities, in particular intelligence, to social position. Thus, they tried to demonstrate that both the lack of social and economic success and the prevalence of social problems such as delinquency among non-whites were primarily due to a lack of intelligence (see figure 50). Although the authors claimed to be "agnostic" with respect to heredity and interethnic differences in intelligence, they forcefully rejected social explanations of the unsuccessful participation of ethnic minorities in American culture, focusing solely on psychological determinants.[60]

5   Conclusion

The path from "savages" to "ethnic minorities" has been tempestuous and troublesome. The early involvement of psychology was a striking feature. In 1802, Péron and his colleagues investigated the people of Marie island using psychological methods, though the research was actually carried out under the banner of medicine and ethnography. In retrospect, the questionnaire employed looks surprisingly modern: the native inhabitants were questioned in detail about their emotions, their cognitions, their child-rearing practices, their habits, and the way they interacted socially.

The systematic study of "the savage mind" was part and parcel of the "civilizing offensive" of the western world, in which the colonial powers had different interests. The French were primarily concerned with the mentality of the indigenous peoples,

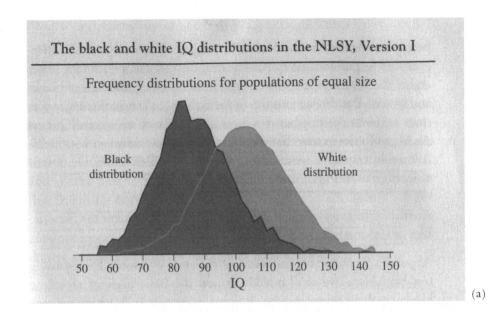

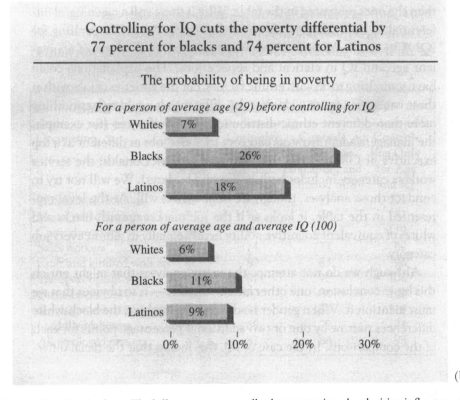

Figure 50 Graphs from *The bell curve*, purportedly demonstrating the decisive influence of ethnic differences in intelligence on social inequality. (a) Intelligence distributions of whites and blacks. (b) Influence of intelligence on levels of poverty. Source: R. J. Herrnstein and C. Murray (1994), *The bell curve* (New York: Free Press).

carrying out research on the cranial capacities of the so-called "primitives." This thoroughly psychological research activity started early in the nineteenth century, and ceased in the early twentieth century when it turned out that cranial size was no indication whatsoever of a less developed brain. The British colonizers focused on the capacity for work and tried to implement measures that would contribute to greater productivity and discipline in the colonies; they were less interested in a psychological approach to the "savage" mind. The measures they took were harsh and crude in their effects, and showed little consideration for local customs and practices.

From the mid-nineteenth century onward till the beginning of the twentieth century, the Germans took a somewhat milder position toward peoples with a different cultural background. They emphasized that the use of language made it possible to educate the native peoples. The notion of *Volksgeist*, or the "spirit of the people," became part of the speculation about aptness for civilization: a proper *Volksgeist* was considered to be a necessary element in the training of the primitive mind. The German approach developed into a focused psychological approach toward primitive peoples, their minds and languages when the *Völkerpsychologie* was institutionalized.

With hindsight, all approaches to the nature of the "savage" mind suffered from schematic thinking in terms of inferiority versus superiority. Judgments about inferiority were clearly implicated in the hereditarian notion of "race," but the culturalist position of the *Völkerpsychologie* also took western superiority for granted. Culture was something the western world "possessed" in the same self-evident and superior way as it once "possessed" the superior Christian faith. Christians had always invaded the unknown territories without really questioning their right to do so. The same happened when the idea of culture had replaced the idea of redemption and faith. Of course, faced with the clearly well-developed cultures of the east, as in China and Japan, it was difficult to maintain the idea of western superiority. In the course of the nineteenth century, artists, writers, and even some scholars were inspired by foreign splendors, and a few exotic aspects of foreign cultures were copied in the west. However, this enthusiasm left the power balance unchanged. Often, "orientalism," as Said has called this attitude toward the east, became part of the imperialist project and could then be as devastating as downright disdain.[61]

From the late nineteenth century onward, western imperialism used science, particularly biology and the new discipline of psychology, to provide evidence for the backwardness of indigenous peoples. Science confirmed that primitive peoples were not fit or not yet fit for civilization, which legitimized the harsh colonial rule. There were, of course, intellectuals and scholars such as Boas who tried to counter the voracious nature of what truly could be labeled "the superiority complex" of the western world, but their attempts remained marginal for a long time. It was not till the late 1920s that the culturalist approaches became a viable alternative to hereditarian inferiority/superiority thought. These alternative approaches, in the footprints of Boas, as well as the social psychology of prejudice gained influence in the course of the century. Particularly after the Second World War, American social psychology made a successful contribution to counteracting blunt racism and outright disrespect for other ways of life. The psychology of prejudice and ethnic relations has been less successful, however, in the design of a multicultural society.

Despite its long experience with the mental make up and cultural heritage of a diversity of peoples, psychology lacks a clear-cut answer to questions about the mutual adaptation of peoples from various cultural backgrounds. In fact, looking at the trajectory from "the mind of the savages" to "ethnic identities," it can be characterized as having been wrought from too little social and behavioral science and too much preconceived, unquestioned belief. For example, hardly anyone took the trouble to investigate what made the western way of life so overpowering and driven to sheer usurpation. In particular, the perception that "we" westerners were highly successful whereas "they" in the south and the east were simply trammeled within cultures that resisted westernization, was seldom challenged.[62] There is no answer as yet, because we are only beginning to ask why the western world was so voraciously preoccupied with its own way of life.

PRINCIPAL SOURCES AND FURTHER READING

Colonialism is the relevant historical context for our discussion of culture and ethnicity. The history and impact of colonialism has been covered in thousands of publications. We found particularly helpful: A. Pagden (1993), *European encounters with the New World: from renaissance to romanticism* (New Haven: Yale University Press). Psychological notions of culture and "exotic" identities were linked inextricably to anthropology; see G. Jahoda (1992), *Crossroads between culture and mind* (New York: Harvester Wheatsheaf). An authoritative account of early anthropology is G. Stocking Jr. (1987), *Victorian anthropology* (New York: Free Press).

G. Richards (1997), *"Race," racism and psychology. Towards a reflexive history* (London: Routledge) covers many relevant developments within the confines of (academic) psychology. E. Herman (1995), *The romance of American psychology. Political culture in the age of experts* (Berkeley: University of California Press) is a good source for the social and political context of the postwar psychology of "ethnic relations."

NOTES

1 J. Jamin (1983), Faibles sauvages . . . corps indigènes, corps indigents: le désenchantement de François Péron, in J. Hainard and R. Kaehr, eds., *Le corps enjeu* (Neuchâtel: Musée d'ethnographie), pp. 61–2.

2 T. Ellingson (2000), *The myth of the noble savage* (Berkeley: University of California Press).

3 *Mundus Novus* is rich in detail, but there are some doubts about its authenticity as a first-hand source. See P. Mason (1991), Continental incontinence: *Horror vacui* and the colonial supplement, in R. Corbey and J. Leerssen, eds., *Alterity, identity, image. Selves and others in society and scholarship* (Amsterdam: Rodopi).

4 According to the Bible, Ham made fun of his drunken father Noah who lay naked in a tent. His two brothers Sem and Japheth covered Noah's shame. When Noah heard what happened he cursed Ham and his descendants, the dark "races" (Genesis 9:20–27).

5 There is a large body of literature about the vicissitudes of colonialism, and imperialism. We employed in particular E. Hobsbawm (1987), *The age of empire, 1875–1914* (New York: Vintage Books), T. Lemaire (1986), *De Indiaan in ons bewustzijn* [The Indian in our consciousness] (Amsterdam: Ambo), and Pagden, *European encounters*.

6   As documented in Basil Davidson (1994), *The search for Africa. History in the making* (London: Currey).

7   R. Hughes (1986), *The fatal shore* (New York: Knopf).

8   C. Herbert (1991), *Culture and anomie: ethnographic imagination in the nineteenth century* (Chicago: University of Chicago Press).

9   E. B. Tylor (1871), *Primitive culture* (New York: Harper); E. B. Tylor (1881), *Anthropology, vols. I and II* (London: Watts); Jahoda, *Crossroads between culture and mind*.

10 The presentation here of three different perspectives was derived from Stocking, *Victorian anthropology*.

11 S. J. Gould (1984), *The mismeasure of man* (London: Pelican Books).

12 Jahoda, *Crossroads between culture and mind*, p. 95. The quotation is from Charles Darwin (1874), *The descent of man* (London: Murray), pp. 127–8.

13 In particular see R. Smith (1997), *The Fontana history of the human sciences* (London: Fontana), pp. 467–77. Also: C. Degler (1991), *In search of human nature. The decline and revival of Darwinism in American social thought* (New York: Oxford University Press); B. Massin (1996), From Virchow to Fischer. Physical anthropology and "modern race theories" in Wilhelmine Germany, in G. W. Stocking, Jr., ed., *Volksgeist as method and ethic. Essays on Boasian ethnography and the German anthropological tradition* (Wisconsin: University of Wisconsin Press), p. 120.

14 Richards, *"Race," racism and psychology*, p. 21.

15 I. Kalmar (1987), The *Völkerpsychologie* of Lazarus and Steinthal and the modern concept of culture, *Journal of the History of Ideas, 48*, 671–90; Massin, From Virchow to Fischer, pp. 97 ff. L. Poliakov's *Le mythe aryen* (Paris: Calmann-Lévy, 1971) offers a detailed discussion of the relation between nineteenth-century philology and racist ideas.

16 W. Wundt (1916), *Elements of folk psychology* (London: Allen & Unwin) summarizes the field in an elaborate and tedious manner.

17 This series of extraordinarily refined statues dated back to the fourteenth to sixteenth centuries, were unrelated to any western artistic tradition and thus indicated an autonomous African development in fine arts.

18 M. Bunzl (1996), Franz Boas and the Humboldtian tradition, in Stocking, ed., *Volksgeist*, pp. 17–78.

19 The Cambridge Torres Strait Expedition is discussed in some detail in Richards, *"Race," racism and psychology*, ch. 3.

20 See Jahoda, *Crossroads between culture and mind*, p. 122.

21 E. B. Tichener (1910), On the ethnological tests of sensation and perception, *Proceedings of the American Philosophical Society, 55*, 204–36. For the equivalence problem, see H. Y. Poortinga (1989), Equivalence of cross-cultural data: an overview of basic issues, *International Journal of Psychology, 24*, 737–56.

22 Richards, *"Race," racism and psychology*, p. 41.

23 As documented in H. A. Diederiks et al., eds., *Van agrarische samenleving naar verzorgingsstaat* [From traditional society to the welfare state] (Groningen: Martinus Nijhoff). In particular on pp. 326–7. Also Hobsbawm, *The age of empire*.

24 As the ominous title of the popular, bigoted volume of eugenicist Madison Grant underlines: *The passing of the great race* (New York: Scribner's, 1916).

25 Both quotes are from: F. Galton (1884/1869), *Hereditary genius* (New York: Appleton), p. 131. For a detailed discussion of Galton and De Candolle see R. Fancher (1983), Alphonse de Candolle, Francis Galton, and the early history of the nature–nurture controversy, *Journal of the History of the Behavioral Sciences, 19*, 341–51.

26 As quoted in Massin, From Virchow to Fischer, p. 118.

27 Massin, From Virchow to Fischer, p. 120.

28   Gould, *The mismeasure of man*, pp. 116–17.

29   L. Zenderland (1998), *Measuring minds. Henry Herbert Goddard and the origins of American intelligence testing* (Cambridge: Cambridge University Press), p. 268.

30   R. M. Yerkes, ed. (1921), *Psychological examining in the United States army. Memoir XV* (Washington, DC: National Academy of Sciences–National Research Council).

31   A. Chase (1980), *The legacy of Malthus. The social costs of the new scientific racism* (Urbana: University of Illinois Press). D. Kevles (1985), *In the name of eugenics* (London: Pelican Books), pp. 127 ff.

32   T. R. Garth (1925). A review of racial psychology (1916–1924), *Psychological Bulletin*, *22*, 343–364; quote on p. 359.

33   Kevles, *In the name of eugenics*; F. Samelson (1978), From "race psychology" to "studies in prejudice": some observations on the thematic reversal in social psychology, *Journal of the History of the Behavioral Sciences, 14*, 265–78.

34   Degler, *In search of human nature*, p. 72; Jahoda, *Crossroads between culture and mind*, p. 102.

35   F. Boas (1966), *Race, language, and culture. Collected scientific papers, 1887–1939* (New York: The Free Press).

36   Chase, *The legacy of Malthus*, p. 181 ff.

37   Boas, *Race, language, and culture.*

38   However, the advance of the nurture perspective did not erase racist psychology between the wars. See Samelson, From "race psychology." General developments are discussed in: R. V. Guthrie (1976). *Even the rat was white: a historical view of psychology* (New York: Harper & Row) and in Richards, *"Race," racism and psychology.*

39   K. Pearson and M. Moul (1925–1926), The problem of alien immigration into Great Britain: illustrated by an examination of Russian and Polish Jewish children. *Annals of Eugenics, 1*, 5–127; see for the context of this publication M. Billig (1981), *L'internationale raciste. De la psychologie à la "science" des races* (Paris: Maspero), pp. 32–3.

40   W. H. Tucker (1994), *The science and politics of racial research* (Urbana: University of Illinois Press).

41   C. G. Jung (1930), Your negroid and Indian behaviour, *Forum, 83*, 193–9.

42   For Jung's relations with Nazism see D. Howitt and J. Owusu-Bempah (1994), *The racism of psychology. Time for a change* (New York: Harvester Wheatsheaf), pp. 80 ff. and Richards, *"Race," racism and psychology*, pp. 169–70. The authoritative source for German Nazi psychology is U. Geuter (1992), *The professionalization of psychology in Nazi Germany* (Cambridge: Cambridge University Press).

43   For anthropology and Fischer's role see Massin, From Virchow to Fischer, pp. 138–41. For psychology see Geuter, *The professionalization of psychology.*

44   T. R. Garth (1930), A review of race psychology (1924–1929), *Psychological Bulletin, 27*, 329–56; quote on p. 348.

45   C. C. Brigham (1930), Intelligence tests of immigrant groups, *Psychological Review, 37*, p. 165.

46   J. Dollard, N. E. Miller, L. W. Doob, O. H. Mowrer, and R. R. Sears (1939). *Frustration and aggression* (New Haven: Yale University Press).

47   R. Benedict (1934), *Patterns of culture* (Boston: Houghton Miffin); A. Kardiner (1939), *The individual and his society. The psychodynamics of primitive social organization* (New York: Columbia University Press).

48   M. Mead (1939), *From the South Seas. Studies of adolescence and sex in primitive societies* (New York: Morrow).

49   The Frankfurt project was published in Paris in 1936 as: M. Horkheimer (ed.), *Studien über Autorität und Familie* (Paris: Librairie Félix Alcan). The US research appeared as T.

W. Adorno, E. Frenkel-Brunswik, D. J. Levinson, and R. N. Sanford (1950), *The authoritarian personality* (New York: Harper).

50   In *The nature of prejudice* (Reading: Addison-Wesley, 1954), G. W. Allport says "Most human characteristics ascribed to race are undoubtedly due to cultural diversity and should, therefore, be regarded as ethnic, not racial" (p. 113). The impact of Allport's *Nature* is illustrated by the fact that 500,000 copies had been sold by its twenty-fifth anniversary in 1979.

51   The statement "The effects of segregation and the consequences of desegregation. A social science statement" was signed by 35 prominent scholars, such as Gordon Allport, Jerome Bruner, Kenneth and Mamie Clark, and Otto Klineberg. Herman, *The romance of American psychology*, briefly discusses the political context of the *Brown v. Board of Education* ruling.

52   The most famous, as well as most controversial, presidential commission was the National Advisory Commission on Civil Disorders, generally known as the Kerner Commission. It was established in 1967. See Herman, *The romance of American psychology*, ch. 8.

53   For example by William Ryan in *Blaming the victim* (New York: Vintage Books, 1971).

54   D. P. Moynihan (1965), The Negro family: the case for national action (Washington, DC: Office of Policy Planning and Research); Guthrie, *Even the rat was white*.

55   R. L. Jones, ed. (1972), *Black psychology* (New York: Harper), p. 44. Richards, *"Race," racism and psychology*, p. 293 covers some important developments in so-called "Black psychology."

56   A. Inkeles and D. Levinson (1969), National character: the study of modal personality and sociocultural systems, in G. Lindzey and E. Aronson, eds. *The handbook of social psychology, vol. 4* (Reading, MA: Addison-Wesley), pp. 977–1027.

57   G. Hofstede (1980), *Culture's consequences: international differences in work-related values* (Beverly Hills: Sage).

58   A. R. Jensen (1969). How much can we boost IQ and scholastic achievement?, *Harvard Educational Review*, 39, 1–123.

59   H. J. Eysenck (1971), *Race, intelligence and education* (London: Temple Smith), p. 99.

60   R. J. Herrnstein and Ch. Murray (1994), *The bell curve. Intelligence and class structure in American life* (New York: The Free Press).

61   E. Saïd (1978), *Orientalism* (New York: Pantheon Books).

62   For an inspiring and promising attempt see J. Diamond (1997), *Guns, germs, and steel. The fates of human societies* (New York: Norton).

6 Delinquency and law

Ido Weijers

Introduction

In a sense, one might say that psychology and criminal law have been intertwined from time immemorial, since both are concerned with the interpretation of human behavior. Fundamental legal concepts such as personal responsibility, liability, honesty, fraud, and default presuppose notions about mental phenomena and processes. However, it was only from the mid-nineteenth century that this intertwining became both more explicit and more complex. Since then, criminal law has become imbued step by step with psychological thinking, in terms, concepts, and practices. This psychologization of criminal law became most visible in the context of philanthropic initiatives for the young and of the emerging recognition of the disturbed criminal. In particular, forensic knowledge concerning mental abnormality in criminal offenders emerged in that period as a field of psychiatric expertise.

Today, psychological assessments are important sources of information in a variety of legal contexts, from criminal courts to juvenile and family courts to civil courts. Among the legal decisions that are assisted nowadays by psychological assessments are criminal court issues, such as competence to stand trial, criminal responsibility, and testimony of eyewitnesses, and mental health law decisions such as competence to consent to or refuse treatment. They have a part to play in juvenile delinquency decisions such as pre-adjudication, detention, and transfer to adult criminal courts, in family law matters such as termination of parental rights and foster home placement, and civil court matters such as evaluation of disability claims.[1] Furthermore, psychological techniques are now provided to train advocates in courtroom skills, and professional psychological expertise is used in courtroom simulations for attorneys and witnesses, and in rehearsing the latter using videotapes.[2] Training programs for all areas of criminal justice psychology, including psychological consultation and practice with law enforcement agencies, the courts, correctional institutions, and legislative bodies, now exist at both the pre-doctoral and post-doctoral levels.[3] In addition to this, psychologists are involved in research programs on risk factors and early prediction of delinquency, and also in a wide range of training activities and therapeutic programs for offenders.

Since there are as yet no thorough studies broadly covering the history of psychology and delinquency in the western world, this chapter does not pretend to give a complete overview; it will sketch only some important turning points in that history. Specific attention will be paid to two questions. First, in the relationship between forensic psychology and its older sister, psychiatry, how far has forensic psychology, gaining influence in the field that had been explored by psychiatry, taken over the psychiatrist's expert model? Second, concerning the relationship between forensic psychology and "psychologization," how far can the rise of forensic psychological expertise, with its interest in objective, scientific knowledge, "hard facts" and "laws," be identified with the rise of a psychologizing view in the field of law?

After a very brief sketch of the early history in section 1, the next section will describe the emergence of the concepts of "moral insanity" and of institutional "re-education." Section 3 will cover the ideas of the popular Italian criminologist Cesare Lombroso on the "born criminal" at the turn of the century, the emergence of forensic psychology in the same period, and the expanding psychological field concerning juvenile delinquency. Section 4 will present the establishment of forensic psychology in the 1950s and 1960s, while section 5 very briefly sketches the vicissitudes of forensic psychology in the last decades of the twentieth century, in the Anglo-Saxon world and in the continental European world.

1 Early history (before *c.* 1800)

It seems that lunacy was recognized at a very early date as a relevant factor in the judgment of criminal acts. More problematic was the insane act of a normal, mentally healthy person. On this point there was a new development in the late eighteenth century when the notion of "irresistible impulse" became accepted by courts. The assessment of the relevance of this notion in actual cases could not be left to the judge but required a special expertise, that of the "medico-psychologist."

1.1 *"Not fully accountable"*

The relevance of lunacy to criminal responsibility was already acknowledged in ancient Hebraic law which stated that idiots, lunatics, and children ought not to be held criminally responsible, because they could not distinguish good from evil. In classical Roman law, lunatics and idiots might be protected from punishment and offenders influenced by strong affects could be held not fully accountable for their actions. For a long time the problem presented by insane violence was solved by the rule that it was the responsibility of the madman's kin to pay for the injuries which he had caused and to keep him out of trouble. Later, insanity no longer exempted anyone from trial; it was for the king to pardon or for the jury to decide that the accused was insane and should be acquitted. The criterion became that the offender did not know what he was doing.

Traditional Anglo-Saxon law stated that it was not proper to punish those "without understanding for their deeds." In practice this rule was interpreted as that the madman might not be able to distinguish right from wrong. "Right and wrong tests" and "wild beast tests" might be applied, whereby a jury had to decide whether the accused exhibited "actions more like animal reflexes than moral choice" which exempted the person from culpability. Seventeenth-century legal thinking was authoritatively expressed by the legal commentator Matthew Hale. He recognized the difficulty of defining the range of exculpatory insanity by drawing attention to "episodic" lunatics, who during "lucid intervals" might be held accountable for their misdeeds. He spoke of "partial insanity." Since he believed that most criminals labored under some degree of partial insanity when they committed their crimes, Hale thought that from considerations of public safety this might not be admitted as an excuse. He held the opinion that for acquittal there had to be a total want of reason, whether permanent or temporary.

1.2   *The insanity defense*

By the late seventeenth century, the insanity defense was firmly in place in general legal thinking, yet, in the courtroom, this defense still had to be established. Though successful defenses on the grounds of insanity were not completely unheard of in the seventeenth century, it was only at the end of the eighteenth that courts began to get accustomed to this kind of defense. It was only then that legal systems began to create the necessary conditions for its use and that lawyers began to acknowledge the authority of medical experts in these cases.

In a famous case in 1760, Earl Ferrers was tried before the House of Lords for the murder of his steward. Ferrers had to conduct his own defense, examining and cross-examining witnesses called by himself and the prosecution and submitting his own written statement in conclusion:

> My lords . . . the ground of this defence has been a family complaint; and I have heard that my own family have of late endeavoured to prove me such (sc. a lunatic). The defence I mean is occasional insanity of mind; and I am convinced from recollecting within myself, that, at the time of this action, I could not know what I was about . . . [4]

The crux of his defense was that not only he but also his uncle and aunt were regarded as lunatics. His key witness was the Physician Superintendent of Bethlem, who had diagnosed his uncle. This trial provides the earliest recorded example of psychiatric testimony in a criminal trial. Ferrers was pronounced guilty by their lordships, who relied on a strict reading of Hale: one might be acquitted in case of a total permanent or total temporary want of reason, but not for a partial degree of insanity. However, this widely known trial made the insanity defense more acceptable.

By the 1780s there can be no doubt that both judges and juries were perfectly ready to give their blessing to a defense of insanity. As a judge said in a murder case in 1784:

> Where men suffer their passions to get the better of their reasons . . . they must answer for the consequences; but rage which is the effect of distemper is brought upon them

by the act of God, and not by themselves, and they are not answerable for what they do in those moments.[5]

With no mention of "wild beast" or the ability to tell right from wrong, here we find the model for the modern but contested notion of "irresistible impulse."

The growing acceptance of insanity as negating criminal responsibility expressed both a new view about criminal proceedings and a changing view of madness. In this period the courts began to develop the modern practices of representing the accused by counsel, of expecting counsel to conduct cross-examination and of looking to expert witnesses for specific purposes. This change in criminal proceedings opened an interesting avenue for an emerging group of new professionals, the psychiatrists or, as they were then called, alienists or medico-psychologists. They were the physicians who in this century started to study lunacy, to describe and classify its symptoms.[6] These pioneers made an issue of the question of the accused counterfeiting madness; they set themselves up as experts whose diagnosis would be vital in court.

2 The concept of "moral insanity" (*c.* 1800–1875)

In the nineteenth century there were at least three new developments that were important in shaping the conditions for the relation between psychology and delinquency at the end of that century. First, there was a famous trial in England in 1800, which drew worldwide attention and which gave the insanity defense a new public legitimacy. Second, the "moral insanity" doctrine gained wide popularity from the 1820s onwards, which strongly enhanced the standing of the medico-psychologists. Third, from the beginning of the century there was growing social attention concerning young offenders, runaways, and rascals, and an enthusiasm for their "re-education" which led to the establishment of special institutions for these young people, where they could be observed, educated, and disciplined.

2.1 The "irresistible impulse" defense

In 1800, James Hadfield, who had fired a pistol at the King and was therefore in danger of the gallows, was provided with counsel to address the court. He was lucky to have a brilliant counsel who said he doubted that Hale's reference to such things as a "total deprivation of memory" could have been intended in a literal sense. The madman, he asserted, reasoned from false premises which were "not false from any defect of knowledge or judgement, but, because a delusive image, the inseparable companion of real insanity, is thrust upon the subjugated understanding, incapable of resistance because unconscious of attack."[7] The counsel succeeded in convincing both judge and jury that Hadfield's crime was the consequence of disease. At the start of the nineteenth century, the Hadfield trial established the doctrine that in order to be excused on the grounds of insanity, the accused need not be shown to have lacked all understanding, or the ability to distinguish between right and wrong, if he could be proved to have suffered from a delusion which prompted his act. The crux was that the accused had been impelled to do what he did by the irresistible force of his impulse.

For the alienists this recognition of partial insanity and the successful rejection of Hale's criticism of that defense meant an affirmation of their expert knowledge, psychological medicine. While the law, at least since the Enlightenment, had predominantly conformed to the voluntaristic tradition, at the turn of the century medical science was increasingly moving toward a contrary conception of human beings. Many doctors were beginning to view people less as mental or spiritual subjects who deliberated morally, and more as biological organisms which were subject to physical derangement. This new model clearly had antivoluntarist and deterministic consequences: physical disease of the brain compelled people to act contrary to their own moral standards. The impetus for this new medical view came from France. It was also in this country where a new scientific basis for the partial insanity defense was created.

2.2   *"Monomania"*

At the beginning of the nineteenth century the authority of medical psychology was represented pre-eminently by the work of Philippe Pinel (see chapter 3).[8] He observed that intellectual clarity persisted in the midst of paroxysms, even those leading to "automatic atrocity." He therefore described a disease called *manie sans délire* (mania without delusion), a state of disordered emotion and volition without disorder of reason:

> Finally the nervous affection gains over the brain, and then the lunatic is dominated by an irresistible desire for violence. . . . He exhibits, however, in other respects, the free exercise of his reason, even during his outburst. He replies directly to questions which one puts to him, and he lets slip no incoherence of ideas or sign of delusion. He feels deeply all the horror of his situation; he is racked by remorse as if he reproached himself with this frantic tendency.[9]

Pinel's period of leadership was followed by that of Jean-Etienne Esquirol, who modified the notion of *manie sans délire* and renamed it as a species of *monomanie* in which some delusion would be present. *Monomanie* was insanity focused on one area of perception or action, in some cases accompanied by extensive lucid periods. It existed nosologically between *mélancolie* and *manie*, the apathetic and maniacal poles of lunacy. In fact, the introduction of the concept of monomania contradicted the working assumption of the legal system, that laymen were competent to identify insanity. A madman was unmistakable to a layman, but the essence of monomania was that it was not a total but a partial insanity, requiring a trained medical eye for its identification (see figure 51).[10]

The vicissitudes of the monomania doctrine may be interpreted both as a boundary dispute with the legal profession and as a political dispute about criminal law. In contrast with the Enlightenment tradition of humanitarian jurisprudence, the French nineteenth-century penal code was unapologetically draconian, based upon the prin-

Figure 51 Cartoon on the monomania defense, by the famous French cartoonist Daumier 1846. "What worries me is that I am being accused of twelve robberies." "Twelve . . . all the better . . . I will plead monomania." Source: Psychology Pictures.

ciple that deterrence was the most reliable means of protecting society against crime. While liberals were pressing for mitigation, the monomania doctrine could function only as a contribution to their position. Notwithstanding its fundamentally contested scientific value and its complicated applicability, the monomania or partial insanity doctrine was internationally valued as one of the examples of French leadership in modern medical thinking. Not only in France, but throughout the western world, monomania became the shibboleth of the growing body of alienists.[11]

The monomania doctrine strongly influenced English and American medical thinking, such as that of James Prichard and Isaac Ray. Prichard, a Bristol physician, anthropologist, and philologist, published *A Treatise on Insanity and other Disorders Affecting the Mind* (1835), which set the trend among British alienists for the rest of the century. Following the line of the French alienists, Prichard stated that in some people "the will is occasionally under the influence of an impulse, which suddenly drives the person affected to the perpetration of acts of the most revolting kind, to the commission of which he has no motive."[12] Thus, for the English-speaking world, Prichard translated the doctrine of monomania doctrine into the doctrine of "moral insanity."

Three years later, Ray, an American doctor, published a book that was to become one of the most influential of the nineteenth century on the subject: *A Treatise on the Medical Jurisprudence of Insanity* (1838). Ray was a general practitioner with a strongly naturalistic and mechanistic view of human beings. Human behavior was an aspect of a person's physical nature: "That insanity is caused by disease, or deranged function of this organ [the brain], is a fact now universally acknowledged by medical men."[13] Ray started from an attack on Hale's statement that partial insanity could not be accepted as sufficient ground for acquittal. Convinced of the correctness of the ideas and observations of his shining French exemplars, he rejected Hale's authority. In his opinion modern medical science had proved that people could intellectually grasp the difference between right and wrong but nonetheless be compelled against their better judgment to behave immorally. According to Ray, all homicidal maniacs possessed an "irresistible motiveless impulse to destroy life," as all kleptomaniacs suffered the "irresistible propensity to steal." While criminals always acted by their own volition and from a clear motive, moral maniacs lost their free will to the action of the disease and acted motivelessly and senselessly in spite of themselves. Ray wanted recognition of medical authority in court; not a public test that would define insanity, but a simple, expert rule, which would give free rein to the medical professional.

However, physicians never acquired this absolute freedom in court. It appeared at first that a famous trial in 1843 allowed medical evidence about insanity to have great potential influence. In 1843 a Scotsman named Daniel M'Naghten shot and killed the personal secretary of the Prime Minister. M'Naghten said that members of the Prime Minister's party were following and persecuting him wherever he went, and that he had become convinced that by killing this man his troubles and those of other working-class men would end. M'Naghten's counsel successfully based most of his defense on Ray's book; the jurors returned a verdict of not guilty by reason of insanity. However, the prominence and suffering of the victim, and the threat from the revolutionary movement of the Chartists with which the offender was associated, created a torrent of public outrage. This prompted the House of Lords to request that the judges announce formally the common law criteria for determining legal insanity. Their answers constituted the "M'Naghten Rules," which for more than a century became the dominant formal framework for administering the insanity defense. However, these rules were, in essence, a repudiation of the M'Naghten verdict: the judges said knowledge that an act was right or wrong was the basic test of insanity! Delusion could also be a defense, but only conditionally.

The new rules eliminated much of the vagueness that had existed in Anglo-Saxon common law before 1843. They formed a landmark for English and American courts till far in the twentieth century, but they did not prevent the clash between law and medical psychology on the point of "irresistible impulse." Judges and barristers accepted serious delusions (and idiocy) as reasons for acquittal, but the ideas of partial or moral insanity continued to raise the question of a person's responsibility for getting into a situation where they might act uncontrollably.

2.3   Re-education

Although it is possible to identify a few institutional precedents in sixteenth-, seventeenth- and eighteenth-century Europe, it is clear that until the early 1800s, families, not institutions, were the principal instrument through which communities disciplined children. There often existed stringent laws, but these were rarely enforced. Very often, judges and juries seem to have determined that neither the interests of justice nor a child's well-being would be served by committing the young offender to an adult penal facility and that exoneration and release would be better than incarceration.

Both this practice of absolving children from punishment, and the negative and depressing situation of children who were nevertheless sent to prison, stimulated grave social concern and fed an interest in establishing separate correctional facilities for juveniles in the early nineteenth century. These motives led to the foundation of special youth prisons and penitentiaries, reform schools and industrial schools, penal and agricultural colonies, and houses of refuge all over the western world. The most well-known examples include Das Raue Haus in Germany; Mettray and Petite Roquette in France (see figure 52); St. Hubert in Belgium and Nederlandsch Mettray in the Netherlands; Parkhurst, Kingswood, and Red Lodge in England; the New York House of Refuge, Ohio's Reform Farm, and the Massachusetts Reform School in the United States; and L'Ile-aux-Noix, St. Vincent de Paul, and the Institut St. Antoine in Canada. Initially having regimes and attitudes toward their inmates that were actually little different from those generally directed toward adults, they became the trailblazers of a new approach in this field.

Punishment was relegated to the background and education, reform, and discipline were emphasized. "Love must lead the way; faith and obedience will follow," the most famous reformer, Mary Carpenter, argued:

> For the spirit of fear, which is usually the controlling one in such Schools, is substituted to a great extent that of love. . . . The boy feels that his master is not a mere officer to

Figure 52   An agricultural colony for juvenile delinquents, Mettray, France (*c.* 1845). Its architecture of separate houses reflected the intention to create a family-like environment. Source: Psychology Pictures/Archives of Dutch Psychology.

watch him and enforce discipline, or a mere instructor to teach him, but is a relation, a friend – to sympathize with him and assist him. . . . With regard to the discipline of the establishment, and the rewards and punishments in use, the principle is, that no part of the boy's conduct, however inconsiderable, be unnoticed or overlooked. . . . But strict as the discipline is, the number of masters and officers, and their continual association with the boys, prevent the occurrence of many faults and infractions of the rules which would else arise.[14]

As Steven Schlossman notes, well before Dickens created the fictional archetype, dire portraits of youthful urban predators were quite common among social commentators who popularized the new image of dangerous street urchins, and campaigned for special institutions to house and rehabilitate them.

. . . "juvenile delinquency" was increasingly used to single out the suspicious activities of groups of lower-class children who occupied a netherworld in the bowels of the nation's growing cities and who were perceived to be either living entirely free of adult supervision or serving as pawns of depraved parents.[15]

From the middle of the nineteenth century the foundation of reform schools and similar juvenile institutions became popular in North America, Great Britain, and continental Europe among modern and educated people. At the Second International Penitentiary Congress held in Stockholm in 1878, for example, it was resolved that delinquent children should not be punished but educated so as to enable them to "gain an honest livelihood and to become of use to society instead of an injury to it."[16]

2.4   Conclusion

The Hadfield trial at the beginning of the century gave rise to the insanity defense. This complicated type of defense in turn required a new kind of expertise in court. The introduction of the monomania concept and consequently of the moral insanity doctrine again clearly enhanced the prominent place of the medico-psychologists in the courtroom. At the same time, the establishment of special institutions for young offenders and rogues not only contributed significantly to the creation of a special status for minors within criminal law,[17] but also helped to create a new field of expertise in the assessment of young offenders for their re-education and assistance. Thus, it prepared a new field for the psychologist in the next century.

3   Early psychologization (*c.* 1875–1930)

At the end of the nineteenth century the general perception of crime and delinquency began to change. The emphasis on reason and free will was seen as too simplistic. A new conviction emerged that much of human behavior was determined by forces over which people had little personal control. First there were biological factors such as physical degeneracy, inherited genetic weaknesses, and defective intelligence. Then there were various mental defects. These again required assessment by medical experts. The birth of forensic psychology, though, came from another field, that is, from its contribution to our knowledge about witness testimony.

3.1   The born criminal

In 1876 Cesare Lombroso, an Italian physician, published *L'uomo delinquente* ("The criminal man"), in which he concluded from observations of prisoners and soldiers that criminals were "atavistic." In his opinion some 40 percent of all law violators belonged to a distinct physical type at birth, possessing physical stigmata that were characteristic of an earlier form of evolutionary development (see figure 53).[18] These ideas attracted wide international attention. Although by the turn of the century there were grave doubts about the validity of the notion of an atavistic and physical criminal type, the seed of this biological explanation had been planted and it was growing rapidly (see figure 54). In 1913 Charles Goring, an English physician who had compared several thousand criminals and non-criminals, discredited Lombroso's ideas. At the same time, he concluded that there was a tendency to criminality which was inherited, and that it was specifically "feeble-mindedness," understood as the outcome of poor heredity, that caused crime. In the same years Henry Goddard, an American psychologist, concluded that most delinquents were mentally defective, or "morons" as he called them (see chapter 2).

Figure 53 The brigand of the Bastille, a picture from the atlas of Lombroso's "Criminal man" (1876), showing the typical features ascribed to born criminals, of huge jawbone, deep-set eyes, and protruding ears and forehead. Source: Psychology Pictures.

Notwithstanding their different emphases, the general theme in all these theories was that lawbreaking was due, at least partially, to factors that offenders could not control. The growing acknowledgment of this idea made it more widely accepted that it would be unjust to punish all delinquents for the acts they committed, which implied a shift in attention from criminal acts to criminal agents.

This emphasis on the person who committed the crime, his personality and individual mental status, was also typical of the International Criminalist Association (IKV), which was active and influential on the European continent from the end of the nineteenth century. The German criminologist Franz von Liszt, his Dutch colleague Gerard Anton van Hamel, and their Belgian colleague Adolphe Prins, who were the leading figures in this movement, pleaded for an active criminal policy, based on the assumption that this would lead to a more effective handling of criminals. They criticized classical law with its focus on the criminal act and argued for a modern science-based legal system, in which punishment and special measures should be adapted to the type of offender involved. They emphasized both greater social safety and a sharper focus on the personality of the criminal. In their opinion, a modern criminal policy demanded that one needed to know whether the lawbreaker was a born criminal. Implementation of these ideas led to the involvement of special experts, including first of all psychiatrists, and to special laws concerning psychopa-

Figure 54 The "stereograph," an apparatus devised by the French surgeon and anthropologist Paul Broca to examine skulls of criminals. Source: Psychology Pictures/Archives of Dutch Psychology.

thy. Disturbed behavior became the main issue in the psychiatric report for the courts, meaning mental deficiency, neurasthenia, epilepsy, hysteria, alcoholism, and "degeneracy." A special psychiatric diagnosis was even created, that of "diminished responsibility."

Throughout the western world in the first decades of the new century, there was increased interest in the subjective aspect of the criminal act. Broader definitions of criminal insanity continued to be accepted by the courts. Psychiatric experts began routinely to observe criminal defendants in order to pronounce them fit or unfit to stand trial. When the accused was found fit to do so, courts regularly requested opinions about the limits of his responsibility and about the prospects of the person's future dangerousness.

3.2 The birth of forensic psychology

Though the nineteenth-century experience of "medical psychology" prepared the field for forensic psychology, the roots of this discipline did not lie in the insanity defense, which was viewed as a medical question at the end of the nineteenth century. Forensic psychology sprang from the psychological laboratory, that is, it arose directly from the work of Wilhelm Wundt. The techniques and instruments Wundt devised and in particular the attraction of their applicability to everyday life inspired students from all over the western world to study under him and to spread the spirit of the methodology of experimental psychology. The law was one of the many fields where this approach was applied: the identification of the offender and the reliability of eyewitness testimony were among the first two issues which attracted the interest of the new psychological researchers.

One of the first places to carry out forensic psychological research was the laboratory of James McKeen Cattell in the 1890s in America. Cattell, who had studied in Germany with Wundt, started experiments in human testimony and published his findings in 1895. These experiments generated considerable interest among other researchers, in particular in Alfred Binet who was one of the founders of the first psychological laboratory in France at the Sorbonne, Paris, in 1889. Having studied both medicine and law, Binet was well placed to apply psychology to legal problems. He replicated and expanded Cattell's work and after some years of research in this field he published a book on the suggestibility of witnesses in 1900.[19] The findings of Cattell and Binet in turn stimulated the German psychologist Wilhelm Stern to do research in this area.[20] In 1902 Stern started the first specialized journal in this field, *Psychologie der Aussage* ("Psychology of testimony"), which changed its name six years later to *Zeitschrift für Angewandte Psychologie* ("Journal for Applied Psychology").

The issue of the identification of the actual offender sprang directly from Wundt's experimental work. Completely independently of each other, Max Wertheimer and Carl Jung recognized simultaneously that Wundt's experiments might have the potential to be used for the identification of the actual perpetrator of a crime under investigation. Wertheimer did experiments at the laboratory of Külpe at Würzburg, where he concluded that concomitant involuntary bodily responses to stimulus words could also be simultaneously monitored by psychophysiological means. He suggested the use of the pneumograph, the sphygmograph, and Sommer's tremometer. At the same time Jung collected material on "associations," and conducted a series of experiments at the Burghölzli psychiatric hospital in Zürich, under the psychiatrist Eugen Bleuler. He also inferred that the use of psychophysical measures such as respiration and skin conductance response would increase the reliability of identification of the offender.[21]

These subjects were discussed at different venues in the first decade of the new century. In Europe, psychology entered the courtroom at the end of the nineteenth century. One of Wundt's students, Schrenk-Notzing, is generally acknowledged as the first "forensic psychologist." He was requested in 1896 to testify concerning the credibility of witness testimony in a murder case in Munich. His involvement in this trial enabled him to present the findings of laboratory experiments on suggestibility and errors of recall, which remained one of the key activities of psychologists in court.

Schrenk-Notzing drew attention to the pre-trial publicity about the case and made a plausible argument that the witnesses had failed to distinguish between what they had actually seen happen and what they had heard from the press.

In 1911, another of Wundt's pupils, Karl Marbe, appears to have been the first expert psychologist in a civil trial. He became well known by demonstrating in court the phenomenon of reaction time, proving that an engine-driver assumed to be responsible for a railway accident could not have stopped the train in time to avert disaster. In the same year, a Belgian psychologist, J. Varendonck, testified in a murder trial. Whereas Binet and Stern believed that errors in recollection, whether by children or adults, were primarily a reflection of leading, suggestive courtroom questioning, this psychologist believed that children's recollection was useless in court because their suggestibility seemed inexhaustible. In America, this kind of courtroom appearance was still impossible, as in that same year an American court had confirmed that only medical experts could testify on the question of insanity.

In the US a very important, integrative but controversial contribution to the rise of forensic psychology was made by another American pupil of Wundt, Hugo Münsterberg. Münsterberg set up a psychological laboratory at Harvard in the 1890s, and published a number of essays on psychology and the law in popular magazines, collected together in the book *On the witness stand* (1908).[22] He stated that American lawyers, judges, and juries were convinced that they did not need psychological expertise, and he formulated his purpose of alerting thinking people to an "absurdly neglected" field which demanded the full attention of the public. He criticized the adversarial legal system in America, which appeared to constrain the acceptance and admissibility of experimental psychological knowledge and he passionately advocated the introduction of new technical forensic evidence into court, such as that obtained by hypnosis.[23] However, his book was severely criticized by leading authorities in this field of law.

Psychological expert testimony developed relatively late in the US compared with continental Europe. In 1922, William Marston, a pupil of Münsterberg and the inventor of the "lie detector," became the first American professor of legal psychology (see figure 55).[24] The first published case where an American psychologist actually qualified as an expert witness in court had occurred only one year earlier. The psychologist had been conducting research into juvenile delinquency and concluded that the 12-year-old victim of attempted rape in the case was a "moron" and could not be believed. This psychological testimony was rejected by the court that noted: "It is yet to be demonstrated that psychological and medical tests are practical, and will detect lies on the witness stand."[25] Again, this court's rejection of the psychological evidence may have discouraged other psychologists in the US for some decades from testifying, and it was not until the early 1950s that psychologists began to testify regularly in the American courts.

3.3   Delinquent youth

Nevertheless, psychologists had already been making inroads into other forensic areas, most notably concerning the problem of diagnosing the degree of responsibility of

Figure 55 A lie-detector test (*c.* 1930s). On the right is the inventor of the device, William M. Marston, the first professor of forensic psychology. Source: W. M. Marston (1938), *The lie detector test* (New York: R. R. Smith).

juvenile delinquents. Around the turn of the century, the idea that delinquent youth required an approach fundamentally different from other criminals resulted in the foundation of specialized juvenile courts.[26] The mission of these courts was first of all rehabilitative: they operated from a conception of *parens patriae*, that is, the responsibility of the state to act as a parent, providing corrective programs rather than punishment. This resulted in a renewed interest in the causes of and potential remedies for juvenile delinquency, already an area which involved psychologists. Some psycho-educational clinics extended their practice to include children brought before juvenile courts. Alongside this, some specialized institutes for the assessment of juvenile delinquents were established, mostly led by a psychiatrist but also including psychologists on their staff.[27]

The most renowned example was the Juvenile Psychopathic Institute in Chicago, founded in 1909. Here, clinical psychologist Grace M. Fernald worked with psychiatrist William Healy to develop the first clinic specifically designed for young offenders, and created to serve the newly established Juvenile Court of Chicago. This model of offering clinical diagnoses of problem children under the supervision of a psychiatrist was soon followed in other states and in many European countries. To a certain extent, the Chicago approach was an extension and refinement of the approach of the reformatory institutes we discussed earlier, the major difference being that the emphasis lay on diagnosis rather than treatment. Thus, every child referred to the institute was subjected to a highly detailed, thorough assessment, focusing on mental and moral development as well as family history, school history, and social environment. Healy and Fernald used the relatively new American version of the Binet–Simon Intelligence Scale, the Stanford–Binet, but they soon realized the importance of obtaining "performance" measures as well. This prompted them to develop their own, the Healy–Fernald series of 23 performance tests (see figure 56).[28]

In the 1920s and 1930s, sporadically, there was heavy criticism from within the new institutions which drew attention to a lack of theoretical foundation for the emerging juvenile justice system. This criticism led to a new orientation toward psychology and to psychoanalysis in particular. In Europe, the psychoanalytic experiments of August Aichhorn in Oberhollabrun (1918, Austria) became well known in the following decades. His point of departure was that all deviant behavior of young people must be seen as a symptom of insufficient inner growth resulting from a lack of love in early youth or from emotional neglect. These ideas took off after the Second World War, when they were combined with developmental psychology and phenomenology. The "endangered child" was conceptualized now as a victim of poor treatment psychologically and of educational neglect rather than as a product of social and biological factors. Increasingly, attention was paid to the relationship of the "child-in-danger" with the parents. Re-education meant giving trust and new chances

Figure 56   The Picture Completion Test. One of the diagnostic devices developed by Healy and Fernald for the examination of juvenile delinquents. Source: Archives of the History of American Psychology, University of Akron.

to the children, listening to their stories, and entering into their emotions and life-worlds.[29]

3.4 Conclusion

Crime and delinquency were viewed from a new perspective at the turn of the century. The idea became widely accepted that most delinquent behavior was not so much determined by reason and free will but by forces over which people had little personal control; these might be biological factors, or mental defects, but could also be psychological. The field where the dominant role of psychological forces in determining problematic and delinquent behavior was stressed most emphatically and successfully was the juvenile justice system. Alongside this, the problem of witness testimony provided another avenue for psychologists into the legal setting.

4 Forensic psychology (*c.* 1945–1970)

A complex of social factors, with different national influences and meanings, seems to have prepared the ground for a psychological perspective to flourish in legal systems in the middle of the twentieth century. First of all there was a broader acceptance of the notion of partial insanity. If this reflected primarily on the role of psychiatrists in the courts, psychologists also managed to find some avenues into the legal system. Because of opposition from psychiatrists, it was only in the 1960s that forensic psychology acquired some autonomy.

4.1 Partial insanity

While the notion of partial insanity had been broadly accepted in continental western Europe since the beginning of the century, partly due to the activities of the International Criminalist Association, a new situation emerged in the 1950s in the Anglo-American world. It was in 1954 that Judge David Bazelon of the US Court of Appeals, District of Columbia Circuit, announced the first major deviation from the M'Naghten Rules in any American jurisdiction. Reviewing the history of the "right or wrong" test, Bazelon cited the criticism voiced by Ray in the 1830s, many justices' complaints about the standard, and a devastating report from Britain by a Royal Commission on Capital Punishment. The Court of Appeals specified the rule, to become known as the Durham Rule, that "an accused is not criminally responsible if his unlawful act was the product of mental disease or mental defect." Knowledge of right and wrong therefore lost its central role in the determination of responsibility. This announcement broadened the range of exculpatory conditions embraced by the insanity defense.

A similar change happened in Great Britain. Here it was the Homicide Act in 1957, which introduced the plea of diminished responsibility. This gave the judge discretion in sentencing, and this appeared to mark the legal recognition of a medical

truth, that mental disorder existed in every degree. The plea of diminished responsibility enabled the courts to sidestep the apparently rigorous test embodied in the
M'Naghten Rules, and allowed "abnormality of mind" of whatever kind, if a jury
could be convinced that it substantially affected responsibility, to affect the verdict.

4.2   Forensic psychology

The acceptance in Great Britain and the United States of the idea of partial insanity
mainly affected the role of psychiatrists in court. However, psychologists saw an
expansion of their role as well. The contribution of psychologists to the war effort,
and the increased use of their expertise in other settings, gradually diminished the
skepticism of judges regarding its validity. In due course, it became acceptable to
introduce psychological test results into the courtroom. Clinical and educational psychologists began to find themselves frequently providing evidence for courts, albeit
vicariously, as part of their routine duties. Quantitative psychological data about those
who appeared in court, commonly forming part of a more interpretative report at a
doctor or psychiatrist, added a new dimension to the evidence on which judicial decisions were made.[30]

Another factor associated with the successful use of psychology in court was the
fight in the US to end state-sanctioned segregation in public schools. As this struggle reached its climax, the lawyers involved in a myriad of legal battles recruited social
sciences to their cause. Psychologists were prominent among those who eventually
participated in the fight against segregated schooling. Most notable among these
efforts were the studies conducted by Kenneth Clark, a New York psychologist. Clark
examined the impact of segregation on the children who were fighting in the courts
to end their inferior, separate education (see figure 57). His contribution to the legal
struggle received nationwide attention, first at the trial court level and ultimately at
the Supreme Court in its 1954 judgment. Notwithstanding later criticism of Clark's
findings, the Supreme Court's reference to psychological research in such a major
case established the place of psychology as a potentially useful tool in law. This stimulated some psychologists to focus their research efforts on legal issues. As a result,
applied psychological research from diverse areas has been employed in various fields
of law.

4.3   Toward autonomy

The introduction into the courtroom of the expertise of psychologists caused considerable tension between psychologists and psychiatrists. Initially, psychological
findings were often presented as part of medical evidence, that is, by doctors. This
meant that findings which were inconsistent with medical opinion were generally
disregarded. It was only in the course of the 1950s that this situation altered and
psychologists gained an autonomous position as expert witnesses.

Forensic praxis in each country is often formed more by the restrictions imposed
by its procedural rules than by the qualifications of its psychologists.[31] In West

Figure 57 The psychologist Kenneth Clark testifying in court about the effects of segregation in schools, 1952. Source: Archives of the History of American Psychology, University of Akron.

Germany a breakthrough came as an outcome of a Parliamentary initiative in 1954 for a complete revision of the Criminal Code. With regard to the rules for lack of, or diminished, criminal responsibility, opinions and proposals were collected from both the German Psychiatric Association and the Psychological Association. After a prolonged and fierce argument between the two groups of professionals, the position advanced by the representatives of psychology prevailed. The condition of "consciousness disorder" was defined as a discrete mental disorder, not attributable to a clinical mental condition and caused neither by a pathological physical condition nor a psychoactive substance.[32] This decision granted the forensic psychologist autonomy in court.

A similar situation occurred in British criminal law in 1958, when a psychiatrist appeared to be unable to answer some questions about data, provided by a psychologist, which were incorporated in a medical report. The judge concluded that this occurrence must be considered to be an infringement of the rule governing "hearsay" evidence. The judge decreed that the psychologist should be called as a "medical witness" in his own right, and once established this decision had wider implications.[33]

Finally, in the US four years later there was an even more far-reaching breakthrough, with the famous case in 1962 of *Jenkins v. United States*. Jenkins, after indictment, was committed for mental examination to determine his competence to stand trial and his mental condition at the time of alleged offences of housebreaking with intent to commit an assault, assault with intent to rape, and assault with a dangerous weapon. Jenkins was examined by several psychologists and psychiatrists, all of whom informed the district court that he was not fit to stand trial. He was then committed to a hospital until he should be mentally competent to stand trial. Here a psychologist concluded that Jenkins was schizophrenic, but two psychiatrists, however, found no evidence of mental disease or defect. A second psychologist administered additional tests and concluded that the schizophrenia diagnosis was correct. The trial court tried to solve this problem of diagnostic incompatibility by instructing the jury to disregard the testimony of the defense psychologists that the defendant had a mental disease when he committed the crimes with which he was charged. When this case came to the US Court of Appeals, the American Psychiatric Association submitted an *amicus curiae* brief, advising the court not to allow psychologists to qualify as experts. However, Judge Bazelon, the same judge who had announced the first major deviation from the M'Naghten Rules in any American jurisdiction eight years earlier, declared that psychologists were entitled to present autonomous expert testimony.[34]

4.4   Conclusion

The Jenkins case made it clear that by the end of the 1950s in America, both psychiatrists and psychologists had a role to play in questions of competency and insanity. Since, apart from assessing eyewitness testimony, such questions represented the main concern of American forensic psychologists, the latter appeared to have at last successfully entered the province of forensic expertise by the 1960s. The Jenkins decision opened the door to the admission of psychological testimony in a multitude of legal areas. Since that time, qualified psychologists have continued to testify routinely in cases involving commitment of individuals to mental hospitals, employment discrimination, eyewitness testimony, neurological injury, juvenile placements, and sentencing arrangements, as well as the insanity defense.

Also in the 1960s, a series of comprehensive theoretical statements on criminal behavior were advanced by psychologists. Starting with Hans Eysenck's *Crime and personality* (1964), a body of psychological literature on matters of criminal behavior emerged, with the studies of Megargee (1966), Toch (1969), and others on violence, aggression, and psychopathy. By 1970, forensic psychology had come of age.

5 Recent developments (*c.* 1970–present)

If the 1950s and 1960s saw a general advance of both the psychological perspective and the role of psychologists in the legal system, the picture which emerged since the 1970s has been more ambivalent. On the one hand there has been the growing influence of a psychological point of view concerning delinquency and legal matters in general, shown by increasing calls for psychological expertise amongst other things. On the other hand, however, with regard to the tolerance often associated with a psychological understanding of delinquency, a change in the tone of public and political debate in the American world since 1970 caused a surprising about-face.

5.1 *The growing cultural influence of psychology*

In the last decades of the twentieth century, forensic psychologists have offered opinions and presented data about subjects as diverse as the influence of pre-trial publicity on potential witnesses and juries, the effects of pornography on adolescents, the effect of some educational practices on children, and the likely influence of advertisements on consumers.[35] Furthermore, in continental western Europe a psychological perspective on crime and delinquency has become widespread, especially regarding delinquent acts which cannot be easily understood otherwise. In general, a psychodynamic view has become dominant in this field.

In the Netherlands in particular, special legal arrangements and institutions for diagnosis and treatment were developed, inspired by the Utrecht School (1950–70) approach to criminal law and forensic psychiatry (Willem Pompe, Ger Kempe, and Pieter Baan). This approach involved teamwork between experts from different disciplines, such as psychiatry, psychology, social work, creative therapy, and so on. The psychiatrist had to and still does integrate the different kinds of information, such as medical details, psychological test results, information about the behavior of the client at group activities, information about family and childhood, to provide a diagnostic report for the court.

Within the context of treatment, the concept of the therapeutic community was developed; in these institutions every aspect of living had to be directed toward reintegration into society. In the 1960s socio-therapy and family therapy were made part of this approach, and the practice and discourse of therapeutic reintegration has become firmly established in the last decades. Nowadays there exists a wide intra- and extramural variety of therapies for people with different kinds of problematic behavior, such as sexual delinquents, mentally retarded offenders, or young aggressive offenders.[36]

5.2 *A move backward*

But there is also another, more puzzling side to the recent success story of forensic psychology. This has to do with the role of psychology in the changing public and political climate since the 1970s, in particular in the United States. The Durham Rule of 1954, which accepted the idea of partial insanity, caused much controversy. In many states in the US, it was not accepted and many judges tended to retain the language of the M'Naghten Rules. In 1972, the Durham Rule was replaced by an improved version, known as the Brawner Rule. It stated that a defendant who, as a result of mental disease or defect, lacked "substantial capacity either to appreciate the wrongfulness of his conduct or to conform his conduct to the requirements of the law" was not responsible for criminal conduct.

The Brawner Rule provided a standard for the insanity defense in the federal courts for more than a decade. But as the political climate began to shift in the 1980s, the support for this rule, taken as a typical humane, liberal rule, began to weaken. In 1984, as part of the Comprehensive Crime Control Act, passed by Congress and signed into law by President Reagan, the approach was completely reversed: the definition of a valid insanity defense reverted to the "right and wrong" doctrine! Insanity may now be used as a defense only if the defendant is unable to understand the nature and wrongfulness of his acts.[37]

This about-face might indicate that the understanding, psychologizing view of delinquency which was representative of the changes in systems of justice in continental Europe in the twentieth century was less so in the Anglo-American world. Although since the 1950s psychology may have entered American courtrooms more energetically and all-embracingly than on the European continent, the tolerant, psychological, understanding discourse of delinquency, and its causes and motives, seems to have taken root more firmly in the European law tradition. This difference might be connected to and even be explained by, at least partly, fundamental differences in systems of criminal law.

Whereas Anglo-American law is characterized by adversarial criminal justice, continental European law has inquisitorial criminal court procedures.[38] In the adversarial system each side instructs their own experts, which not only means that the expert is potentially susceptible to bias and to manipulation by lawyers to produce a report favorable to their side, but also that forensic expertise always has a fundamental problem with claiming objectivity. In this system, the forensic expert acts in the service of either the prosecution or the defense. In contrast, the inquisitorial criminal court procedures use court-appointed experts. This system not only presupposes that more objectivity and impartiality is accorded to forensic expertise, but also that it is first of all in court that an attempt is made to get an objective understanding of the person and personality of the offender. European judges want to understand what happened and why. They began to ask for forensic reports at around the beginning of the twentieth century because they wanted to know how to understand disturbed criminal behavior and how to react adequately. In the twentieth century they have also made themselves familiar with psychological contributions concerning delinquency.

6   Conclusion

The birth of forensic psychology was made possible by the emergence of new ideas and practices concerning delinquency in the nineteenth century. In that century was seen both a new interest in the delinquent child and a strong medical interest in the relation between madness and delinquency. New institutions for delinquent and deviant youth were created, and at the beginning of the twentieth century, with the foundation of juvenile courts, a special juvenile justice system was created. Within this setting, psychologists were able to create new fields of expertise, first in testing, and then in therapy and supervision. At the same time, by the end of the nineteenth century, the medical view of madness had begun to be widely accepted by the criminal courts. The growing cultural influence of psychiatry in matters concerning delinquency prompted a new attitude toward disturbed criminal behavior and an interest in the individual offender.

The emergence of forensic psychology at the end of the nineteenth century must be understood within this context. In the twentieth century the role of the psychologist in the field of law has been continuously extended. The real breakthrough for psychological expertise, though, came only in the middle of the century. The decades immediately following the Second World War were a crucial time for the wider acceptance of psychological forensic expertise. While in western society the psychologizing, individualizing discourse on delinquency had already imbued large parts of criminal law thinking by 1950, it was only then that forensic psychologists seem to have appropriated this discourse. Once psychological testimony had been recognized, forensic psychology rapidly expanded to encompass a broad field of professional activities.

However, whereas forensic psychology had gained influence in the field that had been explored by psychiatry, in the United States especially, the favored expert model was science rather than psychiatry. In contrast to the medical perspective on delinquent behavior, many forensic psychologists were and still are interested primarily in what they see as the objective facts of test results, general laws of delinquent behavior, and demonstrable reliability of eyewitness testimony. Consequently, the advance of forensic psychology as a field of expertise does not by definition represent a more understanding, "psychologized" perspective on crime.

PRINCIPAL SOURCES AND FURTHER READING

There is no comprehensive, up-to-date literature on the topics discussed in this chapter. Authoritative resources for early eighteenth- and nineteenth-century developments are: N. Walker (1968), *Crime and insanity in England, vol. 1: the historical perspective* (Edinburgh: Edinburgh University Press); R. Smith (1981), *Trial by medicine. Insanity and responsibility in Victorian trials* (Edinburgh: Edinburgh University Press); J. S. Hughes (1986), *In the law's darkness: Isaac Ray and the medical jurisprudence of insanity in nineteenth-century America* (New York: Oceana Publications); and J. E. Goldstein (1987), *Console and classify: the French psychiatric profession in the nineteenth century* (Cambridge: Cambridge University Press).

An interesting collection of essays on the history of forensic psychology is A. Trankell, ed., (1982), *Reconstructing the past. The role of psychologists in criminal trials* (Deventer: Kluwer). Brief introductions are W. D. Loh (1981), Perspectives on psychology and law, *Journal of Applied Social Psychology, 11,* 314–55; C. R. Bartol and A. M. Bartol (1987) History of forensic psychology, in I. B. Weiner and A. K. Hess, eds., *Handbook of forensic psychology* (New York: John Wiley), pp. 3–21; A. J. Tomkins and K. Oursland (1991), Social and social scientific perspectives in judicial interpretations of the Constitution. A historical view and an overview, *Law and Human Behaviour 15*, 101–20; J. R. Ogloff, A. J. Tomkins and D. N. Bersoff (1996), Education and training in psychology and law/criminal justice. Historical foundations, present structures, and future developments, *Criminal Justice and Behaviour, 23*, 200–35; and G. H. Gudjonsson and L. R. C. Haward (1998), *Forensic psychology* (London: Routledge), pp. 6–23.

General introductions to the history of juvenile justice and child protection are: R. Mennel (1973), *Thorns and thistles: juvenile delinquents in the United States, 1825–1940* (Hanover, NH: University Press of New England); T. Platt (1977), *The child savers: the invention of delinquency* (Chicago: University of Chicago Press); T. J. Bernard (1992), *The cycle of juvenile justice* (New York/Oxford: Oxford University Press); L. T. Empey, M. C. Stafford and C. H. Hay (1999), *American delinquency. Its meaning and construction* (Belmont: Wadsworth Publishing Company); K. W. Jones (1999), *Taming the troublesome child. American families, child guidance, and the limits of psychiatric authority* (Cambridge, MA: Harvard University Press). For a short history of the reform school, see S. Schlossman (1995), Delinquent children. The juvenile reform school, in: N. Morris and D. J. Rothman, eds., *The Oxford history of the prison. The practice of punishment in western society* (New York/Oxford: Oxford University Press), pp. 363–89.

NOTES

1   See T. Grisso, (1986), Psychological assessment in legal contexts, in W. J. Curran, A. L. McGarry and S. A. Shah, eds., *Forensic psychiatry and psychology. Perspectives and standards for interdisciplinary practice* (Philadephia: F. A. Davis), pp. 103–28.
2   M. T. Nietzel and R. C. Dillahay (1986), *Psychological consultation in the courtroom* (Oxford: Pergamon Press).
3   C. D. Spiegelberger, E. I. Megargee, and G. Ingram (1973), Graduate education in the psychology of crime and delinquency, in S. Brodsky, ed., *Psychologists in the criminal justice system* (Urbana, IL: University of Illinois Press), pp. 117–34.
4   Walker, *Crime and insanity*, p. 59.
5   Quoted in Walker, *Crime and insanity*, p. 64.
6   K. Jones (1993), *Asylums and after. A revised history of the mental health services: from the early 18th century to the 1990s* (London: The Athlone Press).
7   Quoted in Walker, *Crime and insanity*, p. 77.
8   M. Foucault (1965), *Madness and civilization: a history of insanity in the age of reason* (New York: Pantheon Books).
9   Quoted in Smith, *Trial by medicine*, p. 36.
10 Goldstein, *Console and classify*, pp. 169–70.
11 Goldstein, *Console and classify*, p. 189.
12 Quoted in Smith, *Trial by medicine*, p. 39.
13 Quoted in Hughes, *Law's darkness*, pp. 37–8.
14 M. Carpenter (1851/1970), *Reformatory schools for the children of the perishing and dangerous classes and for juvenile offenders* (Montclair: Patterson Smith), pp. 325–27.
15 Schlossman, *Delinquent children*, p. 365.
16 Quoted in Platt, *Child savers*, p. 50.

17 J. Trépanier (1999), Juvenile courts after 100 years: past and present orientations, *European Journal on Criminal Policy and Research*, 7, 3, 303–27.

18 D. Draaisma (1995) De Hollandse schedelmeters. Lombroso in Nederland [Dutch craniometrists. Lombroso in the Netherlands], *Feit & Fictie*, *11*, 2, 50–73.

19 A. Binet (1900), *La suggestibilité* [Suggestibility] (Paris: Schleicher).

20 In 1910 Stern published his findings in English: L. W. Stern (1910) Abstracts of lectures on testimony, *American Journal of Psychology*, *21*, 273–82.

21 C. G. Jung (1905), Zur psychologischen Tatbestandsdiagnostik, *Zentralblatt für Nervenheilkunde und Psychiatry* 28, pp. 813–15 [reprinted in English translation in C. G. Jung (1972) *Collected works, vol. 1*, London: Routledge & Kegan Paul, pp. 219–21].

22 H. Münsterberg (1908), *On the witness stand* (New York: McClure).

23 M. Hale (1980), *Human science and social order: Hugo Münsterberg and the origins of applied psychology* (Philadelphia: Temple University Press).

24 For Marston and the history of the lie detector, see G. Bunn (1997), The lie detector, Wonder Woman and liberty: the life and work of William Moulton Marston, *History of the Human Sciences*, *10*, 91–120.

25 Quoted in Bartol and Bartol, *History of forensic psychology*, pp. 11–12.

26 L. T. Empey, M. C. Stafford and C. H. Hay (1999), *American delinquency*.

27 Jones, *Taming the troublesome child*; D. S. Napoli (1987), *Architects of adjustment. The history of the psychological profession in the United States* (New York: Kennikat Press), p. 17.

28 Jones, *Taming the troublesome child*, p. 8.

29 I. Weijers (1999), The double paradox of juvenile justice, *European Journal on Criminal Policy and Research* 7, 3, 329–51.

30 Gudjonsson and Haward, *Forensic psychology*, p. 14.

31 Trankell, *Reconstructing the past*, p. 11.

32 U. Undeutsch (1992), Highlights of the history of forensic psychology in Germany, in F. Lösel, D. Bender and T. Bliesener, eds., *Psychology and law. International perspectives*, (Berlin/New York: Walter de Gruyter), p. 516.

33 Gudjonsson and Haward, *Forensic psychology*, pp. 16–17.

34 See S. R. Smith and R. G. Meyer (1983), *Law, behaviour, and mental health: Policy and practice* (New York: New York University Press), p. 544.

35 Bartol and Bartol, *History of forensic psychology*, p. 14.

36 F. Koenraadt, ed. (1991), *Ziek of schuldig? Twee eeuwen forensische psychiatrie en psychologie* [Ill or guilty? Two centuries of forensic psychiatry and psychology] (Arnhem: Gouda Quint); T. I. Oei and M. S. Groenhuijsen, eds., (2000), *Forensische psychiatrie anno 2000. Actuele ontwikkelingen in breed perspectief* [Forensic psychiatry in the year 2000. Recent developments in broad perspective] (Arnhem: Gouda Quint).

37 L. S. Wrightsman (1987), *Psychology and the legal system* (Pacific Grove: Brooks/Cole Publishing Company), p. 267.

38 E. Fairchild and H. R. Dammer (2001), *Comparative criminal justice systems* (Belmont: Wadsworth), ch. 7.

7 Social orientations

Jaap van Ginneken

Introduction

What is the relation between psychology, individualization, and social orientations? Did social psychology provide specific tools for social management? It is in the nature of psychology, or at least in the nature of the most prevalent view of psychology, that it is primarily preoccupied with people as individuals: with their development, their capacities, their malfunctions. Yet man is also, and most of all, a social being. Psychology has always wrestled with the question of how to conceptualize the social orientations of man. As early as the late nineteenth century, new sub-disciplines such as the psychology of nations or peoples and the psychology of crowds or masses, tried to get to grips with certain aspects of this question.[1] In the earliest years of the twentieth century, the new sub-discipline of social psychology was put on the map and on the agenda, followed by economic psychology, political psychology, and similar fields.[2]

These proposals and initiatives arose from a widespread feeling that the social orientations of individual people were problematic, and increasingly so. I intentionally use the word "social orientations" as a generic, somewhat vague, and non-technical term for the complex amalgamation of ideas, feelings, and predispositions an individual holds toward groups. In different domains, there was a need to make these social orientations amenable to new "scientific" conceptualizations, and ultimately to measurement, prediction, and, if not control, at least a certain degree of management through information, communication, and persuasion. By making people see things in a particular way, one could also manage the probability that they would react in a certain way. It should be added that this need on the part of social institutions was of course met halfway by a corresponding need on the part of individuals themselves. They, too, felt increasingly disoriented and were looking for new forms of guidance, through institutions and mass media. On "essential" subjects such as political ideology, or "trivial" subjects such as fashion, they were looking for cues on such questions as: "what are the limits of acceptable discourse?" or "what are the limits of acceptable appearance?"

In this chapter, then, we will investigate some of the long-term trends which gave rise to these new psychological realities and frameworks. After an outline of the historical construction of social orientations, we will delve somewhat deeper into developments within psychology and sociology which gave rise to the inter-discipline of social psychology. We will focus on the notions of opinion and attitude, and on the subsequent emergence of a specific "O&A" technology in research.[3] We will show that these notions long remained, in the words of McGuire, "names in search of a distinction, rather than a distinction in search of a terminology," but also that research methodology became the cornerstone of the new polling industry.[4] After that, we will take a closer look at the invention of "the public," that is at the ways in which the public and public reactions were habitually constructed.

1 Early history (*c.* 1775–1914)

In what ways had social orientations changed over the centuries which preceded the rise of modern social science? Between the Middle Ages and Renaissance on the one hand, and the Enlightenment and Industrial Age on the other, western Europe gradually shifted from a "traditional" society to a "modern" one dominated by individualist ideologies and practices. Within the framework of the former society, most people's convictions, allegiances, and fates were largely predestined by their faith and birthplace, position, and profession. Within the framework of the latter, by contrast, people's convictions, allegiances, and fates seemed to become much more volatile. They changed or lost faith, and adhered to secular ideologies. They moved freely from one place to the next, and back. Many people lost their social status (for example, aristocrats), others acquired one (for example, bourgeois). Fewer people took up the trade of their parents, more chose to take up entirely different activities. The social orientation of individuals was increasingly problematic – it had to be guessed time and again.

1.1 From "traditional" to "modern" society

Whereas traditional institutions lost their hold, modern institutions gained ground, particularly during what is often labeled as the "long nineteenth century," between the French Revolution (1789) and the beginning of the First World War in 1914. The state became well defined, on national, regional, and local levels, by its borders, its competence, and its rules. The army, the police, and the judiciary were organized along various lines. Large-scale voluntary organizations sprang up, including political parties, trade unions, associations, and interest groups. The family firm was gradually superseded by the national (or even the transnational) corporation.

All these new structures grouped hundreds or thousands, and sometimes hundreds of thousands, of people. They were usually controlled from the top down, but open from the bottom up. They had to deal with prospective recruits or with relevant audiences. Yet the spatio-temporal distance between policy makers and their subjects had become increasingly large and impersonal. For all these reasons, then, various new forms of management of individual and collective subjectivity were called for.

Over the centuries, therefore, a kind of double shift took place, a complementary movement. People's roles within their groups became less given, predetermined, or self-evident. They were increasingly supposed to discover what their own specific talents, opportunities and inclinations were – and therefore what their roles in society could and would be. At the same time, institutions and procedures and their enforcement became both more solid and more subtle. People were increasingly seen and managed as individuals rather than as representatives of larger groups or categories. A more psychological view of themselves and others was first promoted through art and literature, in particular in realist and naturalist novels, and then – from the late nineteenth century onward – by the new psychosocial sciences as well. This process began within the upper classes, and trickled down to the middle and lower classes. People gradually employed a psychological vocabulary to define themselves, for instance, and also received social feedback in psychological terms. Their social orientations were less given and more negotiable. They were confronted with a whole range of models and impulses every day, through urban life and the mass media. They would learn, for example, that certain fashionable products were desirable, that certain poor groups posed a problem, that certain neighboring countries posed a threat. The whole field of social orientations became more dynamic and also more volatile. Efforts got under way to make better sense of these seemingly chaotic processes. After the proclamation of human rights and political freedoms in the American and French bourgeois revolutions, individual citizens were considered sovereign. Their individual freedom was, however, coupled with an increasing emphasis on social management. The authorities tried to guess what citizens preferred and what they would freely choose, in order to anticipate their moves, so as to be able to manage change.

All this held for most major western nations, but the time, speed, and nature of the shift differed considerably between them. Great Britain had been the first to embark upon the Industrial Revolution, and had the longest time to adapt to it. The island nation did not see its social stability also decisively threatened because of its head start and privileged position. On the unruly European continent, however, things were different. France was the second major nation to embark upon the Industrial Revolution, and suffered much greater adaptation problems. Between 1789 and 1889, it went through half a dozen wars, revolutions, and regime changes, before settling for a more or less stable republic. Germany came late to unification, and was the third major nation in Europe to embark upon the Industrial Revolution, but quickly caught up with the others. The amount of disruption in terms of wars, revolutions, and regime changes was even greater there.

As a settler state, the United States had never been a "traditional" society at all, and had soon become the "modern" individualist society *par excellence* – increasingly so after the Civil War. Newly arrived immigrant groups, whether in the mid-western cities or in the "far western" countryside, did not so much share the experience of a common past but much more the view of a common future. The pragmatic dictum "true is what works" became the leading ideology for many Americans.

1.2   Economy and society, politics and the military: the role of information

In order to understand how opinion and attitude "technology" came about, we must delve somewhat deeper into the different social domains where "social orientations" of groups became a source of concern – both for people themselves and for the institutions trying to deal with them. Social orientations could no longer be taken for granted. At the same time, long-term planning and the large-scale mobilization of resources became more important. Thus there was a need to discover new ways of finding out how people felt, about products and other people, institutions and issues, and to anticipate their possible reactions. This kind of knowledge would contribute, it was thought, to more adequate policy-making and organizational guidance. Let us look at what happened in some of the most relevant domains, particularly from the end of the nineteenth century onward.

The economic domain. The arch model of an individualized society is that of the "free" market of sellers and buyers. The Industrial Revolution had led to mass production of consumer goods. They could be made in ever larger quantities and ever better quality. New forms of conservation and packing made it easier to transport and store such products over larger distances and longer periods. The direct encounter and feedback between producer and consumer, however, began to erode from the late nineteenth and early twentieth century onwards. The small shop was increasingly superseded by department stores and large chains. The practice of "branding" developed, in order to restore some kind of privileged psychological relation between supplier and client. A brand or trademark guaranteed the quality of a product and often provided "surplus satisfaction." An extra investment in promoting and maintaining the solid reputation of a brand usually paid off in steady sales and price benefits. Marketing and advertising thus came to the fore, including more systematic approaches and research techniques.[5]

The social domain. The state, of course, had a stake in maintaining social stability. For some time, the Industrial Revolution sharpened the conflict between the capitalist "haves" and the proletarian "have-nots," and stirred rebelliousness. Around the beginning of the twentieth century, socialist parties, syndicalist unions, and anarchist groups caused widespread social unrest, with demonstrations, strikes, or bomb attacks. Liberal campaigners favored limited reforms to keep the peace. But in order to be able to take adequate measures, policy makers first had to know who was worst off, in what sense, and how they felt about it. Census data had gradually become more complete, but often had to be supplemented by more specific research about the living and working conditions of the poor, their health, and their education. Such social surveys were carried out in all major countries. The best known English examples are Charles Booth's *Life and labour of the people of London* (1889–1903), and Rowntree's subsequent investigation in York (1903).[6]

The political domain. After the concepts of popular sovereignty and the "general will" had been introduced, there was a shift in the balance of power, which accelerated toward the end of the nineteenth century. Increasingly, absolute monarchs and inherited aristocracies were forced to cede their prerogatives to bourgeois leaders, elected governments, and parliamentary assemblies. At first, these were chosen only by a small elite of well-to-do adult male citizens. But gradually the suffrage criteria were widened to include ordinary people, younger people, and ultimately women as well. Parties and candidates tried to calculate which districts they could carry. Governments changed rules and districts in attempts to influence the results. By

1900, electoral geography became an art and a trade; it proved worthwhile to study the details of past results in order to predict future outcomes. Newspapers began to interview both opinion leaders and the "common man" to foresee possible future shifts in popular mood. "Straw voting" and other ways of "pre-scientific" sampling of opinions came into the picture.

The military domain. Mercenary or professional armies were gradually replaced or enlarged by conscript armies. Compulsory service prepared all adult men to be drafted whenever the need arose. They had to be indoctrinated with patriotism and drilled. Increasingly, furthermore, wars were not limited affairs decided on the bat-tlefield alone. The front line was supplied with weapons and ammunition by the industrial home base. Firepower became decisive. When adult men left for the front, women and youngsters replaced them in the factories. By 1914, major international alliances had formed to fight the first "world" war. The battle for the hearts and minds of the public became important: not only at home, but also in neutral coun-tries. When the huge and distant US gave up its initial neutrality, and decided to join Britain and France, for example, this proved decisive. During the war, atrocity prop-aganda on both sides took on massive proportions. Social psychologist Kimball Young noted that these "paper bullets" may not have decided the war, but they played a major role.[7] After peace returned, the apparent gullibility of the media and the public remained a major source of concern, and inspired major studies on public opinion and communication, in the United States, for instance, by pioneers such as Lippman and Lasswell.

The domain of the media. Meanwhile, the media had become both more massive and more impressive and acquired a key role in the production of social orientations. As education spread, several major countries now sold an average of one or more daily newspapers per household. Magazines began to use color, and drawings were gradually supplemented with screened photographs (although color pictures came only later). After the First World War, sound recordings were introduced with the gramophone, and moving images with the cinema. Radio introduced "live" news reporting and soap operas. Film came to feature sound and later color. After the tran-sition from military to civilian production, and with the popularization of a new range of more expensive household convenience goods (bicycles, sewing machines, vacuum cleaners, refrigerators, etc.), marketing and advertising campaigns received a further boost. It became imperative to test products and advertisements before they were introduced. Scientific methods were deployed, as well as the findings of psy-chophysiology and experimental research (see figure 58). In the course of the 1920s, market and media research became more focused and targeted. For example, the

Figure 58   The psychology of advertising, *c*. 1920s. Based on experimental research on per-ception, psychologists argued that the picture at the bottom would have the greatest impact: reducing the drawing to its essentials would make the message clearer, and the reversal of black and white would attract more attention. Source: Psychology Pictures.

Heimlicht = das Kino im Hause!

Heimlicht = das Kino im Hause!

technique of "paired comparisons" was developed which later became the basis for "attitude measurement" – as we will see below.[8]

Information and public relations in general. In ever-increasing numbers, institutions came to hire professional spokespeople, such as press and information officers, in order to handle relations with the news media, with opinion leaders, and with relevant audiences.[9] These experts, too, needed scientific guidance. "Robber baron" tycoons had been exposed by "muck-raking" journalists in the US. But from the First World War onward, their "public relations" became smoother. The super-rich set up foundations. The Carnegie, Rockefeller, and Ford foundations did not limit themselves to philanthropy, furthermore, but became major sponsors of social research. Companies also began to run publicity departments. Utilities initiated information campaigns. Pressure groups, social organizations, political parties, individual candidates, and many others joined the widening battle for the hearts and minds of the public.

1.3   Conclusion

Toward the end of this period, then, there was a mounting preoccupation with the social orientations of masses of individuals, whereas those individuals themselves were also increasingly looking for guidance through the media. Opinion, communication, and persuasion processes were thus gradually "problematized."[10] To the public itself (as the outcome of an election or a war might depend on it), and to the major institutions in these fields (as the success of a product or a newspaper depended on it), winning over public opinion seemed to hold the key to everyone's success. Substantial budgets were allocated for the elaboration and application of new scientific concepts and techniques.

Two things were needed. On the one hand, a new and specific discipline or interdiscipline for the study of the social orientations of individuals, a field of social psychology, was required. And on the other hand a series of techniques, which would make these social orientations amenable to measurement, prediction, and control, such as opinion-sampling and attitude-scaling, were also needed. Although the ground had been prepared from the late nineteenth century onward, these developments only really took off during the interwar period and crossed a threshold between 1925 and 1935.

2   A psychological perspective (*c.* 1900–1930)

From the late 1800s onward, social orientations became a field of interest for both psychologists and sociologists. Almost all the scholars of the time agreed that the theme required cooperation between these disciplines. Nevertheless, to this very day, a genuine interdiscipline of social psychology has never really become viable. By this is meant a genuine link between two disciplines, where psychologists and sociologists would work as equals to bridge the gap between their respective disciplines, frames of mind, and conceptual approaches. There always remained a social psychology of psychologists, which mostly focused on individual processes. In certain respects it became the prime claimant to the term, since "social psychology" seemed to refer to a special branch of psychology. It is on the development of this psychological social psychology that we will primarily focus: that is to say on the emergence of a psychological perspective on the social orientations of individuals.

Yet there also developed a sociological social psychology, a psycho-sociology so to speak, in the United States, for example, within the so-called Chicago School (Park) and the subsequent symbolic interactionist approach (Blumer).[11] It was much more concerned with small-scale everyday social processes, with the negotiation of meaning and "frame analysis" (Goffman). In academe, the two sub-disciplines continued to drift apart. As there was no way to study social psychology as such, students and scholars were forced to choose either psychology or sociology, and then a certain specialization within the framework of that field. It was only in interdisciplinary projects for practical purposes in the world outside the academic sphere (for example, during the war) that the disciplines truly came to collaborate. Elsewhere, they largely continued to speak their own language, and each found it hard to understand what the other was talking about. But let us first go back again, to the origins of the field of social psychology.

2.1 The problem area: between psychology and sociology

Empirical psychology had become a noteworthy enterprise from the late 1870s onward, and empirical sociology from the late 1880s. But in the course of the 1890s it became increasingly clear that they did not get along satisfactorily. They employed different notions and methods, and often found it hard to agree on what united rather than separated them. Similar problems recurred in adjacent disciplines, such as ethnology and criminology. Were individual processes in these fields the result of social processes, were social processes the result of individual processes, neither, or both? Such discussions raged in all major western countries, and were of course closely related to professional claims to intellectual territory and exclusive expertise.

In France, for example, such debates pertained to demographic· statistics on suicide, and also murder and other crimes. In a famous study, one of the founding fathers of empirical sociology, Émile Durkheim, set out to demonstrate that suicide rates were the result of social factors rather than of individual tendencies. One of the founding fathers of empirical criminology, Gabriel Tarde, by contrast, had demonstrated in an earlier study that imitation played a major social role as well. They held a series of public debates, which soon soured into a fiery polemic. It illustrated that the sociological approach and the psychological approach were drifting apart, and that the links between them were gradually almost severed. A "social psychology" should obviously fill the gap, but on what basis?

Whereas Durkheim developed his notion of "collective representations," Tarde went on to develop the groundwork of an interactionist theory of public opinion. He developed a two-factor theory of attitudes (around beliefs and desires) and even suggested that they might ultimately be "measured."[12] He published a book titled *Études de psychologie sociale* ("Studies of social psychology") as early as 1898 (that is to say a full decade before the first major Anglo-American texts included that term in their titles), and also a book titled *Psychologie économique* ("Economic psychology") as early as 1904. Tarde's influence in France remained rather limited, but many of his key ideas were subsequently picked up by Anglo-American pioneers of social psychology, such as McDougall, Ross, and many others.[13]

This early social psychology, however, was caught between an empirical psychology which tried to derive its legitimacy from a close association with biology and medicine, with neurophysiology and psychophysiology, and an empirical sociology which tried to derive its legitimacy from a close association with established studies of culture and religion, but also the rapidly expanding field of social statistics. The question of whether one should understand social orientations as a purely individual or as an intrinsically social phenomenon remained at the heart of these controversies.

William McDougall moved from psychophysical anthropology to social psychology, and from Great Britain to the United States. His "hormic" psychology was derived from a theory of instincts. In 1908, in his *Introduction to social psychology*, McDougall said instincts shaped "knowing, feeling as well as doing" – later identified by others as the "three factors" underlying attitudes (pp. 19 ff.). His later book on *The group mind,* which claimed that crowds, nations, and races all tended to develop some kind of collective consciousness (p. 31), rekindled the discussion on collectivist versus individualist "fallacies" in social psychology – as critics accused him of "reifying" such supra-individual entities.

American sociologist Edward Ross, by contrast, had moved from economics to sociology. The marketplace of goods was an implicit model for "the marketplace of ideas." His earlier book, *Social control,* was already heavily indebted to Tarde, and so was his 1908 *Social psychology – An outline.* Just like Tarde, Ross gave a key role to interaction and to public opinion as an ongoing "discussion that attracts general attention" (p. 346).

Psychological social psychology, by contrast, came to be much more firmly rooted in a purely individualist approach to social orientations – which also happened to square reasonably well with the subsequent hegemony of behaviorism. The key to this psychological social psychology lay with the Allport brothers. The elder brother, Floyd Allport, vehemently rejected McDougall's "group mind fallacy," and defined social psychology as the "study of social behavior and the social consciousness of the individual." As an editor of the *Journal of Abnormal Psychology,* he soon inserted "*and Social*" into the title, and later became editor of the first *Journal of Social Psychology.*

Allport's book, *Social psychology,* published in 1924, became the first real textbook of the new sub-discipline; it was aimed at junior academics and students, and already included a full section on attitudes.[14] From the 1920s onward, then, the new sub-discipline really took off. Ten years later the younger brother, Gordon Allport, could already count no fewer than 52 books on social psychology, and 16 definitions of the key notion of attitudes.[15] But let us first take an even closer look at that key idea.

2.2   Concepts of opinion and attitude

The core idea of attitudes tended to be conceptualized and researched in rather different ways. The common idea was that people's social orientations could be inferred

– not only from their overt behavior, bodily gestures and facial expressions, but even more easily from their verbal expressions. There were basically two ways of using the latter as a point of departure. At one extreme, one could collect a wide range of such verbal expressions as they had been freely produced in the past, and had been recorded in some way in writing, through letters and diaries, testimonies, and life histories. This usually produced a vast array of discursive material which was varied and natural, but not easy to reduce to clear-cut elements. The other extreme was to elicit unequivocal reactions to isolated statements prepared in advance. This was of course much more artificial, but had the advantage of producing "clear-cut" results. The latter approach therefore gradually gained the upper hand, or at least within mainstream social psychology.[16]

The next question concerned what ought to be inferred from these verbal expressions. One could of course ask for quasi-factual information: what, when, where? But this did not necessarily tell one much about people's social orientations. It seemed more interesting to ask people their evaluation of things: how do you feel about this, that, or the other? Yet it seemed that a further distinction should be made. Did the statement only say something about the present state of mind, a superficial and temporary social orientation; was it "just another opinion"? Or did the statement also say something about a probable future state of mind, a supposedly deeper and more stable predisposition? Of course there was a definite preference for the latter concept, even if it would largely remain a hypothetical construct. There was a definite need for a stable psychologization of social orientations. That is how the everyday concept of "attitude" acquired a new meaning and a key significance for the social psychology that emerged.

The word "attitude" was of course not new, but had gradually acquired a more precise meaning in various fields.[17] On the one hand, in the cultural domain, "attitude" emerged as a concept in the discourse about art because visual arts and the theater were profoundly concerned with making inner states visible. In fact, the artefacts were assumed to express an inner reality in an outwardly visible form. This approach could well, of course, be extended to literary characters, or to real-life people for that matter. On the other hand the word "attitude" had gradually acquired a more precise meaning in the scientific domain, for instance in the works of Charles Darwin, where "attitude" referred to the organized motor activities of the organism which constituted the expression of an emotion, or in the work of the neurophysiologist Charles Sherrington. Such references also seemed to make the construct legitimate and appealing to functionalist psychologists and behaviorists.

Yet, the first explicit use of "attitude" as a key notion in the framework of an emerging social psychology was by the American sociologist William Thomas. He had received funds to do a major study on the acculturation of immigrants, and recommended that verbal utterances such as private letters, diaries, court and church records, sermons, and school curricula be used as data. This resulted in a work of no fewer than 2500 pages on *The Polish peasant in Europe and America* (1918–20), co-authored with his younger Polish collaborator Florian Znaniecki. A lengthy "methodological note" served as an introduction, in which they presented two fundamental problems: "(1) the problem of the dependence of the individual upon social organization and culture, and (2) the problem of the dependence of social organization and culture upon the individual." Thomas and Znaniecki continued by putting forward attitudes and values as the relevant data:

> By attitude we understand a process of individual consciousness which determines real
> or possible activity of the individual in the social world . . . By a social value we under-
> stand any datum having an empirical content accessible to the members of some social
> group.

But the two should always be seen as interconnected, they argued, and attitudes
should not be disconnected from the study of social life as such.[18]

Yet contemporary psychologists obviously held a different view. The aforementioned first major textbook, *Social psychology*, published in 1924 by Floyd Allport,
stressed that "there was nothing in human social life, except *separate individuals* and
their reaction to each other as external stimuli" [emphasis in the original]. It defined
an attitude as "a preparation in advance of the actual response" of social behavior
or even as "neural settings" (p. 320). His younger brother and colleague Gordon
Allport later defined an attitude as "a mental and neural state of readiness, organized
through experience, exerting a directive or dynamic influence upon the individual's
response to all objects and situations with which it is related." He also noted that
several early writers even went so far as to simply define social psychology as "the scientific study of attitudes."[19]

As the historian of psychology Kurt Danziger has demonstrated, such definitions
of attitudes as enduring predispositions implied three assumptions.[20] First that attitudes were learned (and could therefore possibly be unlearned as well). Second that
they were an individual attribute and not an intrinsic part of social (and discursive)
reality. And third that they were inner states which could be inferred from their outer
expression. Thus psychologists gradually reified attitudes as "things inside," which
could be measured, predicted, and controlled (or at least tentatively influenced). That
was both the weakness and the strength of the attitude concept, or in advertising and
marketing language, its "unique selling proposition."

It was hoped that the quantitative approach might lead to widespread, and unfore-
seen, applications and success in the wider world, as had already happened with the
concept of intelligence. If one could measure attitudes, one could also measure individual differences in social orientations before and after a communication campaign,
and thus the effectiveness of the information and persuasion efforts, which had continued to become ever more widespread. This indeed held the key to societal success,
as developments were quick to show.

2.3   Conclusion

As we have seen, by the end of the nineteenth century, and at the outset of the twentieth, a new type of society had emerged in western Europe and North America.
Freedom and popular sovereignty spread, within markets and states. Yet the choices
which people tended to make (whether as consumers or citizens) had to be anticipated somehow. Their social orientations were thus problematized within the framework of a new interdiscipline, which had to find its place between psychology and
sociology. It soon focused on eliciting people's opinions about relevant subjects, and
on postulating underlying enduring predispositions which could somehow be derived

from them. Those "attitudes" were thought to hold the key to the prediction of future choices.

The shift toward, and breakthrough of, the term "attitude" has been traced in detail by Kurt Danziger who concluded:

> Whereas the use of the term "attitude" had been unusual in sociological, psychological and social psychological textbooks prior to 1920, it occurs in half of the texts published between 1920 and 1925; between 1925 and the beginning of the 1930s that figure rises to 80 percent.

This success story of the new concept continues to this very day, he added:

> during the most recent twenty-year period over 34,000 published studies addressed attitudes in some way.[21]

To sum up, "attitude" became a key notion in the new field of study of the social orientations of individuals and never disappeared from the scene.

3   New instruments and practices (*c.* 1935–1960)

Postulating opinions and attitudes was all very well, but how could they be made "operational"? It would of course be nice to have instruments to "measure, predict and control" (or at least influence) them. Questionnaires had been developed, but they did not always yield precise results. Also, it was impossible to ask entire populations for their opinions, so sampling techniques had to be further developed. The answers in their turn were often complicated and unwieldy, so scaling techniques also needed to be refined. The major breakthroughs on both scores occurred somewhere between 1925 and 1935, and the new practices then began to spread on the eve of the Second World War.

3.1   Scaling and sampling

In the wake of the gradual "fleshing out" of the attitude concept, various psychologists attempted to develop ways in which attitudes could be "measured." One obvious way to do this was to produce a series of statements about an issue, and have them ranked from weak to strong, or from negative to positive. The interviewer could either order the statements himself, or have them ordered by the interviewees. One could have them ordered in categories, or by paired comparison. Within the framework of psychophysiology, similar methods of ordering the "subjective" experience of "objective" stimuli had already been in use for some time. Statistical methods had also been developed to translate the ordering process into quantitative scores, either for (the experience of) the stimuli themselves, or for (the position of) the interviewees. They could be arranged along a continuum, on the (often unproven) assumption that there was a single underlying dimension.

Chicago sociologist Robert Park inspired the earliest attempts at some kind of atti-tude-scaling by sociologist Emory Bogardus, author of an earlier book about social psychology.[22] By 1925, Bogardus proposed a method to measure what he called "social distance" by having people judge whether they would accept a member of another national or ethnic group (ranging from "Canadians, English, Scots and Irish" to "Turks, Hindus, Mulattos and Negroes") as a compatriot, neighbor, chum, or family member.[23] Work by the psychometrician Cattell had preceded early attempts by the aforementioned psychologist Floyd Allport. By 1925, Cattell and his colleague Hartman had published a list of statements that represented current opinions on political issues, for example, Prohibition (of alcohol), which was a very controversial topic in the twenties.[24]

This set the stage for the next and decisive step made by Leon Thurstone (origi-nally Thunström): an American of Norwegian descent, but also a psychologist with a background in engineering and a training in mathematics. He later remembered:

> Our work on attitudes was started when I had some correspondence with Floyd Allport about the appraisal of political opinions, and there was discussion here at the time about the concept of social distance which had been introduced by Bogardus. It was in such a setting that I speculated about the possible use of the new psychophysical toys.[25]

Note, by the way, that Thurstone's key article "Attitudes can be measured," which became a kind of manifesto for psychologists, was published in the *American Journal of Sociology* in 1928. So although the disciplines of psychology and sociology were drifting apart, particularly with regard to attitudes, they were still on speaking terms.[26] At the same time it should be added that similar but crude techniques were already widely used within the extra-academic framework of marketing, advertising, and media research, from where they also spilled over into practical opinion research.

But there was still another problem to be solved: that of sampling larger popula-tions. By 1928, the introduction of the first national commercial radio network in the United States posed a specific challenge. With newspapers and magazines, adver-tisers had counted on feedback through circulation figures and return coupons. But how could the nature of the audience for radio be established, and the ratings, or even reasonable advertising rates? This could only be done by interviewing repre-sentative groups, either in person or by telephone. This implied a refinement of existing methods of random and quota sampling, which had in turn already been under development within the framework of population censuses.

The broader social context was decisive in other respects, too. The "roaring twen-ties" had been a period of rapid economic and financial growth, characterized by social and political optimism. The stock market crash of late 1929, however, led to economic and financial depression, and social and political instability. In order to counter these trends, president Herbert Hoover began to strengthen social research, social planning, and social programmes.[27] The emerging O&A technology tended to become a key element within this newly emerging field of social management.

This practice of social management was further reinforced when Democratic pres-ident Franklin Roosevelt came to power in 1932, and embarked on the New Deal. At the time, George Gallup had already done some voter research for his mother-in-law, a candidate at state level.[28] At the following election, Republicans hoped for a backlash, and expected their presidential candidate to win back the highest office in 1936. The magazine *Literary Digest* once again organized a "straw vote" of more than a million people, and predicted a Republican victory. But market and media researchers such as Elmo Roper, Archibald Crossley and most of all George Gallup, interrogated much smaller "representative" samples and foretold a Democratic victory instead, and what is more, their new "scientific approach" came up with the correct prediction.[29]

This breakthrough in sampling techniques completed the basic framework of a genuine O&A technology. The first textbooks appeared, and the very next year, the founding of the *Public Opinion Quarterly* marked the establishment of a new field. Research institutes were founded, and polling results were stored for secondary analysis.[30] At the same time, Gallup's American Institute of Public Opinion (AIPO) set up the British Institute of Public Opinion (BIPO) in 1936,[31] whose results were published in newspapers such as the *News Chronicle,* and later in the *Daily Telegraph.* The BIPO was the first overseas branch of what was to become the first of several international networks of polling agencies.[32] France followed in 1937, there even was an interest in Germany, but further development of this key element of "democratic management" on the European continent soon stalled. In 1939 the war broke out, and in 1940 most of the continent was occupied. Free markets and free elections were wiped out by totalitarian regimes.

Although there was experimentation with the new techniques, their full blossoming on the continent had to wait until peace had returned in 1945. From that moment on, the new technology quickly spread to all major countries. Opinion polling and attitude measurement became the latest scientific "trick of the trade," although psychologists shared its use with sociologists, economists, political scientists, and their like. By the late 1940s, the Gallup organization claimed affiliates in a dozen different countries; and by the early 1970s in even more than thirty. At that point, its founder reported that "since the establishment of the [Gallup] Poll, approximately 20,000 questions have been asked of more than two million people."[33]

3.2 European approaches and migration

We have seen that the new techniques of opinion and attitude measurement emerged in the US around 1935. Yet it is important to note that the tendency to "psychologize" social orientations was not exclusively American. Similar trends could be seen throughout the free market and "open democratic" societies of the western world, and increasingly so as these societies were threatened by crisis and war. It is notable that other similar efforts had already been underway when O&A technology took over as the most practical method of monitoring the evolution of collective subjectivity (albeit as a mere aggregate of individual subjectivities). So let us take a brief look at some contrasting earlier techniques, and at some similar contemporaneous techniques which emerged elsewhere.

One particularly interesting alternative technique that rose and declined during this very same period was the British Mass Observation (M.O.) project. It was aimed at the systematic observation of public behavior, and the systematic reporting of public exchanges, on certain topics. Similar efforts had of course been undertaken by the internal security agencies of some countries at home (for example, in revolutionary and Napoleonic France), and abroad by colonial field researchers (as well as by animal watchers). M.O. was initiated by the self-styled ornithologist and anthropologist Tom Harrison, the poet Charles Madge (who later became a sociologist), and the film-maker Humphrey Jennings.

They employed large numbers of full-time observers and volunteers. Their first report was on the public reactions to the coronation of George VI. Subsequent reports focused on leisure, dancing, pubs, and smoking, but also on religion, politics, and the war. Intermittent sponsors ranged from the Ministry of Information to private companies. But after peace returned, interest in the rather elaborate technique faded away, and it was gradually replaced by opinion polling.[34]

At the same time it should be recognized that the techniques of systematic interviewing and the opinion polling of sample groups had been gradually been developing generally, not only in the fields of market and media research, but also in those of social and political investigation. In the Germanic world, for instance, they also developed at the intersection of the academic world and the workers' movement. In Vienna, a socialist student of psychologists Karl and Charlotte Bühler had set up a social research institute, which carried out a major survey among the unemployed in the suburb of Marienthal as early as 1930, and which was favored by the trade unions. This individual, Paul Lazarsfeld, then received a Rockefeller grant for study in the US, migrated there, became involved in early radio research, and subsequently played a key role in the further refinement of opinion and attitude research.[35]

The Bühlers had also collaborated with the Frankfurt Institute of Social Research. This left-leaning institute initiated a series of major studies on the evolution of the mentality of workers and employees under the Weimar Republic. After the Nazis came to power in Germany in 1933, the Institute moved (via Geneva) to Paris, where its pioneering *Studies on authority and family* were published in German in 1936 under the direction of Max Horkheimer, with major contributions from, for example, Erich Fromm and Herbert Marcuse. Meanwhile, the Institute had moved on to New York. In the US, the Frankfurt researchers became involved in a major study of anti-semitism, which ultimately resulted in the famous attitude survey on *The authoritarian personality* by Adorno and his colleagues (see figure 59).[36]

3.3   *Wartime management of social orientations*

As soon as it had become clear that America would be drawn into the European and Asian wars, a huge effort got underway to mobilize all industrial, technological, and scientific resources for the largest confrontation ever. Applied psychology and sociology also came to play a major role, especially social psychology, in all kinds of O&A studies of civilian and military morale. As one well-known social psychologist later put it, this "was total war involving the participation of civilian populations as never before . . . To develop overwhelming military power, a task of social organization was required unparalleled in history."[37] Social psychologists and O&A specialists were

TABLE 4 (IV)

THE TOTAL ETHNOCENTRISM SCALE

Public Opinion Questionnaire E

The following statements refer to opinions regarding a number of social groups and issues, about which some people agree and others disagree. Please mark each statement in the left-hand margin according to your agreement or disagreement, as follows:

+1: slight support, agreement   −1: slight opposition, disagreement
+2: moderate support, "   −2: moderate opposition,   "
+3: strong support,   "   −3: strong opposition,   "

_____ 1. The many political parties tend to confuse national issues, add to the expense of elections, and raise unnecessary agitation. For this and other reasons, it would be best if all political parties except the two major ones were abolished.

_____ 2. If there are enough Negroes who want to attend dances at a local dance hall featuring a colored band, a good way to arrange this would be to have one all-Negro night, and then the whites could dance in peace the rest of the time.

_____ 3. Patriotism and loyalty are the first and most important requirements of a good citizen.

_____ 4. Certain religious sects whose beliefs do not permit them to salute the flag should be forced to conform to such a patriotic action, or else be abolished.

_____ 5. The Negroes would solve many of their social problems by not being so irresponsible, lazy, and ignorant.

_____ 6. Any group or social movement which contains many foreigners should be watched with suspicion and, whenever possible, be investigated by the FBI.

_____ 7. There will always be superior and inferior nations in the world and, in the interests of all concerned, it is best that the superior ones be in control of world affairs.

_____ 8. Negro musicians are sometimes as good as white musicians at swing music and jazz, but it is a mistake to have mixed Negro-white bands.

_____ 9. Although women are necessary now in the armed forces and in industry, they should be returned to their proper place in the home as soon as the war ends.

_____ 10. Minor forms of military training, obedience, and discipline, such as drill, marching and simple commands, should be made a part of the elementary school educational program.

_____ 11. It would be a mistake to have Negroes for foremen and leaders over whites.

_____ 12. The main threat to basic American institutions during this century has come from the infiltration of foreign ideas, doctrines, and agitators.

_____ 13. Present treatment of conscientious objectors, draft-evaders, and enemy aliens is too lenient and mollycoddling. If a person won't fight for his country, he deserves a lot worse than just a prison or a work camp.

_____ 14. Negroes may have a part to play in white civilization, but it is best to keep them in their own districts and schools and to prevent too much intermixing with whites.

_____ 15. One main difficulty with allowing the entire population to participate

Figure 59 An ethnocentrism scale. From T. W. Adorno et al. (1950), *The authoritarian personality* (New York: Norton).

employed by the intelligence services and many other bodies in the information, communication, and persuasion fields.

Most relevant for the full blossoming of O&A technology was the United States Office of War Information, which came to employ close to six thousand people. In addition, the Information and Education Division of the US Army had a Research Branch, supervised by Samuel Stouffer. This department included a survey section headed by Leonard Cottrell, and an experimental section headed by Carl Hovland, who was assisted by Nathan Maccoby, and advised by university professors such as Hadley Cantril (Princeton), John Dollard (Yale), Robert Merton (Columbia), Frank Stanton (CBS), and Kimball Young (Queens College). After the war, Stouffer edited a multi-volume overview, which noted that between Pearl Harbor and the end of the war "more than half a million soldiers were to be questioned . . . in all parts of the world. Over 200 different questionnaires, many of which contained 100 or more separate items, were to be administered." He also noted that "in the files of the war department are more than 300 manuscript reports prepared on a great variety of subjects."[38]

In other words, there was a massive mobilization of brainpower. Almost anybody who was (or was to become) somebody in psycho-social science came to be involved in some way in psycho-social research for the war effort. They generated entirely new techniques and notions, such as content analysis (of enemy propaganda), group morale (under hostile attacks), modal personality (in foreign cultures, see chapter 6), and many more. After peace had returned, there was a brief lull, but as soon as the Cold War had begun, in its turn, new projects were started. Institutions such as the Rockefeller and Carnegie foundations co-sponsored studies of international opinion, ranging from *How nations see each other* (1948) to *The appeals of communism* (1954).

The O&A technology played a key role in all fields where attempted or actual social management surfaced in any fashion. Marketing and advertising research developed new concepts such as consumer lifestyles and values, and new technologies to try to gauge the public response to new products, advertising campaigns, radio programs, and the like (see figure 60). Policy research tested government plans before they were made final and implemented. Voting and election research came to be a standard feature of the democratic process. Paul Lazarsfeld and his colleagues initiated the Columbia tradition, which resulted in early studies such as *The people's choice* (1944) and *Voting* (1954). Angus Campbell, Philip Converse, and colleagues started the Michigan school, leading to studies such as *The American voter* (1960). Newspapers and broadcasters became eager to publish poll results, which in turn stimulated public discussion on issues and candidates.

Opinion and attitude research became a profession and a trade, not only in the US, but in all western countries. The American Association of Public Opinion Research (AAPOR), founded in 1946, soon had several hundred members. On an international level, it was followed by the creation of a World Association of Public Opinion Research (WAPOR), and the European Society for Opinion and Market Research (ESOMAR). Market and advertising research became the real locomotives pulling the entire O&A train; despite their high media profiles, social and political surveys often worked with much lower budgets, and often even at a loss. Purely academic research trailed behind for a long time, except in certain specialized fields.

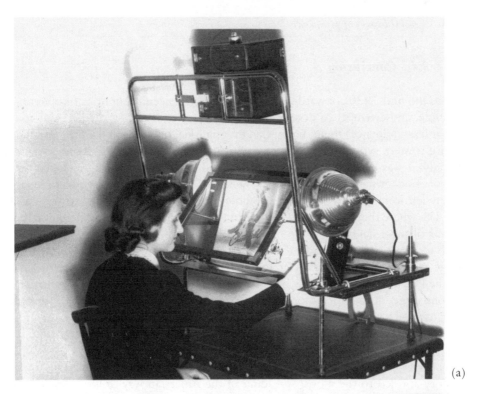

Figure 60 New technologies for investigating the response of the public. (a) The Purdue eye-camera (*c*. 1940). This apparatus was used by advertisers to monitor eye-movements of individuals when they were leafing through a magazine. Source: Archives of the History of American Psychology, University of Akron. (b) The "Program analyzer" was devised in the 1950s to register the opinion of a panel about a radio or television program. From A. Anastasi (1964), *Fields of applied psychology* (New York: McGraw-Hill). Courtesy Columbia Broadcasting Company.

3.4   Conclusion

From the mid-1930s onwards, social psychology, its central notions of opinion and attitude, and attempts to develop new techniques to measure, predict, and control (or at least influence) them, became an international phenomenon which affected the entire western world. The alternative British approach of Mass Observation faded because it was deemed to be less practical and exact. Approaches developed on the European continent were blocked by the rise of fascism and the wartime occupation. Many left-leaning and/or Jewish psychologists and sociologists fled to the UK and the US, where they contributed further to the conceptual and methodological refinements of these fields.

It took two or three decades for O&A technology to spread globally. During the first stage, until the Second World War, fully fledged applications had been primarily limited to the US, followed tentatively by a few other developed Anglo-Saxon countries. The second stage, during the Second World War, saw the further elaboration and application of these techniques to a wide range of problems directly related to the war effort of those same countries, such as the monitoring of military and civilian morale. These efforts slowed down when peace returned, but picked up again as the Cold War took over. More important during this third stage, however, was the fact that the American victory also led to the global spreading of the American way of life, companies and goods, management and marketing techniques, and research and planning tools.

4   The psychologization of social orientations

Now let us step back again, and look at this entire canon of O&A technology as it spread after the Second World War. It presented a number of choices on how to proceed. The choices made were no doubt the most practical ones, but could easily be called into question on theoretical grounds (and have intermittently been so challenged to this very day). This is not the place for an elaborate discussion of those issues.[39] But the important thing to note here is that the notions of opinions and attitudes which took shape over the years are socio-historically contingent. "The invention of the public," as I have called it earlier, or the "social construction" of a certain view of collective subjectivity, corresponds with a particular type of society, at a particular stage of its development, and with a particular range of imperatives.[40]

The earliest nineteenth-century social surveys (for instance on poverty, health, and education) had mostly been indirect surveys. That is to say, social dignitaries and "experts," such as social workers, general practitioners, and schoolteachers, who were supposed to be in regular contact with the underprivileged, were asked how the latter lived, worked, and thought. Thus, researchers did not put their questions to the population under investigation, and of course this often produced a certain slant. At some point around the beginning of the twentieth century, however, this indirect approach was gradually replaced by a direct one. In practice this was only feasible insofar as local dialects had gradually been replaced by national languages, and widespread illiteracy had been replaced by elementary schooling. People were now finally permitted to "speak for themselves," but – as we will see below – only to a certain degree.

The earliest surveys had also focused on the gathering of factual information about food, housing, and working conditions, asking the questions which, where, how many? Later surveys placed increasing emphasis on hypothetical "what if?" questions, and on the "how do you feel about . . . ?" type of question. The later surveys were less interested in gathering information about actual situations (which could now increasingly be drawn from social statistics and other means), and focused more on possible developments, often with the aim of predicting future actions and reactions. The evaluation of public moods became important.

The most important next step was that opinions and attitudes were no longer inferred from observed behavior (as in the aforementioned "Mass Observation" surveys), but from verbal statements. This effected a removal from the messy situation of everyday life, and even from the neat procedures of the experimental laboratories. But it also begged the question as to what extent such elicited verbal statements were a good predictor of future behavior. Initial results were frequently disappointing. Very often people did not know how they "really" felt, or why they did so. Also many were reluctant to share their views with an interviewer, who was usually a total stranger. Better interview techniques were designed to circumvent these traps, but they only succeeded in part. Sometimes, people were for instance asked to complete statements or to respond to visual cues or other sensory stimuli, which further "framed" their responses in advance.

It soon turned out that the exact choice of words, the precise phrasing of questions, a methodical succession of themes, was of the utmost importance. Even slight variations could lead to different suggestions and therefore to varying results. This would then hamper the comparability of results between groups, before and after a campaign, or from competing agencies. Questions had to be put in a "neutral" way, one had to make sure that people had the basic information and had formed a definite opinion. Otherwise, the exercise would be vain. Questionnaires were tested for shortcomings during a preliminary round, to identify possible vagueness, ambiguity, or false suggestions. More often than not, however, such precautions were omitted as a result of practical demands such as time pressure.

In order to impose even more clarity upon the unwitting interviewees, they were increasingly confronted with pre-formulated closed answers and limited alternatives. They were given two alternatives ("yes" or "no"), or three alternatives ("yes," "indifferent," or "no"), or were allowed to express their ignorance by including "don't know." It became common practice to present the alternatives as scales. Five-point scales were developed, but also seven-, nine-, and eleven-point scales. Step by step, people were led into and through a maze of seemingly logical choices. But often, this did not follow their own patterns of reasoning and thought; consequently, the reasoning of sponsors was imposed upon them.

Finally, mathematics was introduced in the analysis of research results. Techniques such as systematic comparison, correlation, and factor analysis created a range of ways to make research data both more simple and more complicated. With the slow but steady rise of the computer the statistical techniques became more elaborate and sophisticated; research results could be employed for precise purposes. Social research also became more opaque, since an increasing proportion of researchers, policy makers, and the public did not really understand the implications of all this gobbledegook. This was also clear in the "prediction" of election results. The methods were usually taken for granted whenever they turned out correct, and contested whenever they did not; the latter happened quite frequently, particularly in confrontations between only two major parties or alliances, with a close call between 51 and 49 percent.

It should also be noted that the new O&A technology and its results thoroughly affected the perception of public opinion itself, of what was real or possible or not. Previously, opinion leaders and the media had of course claimed that "public opinion" supported this or that candidate or initiative, but those claims had been rather vague and contestable. From now on, however, public opinion was increasingly equated with mere poll results. This altered procedures for the selection of electoral candidates and of policy alternatives, with the definition of people and proposals as "mainstream" or "marginal." By the early 1960s this identification of poll findings with public opinion profoundly changed the rules of the democratic game.

In the course of time, dozens of other methodological questions emerged. Prolonged debates produced provisional solutions, supported by the larger part of the research community. Yet the very simplicity and practicality of these techniques proved both their usefulness and superficiality. They were successful in identifying and exploring certain psycho-social problems, but often failed to provide more subtle cues and deeper insights, about layered and even contradictory feelings. One recurring question was therefore whether such quantitative results should be further refined by qualitative research.

5 Conclusion

During the second half of the twentieth century, opinion and attitude research expanded to become a major scientific tool and a major global industry, integrating new technologies such as the telephone and, recently, the personal computer and the internet. However, this entire conceptualization of social orientations remained mired in the limitations which had beset it from the outset, particularly in the forms of excessive individualization and psychologization. Almost always, problems of social adaptation were laid at the doorstep of individuals, and were put in psychological terms. Psychologists came to use opinions and attitudes as purely individualistic categories and not as truly social notions. This generally contributed to shielding established institutions. The danger of such one-sidedness had been identified early on by some pioneers in the field of "social orientations." For example, William Thomas, the pioneer of psycho-sociology mentioned earlier, warned: "Any method of research which takes the individual as a distinct entity and isolates him from his social environment . . . finds necessarily only psychical, physical or biological facts essentially and indissolubly connected with the individual as a psychical, physical, or generally biological reality."[41]

Some psychologists had their doubts too. In 1935, Gordon Allport had warned that: "The price one must pay for bipolarity and quantification is, of course, extreme, and often absurd elementarism."[42] Nevertheless, opinions and attitudes were increasingly approached as "things inside our heads," which, furthermore, could easily be "measured, predicted and even controlled" (or at least managed through information, communication, and persuasion). In addition, public opinion at the group level continued to be approached as the mere sum of individual opinions, rather than as an evolving configuration. Yet Cooley, another pioneer of psycho-sociology, had warned that it was not "merely an aggregate of separate individual judgements, but rather an organization, a cooperative product of communication and mutual influence."[43] Allan Barton later put this issue even more provocatively. He said that by using a mere sample of individuals,

> . . . the survey becomes a sociological meat grinder, which isolates the individual from his social context, and guarantees that no one in the investigation interacts with anyone else. A bit like the biologist putting his experimental animals through the hamburger machine, structure and function disappear, all that is left is cell biology.[44]

One of the side-effects of the reification of opinions and attitudes as things inside our heads and of individualist reduction is that non-linear shifts in public opinion and perception cannot be properly understood. Yet in recent years, major institutions with huge research departments have often stumbled into dramatic communication crises, which they proved unable to handle properly. Thus in order to be able to fathom this, one may need to develop radically different approaches in the study of social orientations. The older disciplines of mass psychology and the sociology of collective behavior, reconsidered in the light of the chaos and complexity revolutions, may help to provide alternative conceptual frameworks.[45]

PRINCIPAL SOURCES AND FURTHER READING

The earliest, mass-psychological studies about "social orientations" and their social and political context are discussed in J. van Ginneken (1992), *Crowds, psychology and politics* (New York: Cambridge University Press). M. Bulmer, K. Bales and K. K. Sklar, eds. (1991), *The social survey in historical perspective* (Cambridge: Cambridge University Press) covers the development of early surveys about social abuses. A rather traditional "inside" view of the emergence of academic social psychology is given in G. W. Allport (1954), The historical background of modern social psychology, in G. Lindzey, ed., *Handbook of social psychology, vol. I* (Cambridge, MA: Addison-Wesley), pp. 3–56. Several aspects of the (new) field of public opinion are treated in C. Glynn, S. Herbst, G. O'Keefe and R. Y. Shapiro (1999), *Public opinion* (Boulder: Westview). K. Danziger (1997), *Naming the mind. How psychology found its language* (London: Sage) discusses how much the psychological concept of "attitude" owed to conceptualizations in, for example, related academic disciplines and the arts.

NOTES

1   Van Ginneken, *Crowds, psychology and politics.*
2   J. van Ginneken (1988, 2nd ed.), A cultural history of political psychology, in W. Stone and P. Schaffner, eds., *The psychology of politics* (New York: Springer), pp. 3–22.
3   My earliest attempt to try to come to grips with these themes was a paper with an "Outline of a social history of opinion and attitude research during the American interbellum,"

presented at the 17th Annual Scientific Meeting of the American Cheiron Society for the History of the Behavioral and Social Sciences, in Philadelphia. This was then developed into a chapter for a book on the social history of psychology I edited with J. Jansz in 1986: *Psychologische praktijken – Een twintigste eeuwse geschiedenis* [Psychological practices – A twentieth century history] (Den Haag: Vuga).

4   Quoted in C. A. Kiesler, B. E. Collins and N. Miller (1969), *Attitude change. A critical analysis of theoretical approaches* (New York: Wiley), p. 4.

5   As early as 1924, some 2000 Americans came to participate in the International Advertising Convention in London, which led to the founding of the International Advertising Association. Publication of the journal *Advertising Age* began in 1930. In 1936, the [American] Association of National Advertisers and the Association of Advertising Agencies set up an Advertising Research Foundation.

6   Bulmer et al., *The social survey.*

7   J. A. C. Brown (1963), *Techniques of persuasion* (Harmondsworth: Penguin Books), p. 99.

8   More in: J. M. Converse (1987), *Survey research in the US. Roots and emergence* (Berkeley: University of California Press).

9   A nephew of Sigmund Freud's wife became a major pioneer. See his memoirs: E. L. Bernays (1952, 1980), *Public relations* (Norman: University of Oklahoma Press).

10   On the eve of the Depression, in 1928, there were already 39 American universities offering courses in marketing, sales promotion, and advertising. In 1937, there were only three universities teaching "public relations," but this figure rose tenfold over the next decade. Around the mid-1930s, there were already several universities that taught public opinion and propaganda (or persuasion), for example: Cornell, Rutgers, Ohio State, Brooklyn College, and the University of Minnesota.

11   J. Szacki (1979), *History of sociological thought* (London: Aldwych), chs. 14 and 15. Today this field is also labeled "micro-sociology": see for example: T. J. Scheff (1990), *Microsociology. Discourse, emotion, and social structure* (Chicago: University of Chicago Press).

12   See T. N. Clark, ed. (1969), *Gabriel Tarde on communication and social influence* (Chicago: University of Chicago Press). Tarde's ideas about public opinion were also inspired by the Dreyfus affair which divided the country for more than a decade. See Van Ginneken, *Crowds, psychology and politics*, ch. 5.

13   Van Ginneken, *Crowds, psychology and politics*, pp. 222–9.

14   Also see: F. H. Allport (1937), Toward a science of public opinion, *Public Opinion Quarterly, 1,* 7–23; and also R. I. Evans (1980), *The making of social psychology. Discussion with creative contributors* (New York: Gardner).

15   See: G. W. Allport (1935), Attitudes, in C. Murchison, ed., *Handbook of social psychology* (Worcester: Clark University Press), pp. 798–844; and also: Allport, The historical background. He later developed into one of the foremost scholars in fields such as personality, the study of rumor, and the psychology of prejudice (see also chapter 5, this volume).

16   As was underlined in Allport, Attitudes. For a reflexive view see: F. Samuelson (1974). History, origin myth and ideology. "Discovery" of social psychology. *Journal for the Theory of Social Behaviour, 4,* 217–231. Also see: W. S. Sahakian (1984, 2nd ed.). *History and systems of social psychology* (Washington: Hemisphere).

17   The following analysis of attitude in art and science is derived from Danziger, *Naming the mind.* Also see: K. Danziger (1990), *Constructing the subject. Historical origins of psychological research* (Cambridge: Cambridge University Press) and N. Rose (1990), *Governing the soul* (London: Routledge).

18 W. I. Thomas and F. Znaniecki (1918), *The Polish peasant in Europe and America* (New York: Knopf), pp. 20–3. See also Danziger, *Naming the mind*, pp. 134–57.

19 G. Allport, Attitudes, pp. 810, 798.

20 Danziger, *Naming the mind*, pp. 141 ff.

21 Danziger, *Naming the mind*, pp. 143, 134.

22 E. S. Bogardus (1920; rev. ed.), *Essentials of social psychology* (Los Angeles: University of California Press), p. 9.

23 E. S. Bogardus (1925), Measuring social distances, *Journal of Applied Psychology, 9*, 216–26; and: E. S. Bogardus, *Essentials of social psychology*.

24 Danziger, *Naming the mind*, pp. 148–9.

25 As quoted in Danziger, *Naming the mind*, p. 148.

26 The article was reprinted, along with other key contributions to the development of attitude scaling by, for example, Rensis Likert, Louis Guttman, and Charles Osgood in M. Fishbein, ed. (1967), *Attitude theory and measurement* (New York: Wiley).

27 F. van Vught (1979), *Sociale planning* [Social planning] (Assen: Van Gorcum).

28 C. Roll (1982), Private opinion polls, in G. Benjamin, ed., The communications revolution in politics, *Proceedings of the Academy of Political Science, vol. 34*, pp. 61ff.

29 See for example A. Crossley (1966), The developing years, *Polls, 2*, 1–9; and L. J. Martin (1984), The genealogy of public opinion polling, *Annals of the American Academy of Political and Social Science, 472*, 12–23; also Converse, *Survey research in the US*.

30 H. Childs (the author of several textbooks on the subject) established a first research center and data bank at Princeton University. With the support of the Marshall Field Foundation, Gallup's associate, Field, established the National Opinion Research Center (NORC) at the University of Denver (which later moved to the University of Chicago). Roper teamed up with William College, in turn. Another major center was established at the University of Michigan at Ann Arbor. After the Second World War, Likert came to chair the Institute of Social Research there, and Katona chaired the Survey Research Center.

31 R. M. Worcester (1991), *British public opinion. A guide to the history and methodology* (Oxford: Blackwell).

32 Worcester, *British public opinion*, pp. 3–5.

33 G. Gallup (1972), *The Gallup poll. Public opinion 1935–1971* (New York: Random House), p. v. Also see: G. Gallup (1972), *The sophisticated poll watcher's guide* (Princeton: Princeton University Press).

34 A. Calder (1985), Mass Observation 1937–1949, in M. Bulmer, ed., *Essays on the history of British sociological research* (Cambridge: Cambridge University Press), pp. 121–36; R. A. Kent (1981), *A history of British empirical sociology* (Aldershot: Gower), pp. 117–20. Also see N. Rose (1985), *The psychological complex. Psychology, politics and society in England 1869–1939* (London: Routledge). The Mass Observation archives still survive at the University of Sussex in Brighton.

35 A. H. Barton (1979), Paul Lazarsfeld and applied social research, *Social Science History, 3*, 4–44.

36 T. W. Adorno, E. Frenkel-Brunswik, D. J. Levinson and R. N. Sanford (1950), *The authoritarian personality* (New York: Harper); see also M. Jay (1973), *The dialectical imagination* (Boston: Little Brown).

37 D. Cartwright (1946), American social psychology and the war, *Journal of Consulting Psychology, 10*, 67–72. Also D. Cartwright (1947–48), Social psychology in the US during the Second World War, *Human relations, 1*, 333–52.

38 S. A. Stouffer, E. A. Suchman, L. C. DeVinney, S. A. Star and R. M. Williams Jr. (1949), *The American soldier. Adjustment during Army life, vol. I* (New York: Wiley), pp. 6, 12.

39 Some of the issues are discussed in substantial overviews such as Glynn et al., *Public opinion*, ch. 1. It is significant, though, that the chapter "Sociological perspectives" in this volume does not deal with sociological perspectives at all, but only with (social) psychological perspectives.

40 J. van Ginneken (1993), *De uitvinding van het publiek* [The invention of the public] (Amsterdam: Cramwinckel).

41 Thomas and Znaniecki, *The Polish peasant*, p. 26.

42 Allport, Attitudes, p. 820; Danziger, *Naming the mind*, pp. 141, 150.

43 Cooley, as quoted in C. Fraser and G. Gaskell, eds. (1990), *The social psychological study of widespread beliefs* (Oxford: Clarendon Press), p. 80.

44 Barton in E. Rogers (1995, 4th ed.), *The diffusion of innovations* (New York: Free Press), p. 120.

45 See J. van Ginneken (1999), *Brein-bevingen* (Amsterdam: Boom). English translation in preparation with Erlbaum (Mahwah, NJ, 2003).

Epilogue

Peter van Drunen and Jeroen Jansz

In the introduction to this book, we observed that there is more to the history of psychology than simply the rise of a new branch of science, a new collection of theories, and a new group of professionals. The tremendous growth of "the science of man," we claimed, has pervasively influenced and transformed both society at large and our common understanding of ourselves. As an introductory statement, this claim may have sounded somewhat far-fetched to some of our readers. If so, we hope to have convinced them through our detailed accounts of the vicissitudes of the discipline within the various social domains we examined. Whether we look at child-rearing and education, work, or mental health, psychologists have become major players with respect to the management of social behavior, not only as professional experts, but also as agents who have influenced the way we experience ourselves and each other.

The same holds for the fields we examined in subsequent chapters on ethnicity, delinquency, and social orientations. Although not considered "core disciplines" of professional psychology, these fields have definitely also been influenced by psychological expertise: our behavior as political citizens and consumers is increasingly analyzed (and measured) in terms of "attitudes" and related concepts; our focus on delinquency has turned from crime *per se* to the mental make-up of its perpetrators; and the recurrent heated debates on mental differences between various ethnic groups testify to the importance we have come to attach to these psychological categories, when it comes to the difficult task of dealing with cultural and ethnic differences.

At the end of our historical journey, it is time to try to draw up a balance sheet: what have we learned from the previous narratives regarding the interaction between psychology and society? How can we account for the tremendous expansion of practical psychology? How is it related to academic psychology on the one hand, and developments within society at large on the other? And, perhaps even more importantly: what has practical psychology brought us? Has it contributed to our material and spiritual well-being, as some commentators tend to emphasize? Or has it rather been a new force of oppression and control, as others have argued?

To put these questions into perspective, we will first provide a brief sketch of two opposing perspectives on the relation between psychology and society. After that, we will more or less systematically discuss some of the main issues which are at stake.

1   Psychology and society: perspectives

The tremendous growth of psychology and its increasing impact on western society have not gone unnoticed. Especially in recent decades, they have increasingly been a topic of reflection, not only by psychologists and historians of the discipline, but also by social commentators, some of whom have dubbed "psychologization" as one of the most important characteristics of late twentieth-century western society. Generally speaking, two perspectives can be identified: the "positivist" view, which applauds the rise to prominence of psychology, and the "revisionist" view, which tends to be more critical.

THE POSITIVIST VIEW

Not surprisingly, the positivist view has its most fierce adherents among psychologists themselves. Almost invariably, they emphasize the potential benefits their work may carry for society at large, as well as for its individual members. Some even go as far as to accord psychology a special status among the other sciences. In chapter 1, for instance, we encountered the Dutch psychologist Heymans, who as early as 1909 predicted that psychology held the key to happiness and peace of mind. The same theme reverberates in publications by psychologists throughout the past century. So, for instance, APA president George A. Miller in 1969 urged his colleagues to bring their knowledge to bear on the problems of society, a challenge that was taken up one year later by the publication of a wide-ranging volume on "Psychology and the problems of society." As its significant opening lines stated: "With the growing realization that contemporary society's problems are human, not technological, a troubled society turns to psychology for help."[1]

Of course, psychologists are not alone in this self-confident attitude. With respect to the beneficial nature of science, they stand in a long historical and philosophical tradition, of which the Enlightenment and Comte's philosophy of positivism are only two examples. Moreover, it is almost a defining characteristic of any profession to construct its work as serving the general welfare. Neither is this mere rhetoric to enhance professional prestige, status, and opportunities. Underlying many of the grand schemes and projects of professional psychology has been a genuine belief that the advancement of psychology is to the benefit of society at large – misguided as some of the projects appear in retrospect (think of Watson's behavioristic pedagogy, Terman's eugenics, or the way traditional gender roles and patterns of white domination were legitimized by psychological theory).

Generally, the positivistic view is expressed as an article of faith (or, in current newspeak, a "mission statement") rather than being based on historical analysis. It finds its most succinct expression in the by-laws of the APA and other professional associations of psychologists. So, for instance the APA states that its goal is "to advance psychology as a science and profession and as a means of promoting health and human welfare."

If we take a closer look at positivism, it entails three assumptions. First, practical psychology is assumed to rest on scientific knowledge, that is, theories and methods developed within academic psychology. Secondly, this knowledge is thought to be progressive and "value-free," that is, independent of cultural preconceptions or ideological presuppositions. And thirdly, that "application" of this knowledge is generally to the benefit of society and mankind.

THE REVISIONIST VIEW

If psychologists welcome their growing "jurisdiction," outsiders generally tend to be more skeptical, sometimes to the point of blaming psychology for many of today's problems. Perhaps the most prominent example is the American historian Christopher Lasch, who in his books *Haven in a heartless world* (1977) and *The culture of narcissism* (1979) launched a vehement attack on psychology and related disciplines.[2] According to Lasch, they were to a large part accountable for a growing sense of uncertainty, which he takes to be characteristic of modern culture. Contemporary narcissists, Lasch argues, suffer from emotional shallowness, fear of intimacy, and pseudo-self-insight. As a result of their frantic search for fulfilment they have lost any interest in the future.

Revisionists differ somewhat with respect to the arguments on which their critical assessment rests. Some emphasize that psychology, despite its scientific pretensions, has remained caught in current social preconceptions and ideological bias. In other words, that it is no more than a servant to the powers that be. An example is Stephen Gould's incisive criticism of intelligence testing, showing the influence of eugenics and white supremacist thought on the way psychologists constructed their instruments and interpreted their data.[3]

Others do grant that the discipline has some autonomy, but take issue with its supposed benefits for society at large. A good example of this line of reasoning is a recent study of the social effects of classifications of mental disorders such as the DSM-IV, under the telling title *Making us crazy*.[4] Rather than categorizing existing disorders, the authors claim, the DSM has contributed to an increased medicalization and psychologization of forms of behavior hitherto considered normal, in the process expanding the jurisdiction of psychiatrists and other mental health professionals to include virtually all of us.

An attempt to integrate the two perspectives can be found in the work of the French philosopher Michel Foucault, and those inspired by him, such as the English sociologist Nikolas Rose.[5] On the one hand, their accounts demonstrate how psychology and the other social and life sciences evolved as part of grander schemes of social management and control. On the other hand, they also show how these sciences, psychology included, over time acquired a relative autonomy, thus developing an independent force of their own.

Despite these differences, all revisionist accounts concur in taking issue with the principal tenets of the positivist outlook: practical psychology received its main impetus from social forces rather than academic psychology; while psychological per-spectives change and develop over time, this does not necessarily signify cognitive progress, i.e. the replacement of "false" theories and ideas by superior ones; and psy-chology's part with respect to the general good is considered highly problematic, as historically, its role has been oppressive just as often as it fostered social progress.

We do not claim that history can provide all the answers to the questions raised above – let alone that the preceding accounts in this book provide sufficient ground for that. However, the historical material presented does lend itself to some obser-vations and comments. First, we will discuss the forces that shaped practical psy-chology. After that, we will take a look at its social impact.

2   Shaping practical psychology

What were the forces that shaped practical psychology? One of the tenets of the positivist view is that theoretical and methodological advances within academic psy-chology play a pivotal role. Revisionists, on the other hand, stress societal influences of various kinds.

Explaining our general approach, in the introduction to this book we have already pointed out that practical psychology has a development of its own, and is certainly not just the logical outcome of the "application" of scientific findings. Subsequent chapters have, we think, amply corroborated this viewpoint. Consider, for example, the "grand theories" that guided the academic development of psychology: the Wundtian psychology of consciousness, Watsonian and Skinnerian behaviorism, or modern cognitive psychology. Some of these have left their marks in psychological practice, but none of them was of decisive importance to its development.

On the other hand, if we consider theories and techniques that did make a dif-ference, we see that virtually none of them emanated from academic psychology. Psy-choanalysis, the "practice theory" par excellence in the century that lies behind us, was developed in close interaction with psychological practice. Moreover, it entailed a radical breach with the assumptions of early twentieth-century academic psychol-ogy, specifically, a shift of focus from "consciousness" to the subconscious. The same holds for that other grand practical tradition, of diagnosis and mental testing, specif-ically intelligence testing. As we have seen, the "discovery" of the intelligence test was only possible by breaking away from existing conceptions of individual differ-ences, and taking a whole new approach to the problem of measuring such differ-ences. For a practical psychology to evolve, these examples suggest, academic psychology had to be put aside rather than "applied."

Which brings us to our next question: if practical psychology resulted from "exter-nal," social forces rather than the development of academic psychology, what social forces were involved?

In the Introduction, we identified two major long-term developments as being of relevance. The first we dubbed "individualization": a multifaceted cultural process, encompassing both a growing sense of individuality and a growing attention to the emotional "inner world," the origins of which go back as far as the fifteenth century. Besides this, the nineteenth and twentieth centuries have witnessed the expansion of a second process, which we identified as "social management," that is, attempts to direct, control, or "discipline" the behavior of individuals and social groups.

Of these two processes, social management in particular has been a decisive factor in the rise of practical psychology, as the various chapters amply demonstrate. Almost without exception, practical psychology got its original impetus from new interventionist aims, be they increasing attention to child-rearing practices at home, attempts at improving efficiency in schools and the workplace, monitoring public opinion, or legitimizing existing inequalities between the sexes and between various ethnic groups. Moreover, the practices which emanated from these aims provided the institutional context within which psychologists could develop their professional role.

With respect to the role of individualization, the various accounts are less clear. This is partly a problem of lack of sources: whereas links between social management schemes and the rise of psychology are easily demonstrable, the influence of processes of individualization are by their very nature less tangible. Nevertheless, we think there can be little doubt about their relevance, especially when one considers the strong popular appeal of psychology and its nineteenth-century predecessors, such as physiognomy and phrenology. For example, interventionist motives may have inspired Stanley Hall's project of "child study," but they do not easily account for the enthusiastic participation of parents and educators in the project. Likewise, Galton's interest in mental measurement was firmly rooted in his eugenic program, but this leaves unexplained the massive public interest in his "anthropometric laboratory." Nor can the tremendous popularity of psychoanalysis be easily attributed to the social aims of the mental health movement. In sum: the agenda of practical psychology may have been set by interventionist motives, but its tremendous success cannot be accounted for without referral to a widespread popular fascination, rooted in a growing interest in individuality.

It is important to note that social management and processes of individualization did not only create the circumstances in which professional psychology could emanate and flourish. As has become apparent, they also deeply influenced the concepts and the techniques of the profession. Time and again, we saw how psychological practice was colored by prevailing cultural conceptions. Some of the examples of this influence may have come as a shock to those who believe in the humanitarian ethos of psychology – for example, the downright bigotry inherent in early practices and theories about ethnic differences, and the harsh attitude of eugenically inspired psychologists toward those suffering from mental deficits.

However, the influence of prevailing cultural conceptions is not limited to older practices now considered politically incorrect. We hope to have demonstrated that to this very day psychological practice is to a large extent guided by social norms and preconceptions. This is perhaps most evident in the realm of mental health care, with its successive leading values of adaptation (reflected by revised forms of psychoanalysis), liberation (reflected by Rogerian, non-directive therapy) and pragmatism (reflected by behavioral and cognitive therapies). The same holds, however, for other domains: whether we consider psychological conceptions and practices regarding women, non-white ethnic groups, homosexuals, or the "human resource" within the realm of work and organization, we invariably see a close correspondence between psychological conceptions and the values and ideas which prevail in society at large.

These socio-cultural influences on practical psychology have a direct bearing on two of the central tenets of positivism, that is, cognitive progress and the neutrality of science with respect to values. If cultural preconceptions and value systems are the driving force behind the development of practical psychology, then the distinction between factual knowledge and values becomes problematic. This is not to say that new empirical findings play no role at all in the development of the discipline. However, history suggests that they do so within the confines of existing modes of practice, rather than providing the impetus for radical changes. Culturally prevalent conceptions and value systems lead the way, rather than scientific advances.

Again, there is no reason to assume that this cultural embeddedness is only a thing of the past. Undoubtedly, many of our readers will judge practical psychology to be progressive, in other words, modern modes of practice to be better than older ones. However, this judgment probably rests on its concurrence with present-day values, rather than its empirical superiority.

All this, of course, is not to say that psychology has no "surplus value," that it is just another expression of current social thinking and another mode of existing social practices. The rise of practical psychology has certainly made a difference, and left its mark on contemporary society and culture. It is to this impact that we will now turn.

3   The impact of psychology

Perspectives on the impact of psychology vary as widely as those on the forces that shaped the discipline. Positivists tend to emphasize its benefit for the general welfare; some revisionists see it as a new instrument of social control, whereas others stress the pernicious influence of "psychologization" as such. We will first discuss the social progress versus social control perspective, and then proceed to the relation between psychology and "psychologization."

SOCIAL PROGRESS VERSUS SOCIAL CONTROL

The idea that science has contributed to social progress is one of the cornerstones of the positivist view. With respect to psychology, it is apparent both in the many prospective schemes and programs for the "application" of psychological knowledge, and in many historical retrospects, especially those found in celebratory publications and the introductory chapters of textbooks. Almost invariably, the advent of psychology is depicted as being beneficial, not only to the discipline itself and its practitioners, but also to society at large.

The preceding chapters have shown this optimism to be highly problematic. There is no reason to doubt the integrity of psychologists' humanitarian ethos (although we should not underestimate its sometimes rhetorical purposes). However, our historical journey has made it clear that practical psychology consistently tended to side with the perspective and the socio-political aims of the contemporary social elites. This became particularly manifest in the chapter on ethnic differences. Here, we saw how psychologists and representatives of neighboring sciences almost invariably took

western superiority for granted, depicting those from other cultures as either genetically inferior or historically backward. Somewhat more subtly, the same theme
emerged in other chapters: as part of more general programs of social management,
psychologists' theories, methods, and practical interventions almost without exception were rooted in masculine, middle-class conceptions of social reality. Even if many
of its programs entailed an attempt to "civilize" or "emancipate" members of other
social strata (or of the other gender), the values which guided this attempt were the
dominant social values of the time.

Nevertheless, we think it would be too rash to simply side with those revisionists
who claim that psychologists are merely "servants of power."[6] For one thing, we also
saw how, as time progressed, various formerly "oppressed" groups acquired a "psychological voice" of their own. This was for instance evident in the rise of the Boasian
school in cultural psychology, in the countermovement of anti-psychiatry, and in the
impact of feminism on psychology. More importantly perhaps, "social control" theorists tend to be blind to the way existing social relations were transformed by psychology. While practical psychology may have been rooted in existing socio-cultural
preconceptions and practices, its vast expansion has not left these conceptions and
practices untouched. In many areas, the "psychological perspective" seems to have
acquired a status of its own, transforming the very conceptions and "social agendas"
which initially inspired it. It is to this theme of "psychologization" that we will now
turn.

PSYCHOLOGY AND PSYCHOLOGIZATION

"All the great problems of our age are becoming more and more psychological the
better we understand them," wrote Stanley Hall in 1924. Leaving aside the notion
of "better understanding," the past chapters have certainly demonstrated that "the
great problems" have become more "psychological" – be they differences between
social groups (men and women, whites and non-whites, etc.), matters of illness and
health, education, political opinion, or delinquency and crime.

If Stanley Hall and many other psychologists after him applauded this development, others are more critical. In this respect, Christopher Lasch is certainly not alone
in holding psychology accountable for many of today's problems. In 1978, for
instance, the American journalist and social commentator Martin Gross criticized
"psychological society" for creating a culture of vulnerability:

> Its citizen is a new model of Western man, one who is dependent on others for guid-
> ance as to what is real or false. . . . We have become fascinated with our madness, moti-
> vations and our endless, sometimes wearying search for normality. . . . *The major agent
> of change has been modern psychology* [italics in original].[7]

The most incisive and provocative analysis of this process of "psychologization" is
provided by historians inspired by the thought of the French philosopher Michel
Foucault, most notably the historian of psychology Nikolas Rose. Rose argues that
the modern project of psychologization is a direct offspring of older technologies
of social management: rather than directly supervising and controlling the human

populace, psychologization has seen to it that people have internalized the allegedly "objective" guidelines of psychology, thus facilitating the replacement of outside control and supervision by self-control.[8]

To some extent, Rose's account is corroborated by the previous chapters. Nevertheless, we think some qualifications are in order, especially when considering the relation between psychology as a practical and professional enterprise and "psychologization" as a more general cultural phenomenon. Undoubtedly, it can be concluded from the last section that psychology has become a major force in shaping our conceptions of mental phenomena, be they intelligence, mental problems, attitudes, or the sources of delinquency. Does this also imply, as Rose and others argue, that it is the main agent of the cultural processes of individualization, "emotionalization," and "psychologization," that seem to be so characteristic of our time?

In our opinion, this is a bridge too far. For one thing, as was shown in chapter 1 in particular, processes of individualization and "psychologization" (i.e. a growing sense of the "emotional interior") long preceded the rise of psychology. Secondly, when it comes to more recent developments, the correspondence between the conceptions offered by professional psychology and those embraced by people in general is anything but perfect. Historically the most prominent example of this is psychoanalysis – originally frowned upon by psychologists, but eagerly adopted by the general public. To a great extent, the same holds for other popular psychologies, from Maslowian "humanistic psychology" in the 1960s to the recent notion of "emotional intelligence." Just as practical psychology developed rather autonomously from academic psychology, so popular psychology also seems to have a dynamic of its own.

This having been said, the fact remains that the general cultural fascination with the emotional interior, which seems so characteristic of our time, has accorded psychology and psychologists an important place within modern western society. Just as the importance of health is reflected in the authority of medical doctors, so our fascination with individual differences, emotionality, and the like has contributed to the status of psychologists.

4   Conclusion

Whatever the background of psychologization as a cultural phenomenon, it has resulted in a decisive influence for psychology and psychologists with respect to the way people experience themselves, one another, and their environs. Significantly, even those who are critical of the role of psychology often use a psychological vocabulary to articulate their criticism – see for example Lasch's reference to the Freudian concept of "narcissism," or the development of "feminist" and "critical" psychologies.

But if we cannot fully escape the influence of psychology, it is at least worth trying to take a more detached and critical look at it. Rather than merely documenting the history of psychology, this is what we have aimed for in this book: no definitive answers, but a fresh perspective, which may stimulate further inquiry and critical reflection.

NOTES

1   F. F. Korten, S. W. Cook and J. I. Lacey, eds., *Psychology and the problems of society* (Washington, DC: American Psychological Association). This includes Miller's address of the year before: G. A. Miller, Psychology as a means of promoting human welfare, pp. 5–21.
2   C. Lasch (1977), *Haven in a heartless world. The family besieged* (New York: Basic Books); C. Lasch (1978), *The culture of narcissism. American life in an age of diminishing expectations* (New York: Norton).
3   S. J. Gould (1981), *The mismeasure of man* (New York: Norton).
4   H. Kutchins and S. A. Kirk (1997), *Making us crazy. DSM: the psychiatric bible and the creation of mental disorders* (New York: The Free Press).
5   See in particular M. Foucault (1974), *The order of things: an archeology of the human sciences* (London: Tavistock Publications) (originally published in 1966 as *Les mots et les choses*, (Paris: Gallimard), and N. Rose (1996), *Inventing our selves* (Cambridge: Cambridge University Press).
6   L. Baritz (1960), *Servants of power. A history of the use of social science in American industry* (Westport, CT: Greenwood Press).
7   M. L. Gross (1978), *The psychological society. A critical analysis of psychiatry, psychotherapy, psychoanalysis and the psychological revolution* (New York: Random House), pp. 3–4. In a similar spirit are: J. Pfister and N. Schnog (1997), *Inventing the psychological. Towards a cultural history of emotional life in America* (New Haven/London: Yale University Press); and B. Zilbergeld (1983), *The shrinking of America: myths of psychological change* (Boston; Little, Brown)
8   N. Rose (1996), *Inventing our selves* (Cambridge: Cambridge University Press), especially ch. 5. See also N. Rose (1990), *Governing the soul. The shaping of the private self* (London: Routledge).

Notes on contributors

Ruud Abma (1951) is assistant professor in the Department of General Social Sciences, Communication, Care and Welfare Section, at Utrecht University. He has written a book on the history of the psychological laboratory at the University of Nijmegen, and has published various articles on the history of psychology in the Netherlands. His Ph.D. thesis *Jeugd en tegencultuur* ("Youth and counterculture") (1990) combines psychological, sociological, and historical perspectives. At present, his research is focused on the history of mental health care and its interrelation with cultural change. He has been on the editorial board of *De Psycholoog* ("The Psychologist") since 1997. Address: Department of General Social Sciences, P.O. Box 80140, 3508 TC Utrecht, the Netherlands. E-mail: r.abma@fss.uu.nl

Peter van Drunen (1955) is part-time assistant professor of the history of psychology at Groningen University, the Netherlands. He also works as a self-employed journalist and historian of psychology. He is former Director of the Archives of Dutch Psychology and a former member of the Board of the European Society for the History of the Human Sciences. He is the author of several books and articles on the history of Dutch psychology and the history of psychological testing. Together with Jeroen Jansz, he has edited a Dutch textbook on the history of psychology, *Met zachte hand* ("The gentle force"; Utrecht: Lemma, 1996). Address: Looiersgracht 64d, 1016 VT Amsterdam, the Netherlands. E-mail: pvdrunen@hetnet.nl

Jaap van Ginneken (1943) alternates as an associate professor in the Communication Sciences department at the University of Amsterdam, and as an independent speaker/writer based near Nice, France. After gaining an M.A. in social psychology, and a Ph.D., he taught at various universities and in various disciplines. Three of his major books have also been published in English: *Crowds, psychology and politics* (Cambridge: Cambridge University Press, 1992), *Understanding global news* (London: Sage, 1998), *Collective behavior and public opinion* (Mahwah, NJ: Erlbaum, 2003). He has also published some ten smaller books in Dutch, on applied, economic, political, mass, and media psychology and on public opinion. In addition, he has acted as a consultant for a range of projects in science communication, and for three recent series of national television programs. Address: Department of Communication Science, Kloveniersburgwal 48, 1012 CX Amsterdam, the Netherlands. E-mail: vanginneken@pscw.uva.nl

Eric Haas (1954) has taught courses in the social sciences at the History and Arts Department of the Erasmus University of Rotterdam. He now teaches social sciences at the Social Work Unit of the Ichthus University of Professional Education, and is project leader of the Ichthus Expertise Centre for Urban Development. He has published articles in Dutch on the history of psychology, and wrote *Op de juiste plaats. De opkomst van de bedrijfs – en schoolpsychologische beroepspraktijk in Nederland* ("In the right place. The rise of industrial and school psychological practice in the Netherlands") (Hilversum: Verloren, 1995). Address: Ichthus University of Professional Education, Posthumalaan 90, PO-Box 23145, 3001 KC Rotterdam, the Netherlands. E-mail: e.haas@ichthus-hs.nl

Jeroen Jansz (1958) taught graduate and undergraduate courses in the history and theory of psychology for 15 years at Leiden University. He is now associate professor in the Department of Communication Science (University of Amsterdam) where he teaches the philosophy of science. As well as contributing to Dutch scientific journals, he has published papers on theoretical and historical issues in *Theory & Psychology, Journal for the Theory of Social Behaviour*, and the *Journal for the History of the Behavioral Sciences*. He has co-authored several books in Dutch, including a textbook on the history of psychology, edited with Peter van Drunen (*Met zachte hand* ("The gentle force"), Utrecht: Lemma, 1996). In English, he has published *Person, self and moral demands. Individualism contested by collectivism* (Leiden: DSWO, 1991) and co-authored *Psychology: a European text* (London: HarperCollins, 1995). He is secretary of the International Society for Theoretical Psychology. Address: Department of Communication Science, Kloveniersburgwal 48, 1012 CX Amsterdam, the Netherlands. E-mail: jansz@pscw.uva.nl

Pieter J. van Strien (1928) is professor emeritus at Groningen University, and former president of the board of the Archives of Dutch Psychology and member of the advisory board of two journals on the history of psychology. He started his career as a practitioner in work and organizational psychology, and was a full professor in this field from 1967 to 1980. In 1980 he was appointed to the chair for the Foundations and History of Psychology. He has published half a dozen books and numerous articles on theoretical, methodological, ethical, and professional issues and on the history of psychology, with a special focus on W&O psychology, social psychology, and methodology. With S. Shimmin he wrote a chapter on W&O history in the *Handbook of work and organizational psychology* (1998), edited by P. J. D. Drenth et al. Address: Department of Psychology, Theory and History of Psychology Section, Grote Kruisstraat 2/1, 9712 TS Groningen, The Netherlands. E-mail: p.j.van.Strien@ppsw.rug.nl

Paul Voestermans (1946) is associate professor in cultural psychology affiliated to the University of Nijmegen. As a freelance behavioral scientist, he teaches cultural psychology, the history of psychology, and evolutionary psychology. He has published in New Ideas in Psychology, Theory & Psychology, and in several Dutch psychology journals. He has contributed to books about sexuality, culture theory, the student movement, and evolutionary psychology. Address: The Nijmegen Cultural Psychology Group, Kerkpad 7, 6543 XM Nijmegen, the Netherlands (www.cultpsy.org). E-mail: voestermans@psych.kun.nl

Ido Weijers (1948) is associate professor at the Department of Educational Sciences at the University of Utrecht. He teaches the history and philosophy of education. His current research interests are in the history of Dutch psychiatry and the history and philosophy of juvenile justice. He is the author of books in Dutch on the postwar culture in the Netherlands, on Dutch higher education, on the history of education, and on juvenile justice. He has published several articles, in the *Journal of Moral Education*, *History of Education Quarterly*, *Social History of Medicine*, *Mental Retardation*, *European Journal on Criminal Policy and Research*, and the *European Journal of Crime, Criminal Law and Criminal Justice*. He is editor with Antony Duff of the book *Punishing juveniles. Principle and critique* (Oxford: Hart, 2002). Address: Department of Educational Sciences, Heidelberglaan 1, 3584 CS Utrecht, the Netherlands. E-mail: i.weijers@fss.uu.nl

Index